Armed Drones and the Ethics of War

This book assesses the ethical implications of using armed uninhabited aerial vehicles ('hunter-killer drones') in contemporary conflicts.

The American way of war is trending away from the heroic and towards the post-heroic, driven by a political preference for air-powered management of strategic risks and the reduction of physical risk to US personnel. The recent use of drones in the War on Terror has demonstrated the power of this technology to transcend time and space, but there has been relatively little debate in the United States and elsewhere over the embrace of what might be regarded as politically desirable and yet morally worrisome: risk-free killing. Arguably, the absence of a relationship of mutual risk between putative combatants poses a fundamental challenge to the status of war as something morally distinguishable from other forms of violence, and it also undermines the professional virtue of the warrior as a courageous risk-taker.

This book considers the use of armed drones in the light of ethical principles that are intended to guard against unjust increases in the incidence and lethality of armed conflict. The evidence and arguments presented indicate that, in some respects, the use of armed drones is to be welcomed as an ethically superior mode of warfare. Over time, however, their continued and increased use is likely to generate more challenges than solutions, and perhaps do more harm than good.

This book will be of much interest to students of the ethics of war, airpower, counter-terrorism, strategic studies and security studies in general.

Christian Enemark is a Reader in the Department of International Politics at Aberystwyth University.

War, Conflict and Ethics
Series Editors:
Michael L. Gross
University Of Haifa
and
Daniel Rothbart
George Mason University

This new book series focuses on the morality of decisions by military and political leaders to engage in violence and the normative underpinnings of military strategy and tactics in the prosecution of the war.

Civilians and Modern War
Armed conflict and the ideology of violence
Edited by Daniel Rothbart, Karina Korostelina and Mohammed Cherkaoui

Ethics, Norms and the Narratives of War
Creating and encountering the enemy other
Pamela Creed

Armed Drones and the Ethics of War
Military virtue in a post-heroic age
Christian Enemark

Armed Drones and the Ethics of War

Military virtue in a post-heroic age

Christian Enemark

LONDON AND NEW YORK

First published 2014
by Routledge
2 Park Square, Milton Park, Abingdon, Oxon OX14 4RN

Simultaneously published in the USA and Canada
by Routledge
711 Third Avenue, New York, NY 10017

Routledge is an imprint of the Taylor & Francis Group, an informa business

© 2014 Christian Enemark

The right of Christian Enemark to be identified as author of this work has been asserted by him in accordance with sections 77 and 78 of the Copyright, Designs and Patents Act 1988.

All rights reserved. No part of this book may be reprinted or reproduced or utilised in any form or by any electronic, mechanical, or other means, now known or hereafter invented, including photocopying and recording, or in any information storage or retrieval system, without permission in writing from the publishers.

Trademark notice: Product or corporate names may be trademarks or registered trademarks, and are used only for identification and explanation without intent to infringe.

British Library Cataloguing in Publication Data
A catalogue record for this book is available from the British Library

Library of Congress Cataloging-in-Publication Data
Enemark, Christian.
  Armed drones and the ethics of war : military virtue in a post-heroic age / Christian Enemark.
  pages cm. – (War, conflict and ethics)
  Includes bibliographical references and index.
  1. Military robots–Moral and ethical aspects. 2. Drone aircraft–Moral and ethical aspects. 3. Robotics–Moral and ethical aspects.
  4. Robotics–Military applications. 5. Military ethics–United States. I. Title.
  UG479.E74 2013
  172'.42–dc23
                                                                    2013011447

ISBN: 978-0-415-54052-0 (hbk)
ISBN: 978-0-203-10721-8 (ebk)

Typeset in Times
by Wearset Ltd, Boldon, Tyne and Wear

Printed and bound in Great Britain by
TJ International Ltd, Padstow, Cornwall

For Bree and Henry

Contents

	Acknowledgements	viii
	List of abbreviations	ix
1	Introduction	1
2	Post-heroic war and armed drones	9
3	Drones and the war threshold	22
4	Conducting drone warfare: the case of Pakistan	37
5	Radical asymmetry and the moral equality of combatants	58
6	Drone operators and the warrior ethos	76
7	Autonomous drones and post-human war	97
8	Conclusion	112
	Notes	118
	Select bibliography	141
	Index	143

Acknowledgements

For their valuable advice and feedback, I thank Roderic Alley, Chris Barrie, Alex Bellamy, Richard Brabin-Smith, Paul Dibb, Nick Evans, Shannon Ford, Lawrence Freedman, Jay Galliott, Luke Glanville, Jonathan Herington, Sanu Kainikara, Rick Keir, Margaret Kosal, Katrina Lee-Koo, David Lovell, Chris McNicol, Chris Michaelsen, Chris Roberts, Andrew O'Neil, Mark O'Neill, Malcolm Patterson, Anna Samson, Jason Sharman, Graeme Shennan, Brendan Taylor and Hugh White. Michael Gross, in particular, provided excellent and detailed advice to me. I am grateful also for the patience and professionalism of my publishers, Andrew Humphrys and Annabelle Harris. Most of all, and for countless reasons, I thank my little family.

Abbreviations

AUMF	Authorization for the Use of Military Force
CEP	circular error probable
CIA	Central Intelligence Agency
COIN	counterinsurgency
DFC	Distinguished Flying Cross
FAA	Federal Aviation Administration
ICRC	International Committee of the Red Cross
IDF	Israel Defense Forces
GPS	Global Positioning System
NATO	North Atlantic Treaty Organization
PGM	precision-guided munition
PTSD	post-traumatic stress disorder
UAV	uninhabited aerial vehicle
UK	United Kingdom
UN	United Nations
UNSC	United Nations Security Council
US	United States
USAF	United States Air Force
USIR	*Unmanned Systems Integrated Roadmap*

1 Introduction

On a hot August night in 2009, a man named Baitullah Mehsud lay on the rooftop of his father-in-law's house. The house was in the village of Zanghara in the remote and mountainous region of South Waziristan in north-west Pakistan, close to the border with Afghanistan. The man, a diabetic, was at the time receiving a leg massage as well as an intravenous drip to treat dehydration and stomach problems. Suddenly, the house was engulfed in flame as two Hellfire air-to-surface missiles slammed into it, instantly killing the man and 11 other people. Baitullah Mehsud was the leader of the Pakistani Taliban, and the missiles had been fired from an uninhabited aerial vehicle (UAV) or 'drone' hovering, undetected, about two miles above the house.[1] According to the Government of Pakistan, Mehsud was the mastermind of the 2007 assassination of former Prime Minister Benazir Bhutto and responsible for many suicide bombings across the border in Afghanistan. The decision to kill him, and the pressing of a button to make it happen, reportedly took place almost 7,000 miles away at the headquarters of the Central Intelligence Agency (CIA), a non-military agency of the United States (US) Government.[2] The person who, via satellite, remotely operated the drone and released the missiles was probably either a CIA officer or a former member of the US military working under contract to the Agency. He or she would have been sitting at a console with a keyboard, a steering device resembling a joystick, and three television screens (one with live video feed from the drone flying over Pakistan, one displaying technical data on the drone, and a third showing a navigation map).[3] For hours or days prior to the missile strike on Mehsud, the operator and others would have been watching live, close-up video footage of the house in South Waziristan captured by the drone's powerful camera. This particular drone strike was the last of 15 that had specifically targeted Mehsud,[4] but it is unclear how many deaths (if any) resulted from the previous 14 attempts on his life.

Since 2004 the US Government has been pursuing an undeclared but not-so-secret policy of using armed drones to launch air strikes against human targets inside Pakistan. Details of the circumstances surrounding the killing of Baitullah Mehsud can only be gleaned from media reports citing anonymous Pakistani and US intelligence officials, so the facts are perhaps not precisely as described above. However, this account fairly characterizes the technologies and processes that enable government agents in the United States to transcend time and space in order to kill a particular person at a precise location, virtually anywhere in the world. Unlike a missile, a drone is a reusable weapons platform, and the putative military value for its ground-based user lies not just in its capacity to strike but also in its capacity to observe. This combination manifests in a deadly new form of power projection which rests largely (for the present) in the hands of the most powerful state actor in the world. The financial and operational commitment of the US military to drone warfare is increasing, and the underlying technologies are advancing rapidly. There has not, however, been a commensurate amount of debate over the embrace of something that might be regarded as politically desirable and yet morally worrisome: risk-free killing. The purpose of this book is to contribute to that debate by offering an ethical analysis of the use of armed drones. The analysis focuses on the United States, which has engaged most extensively in the use of this technology (in Afghanistan, Iraq, Pakistan, Libya, Yemen and Somalia), although the lessons to be drawn from US experience are applicable to any other country that uses or seeks to use armed drones.

Drones

Military drones come in a range of sizes – from the 8-inch-long Wasp Micro UAV with a range of five nautical miles, to the 44-foot-long Global Hawk with a range of 5,400 nautical miles[5] – and most are not equipped with weapons. It is also the case that unarmed drones are used by civilian actors for a variety of non-military purposes. For example, the surveillance capability of a camera-equipped drone can assist with such tasks as border monitoring, assessing damage to critical infrastructure (e.g. nuclear power plants), guiding search and rescue workers at natural disaster sites, monitoring weather patterns, searching for persons missing in difficult terrain, and tracking the spread of large-scale fires. From an ethical perspective, there is much that could be written about the use of unarmed drones for surveillance purposes in a domestic context. For example, one important area of concern is public safety. In the dense air traffic environment above major cities, drones need to be airworthy, and capable of avoiding other aircraft, including those carrying a large number of passengers, or stationary objects. In the United States, the Federal Aviation Administration Modernization and Reform Act (2012) requires the FAA to plan for the safe integration of uninhabited systems into the civil airspace 'as soon as practicable, but not later than September 30, 2015'.[6] Safety concerns there had been accentuated in August 2010 when, due to a 'software issue', operators briefly lost control of a US Navy MQ-8B Fire Scout helicopter flying at 2,000 feet which then drifted into the crowded and restricted airspace over Washington, DC.[7] Another issue worthy of ethical assessment is the impact of drone-based surveillance on personal privacy. Remote-controlled and highly mobile sensor platforms enable surveillance (possibly covert) at unprecedented levels of intensity, intrusiveness and endurance. As a result, individuals concerned for their privacy might build up inhibitions about exercising such rights as free movement, free speech, free assembly and free association.[8]

The drones used in civilian contexts tend to be small and light. When it comes to the use of force, however, the size and payload capacity of a drone must be sufficient for carrying weapons. Accordingly, discussion in this book is restricted to drones classified by the North Atlantic Treaty Organisation (NATO) as Class III (weighing more than 600 kilograms), although it is possible that smaller and lighter drones – Class II (150 to 600 kilograms) and Class I (under 150 kilograms) – will carry a lethal payload in the future. The best-known Class III drone is the Predator which, when unarmed, can provide reconnaissance and target-identification capabilities. When equipped with Hellfire missiles, the Predator becomes a platform for both surveillance and strike. A round mounting (known as the Ball) under the nose of this drone carries two television cameras (one for seeing during the day and an infrared one for night time), and a radar device that facilitates viewing through clouds, smoke or dust, but it also carries a laser designator to lock onto any targets detected by the cameras and radar.[9] The operational advantage that armed drones afford was neatly encapsulated by US President Barack Obama in a speech to the White House Correspondents Dinner in May 2010. Purporting to protect his young daughters from the amorous attentions of some young male pop stars in attendance, the president joked: 'The Jonas Brothers are here; they're out there somewhere. Sasha and Malia are huge fans. But boys, don't get any ideas. I have two words for you, "predator drones". You will never see it coming.'[10]

Stand-off military technologies that surprise an enemy are by no means without precedent. Indeed, German torpedoes during World War II provided a great advantage because 'the weapon did not leave a wake and could not be spotted early by defenders to either take evasive or offensive action'.[11] Likewise, long-range artillery, missiles, and inhabited aircraft enable the waging of war over great physical distances and, potentially, beyond the range of retaliation. A question that frequently arises with regard to drones is whether the advent of this technology signals change or continuity. Throughout history, new military technologies – the crossbow, gunpowder, the machine gun, the tank and the submarine, to take just a few examples – have occasioned debate over the changing character of war. Each innovation in its time has prompted a mixture of outrage, awe and soul-searching on the part of users and victims alike. In one sense, therefore, the present degree of scholarly and journalistic attention to the rise of armed drones is nothing new, and there is a strong resonance with reactions to the initial introduction of older and now-familiar military technologies. In another sense, however, the advent of drones really is an unprecedented development because it has achieved the first complete surmounting of physical limits of time and space in military affairs. The aircraft already exists, but it is controlled by an on-board pilot. The long-range missile already exists, but travel-time from launch to impact is measured in minutes. Unlike the pilot of an aeroplane and the launcher of a long-range missile, the operator of a drone – a platform that combines aircraft and missile technology – is able almost instantaneously to kill another person as far away as on the other side of the world. This is genuinely new, even if it is more evolutionary than revolutionary.

Ethically speaking, any observation that 'there is nothing new' about drones is one that misses the point. Even if the use of armed drones does not introduce an entirely new form of killing, such use might still exacerbate or expand existing moral concerns about when and how force may be used. A moral concern need not be novel to be important, so it does not diffuse an ethical debate over the use of drones to argue that these are only as bad as, for example, B-52 bombers. That something equally bad has occurred in the past means neither that the older technology has *become* morally acceptable nor that the newer technology *is* morally acceptable. Later chapters of this book draw comparisons to the use of inhabited military aircraft in the course of exploring the ethical questions of when and how armed drones may be used. However, the fact that drones are uninhabited injects a sufficient degree of newness into airpower as to require fresh ethical consideration. Specifically, if drones cross a line between a mode of killing that entails reduced risk to the killer and a mode of killing that is risk-free, it is worth asking whether war is going on at all. This is a vital question because of the relationship between war and ethics.

War and ethics

When contemplating military technologies, the tendency of many scholars and policy-makers is to think only in terms of what is possible. However, if war is to remain (if ever it was to begin with) a pursuit more virtuous than organized murder, it is vital also to think in terms of what is permissible. War is a state of affairs, but 'war' is also a political term of art that 'gives a certain status and connotation to violence' as actors attempt to 'legitimize and formalize the violence in which they engage'.[12] Ethics is thus constitutive of the practice of war as a form of violence that is (or is held to be) morally distinguishable from other forms (for example, violence carried out for law enforcement or murderous purposes). Colin Gray has observed that states conducting their international affairs 'have always felt the need to provide moral justification for their acts', and that the credibility of moral claims 'can be a potent source of strategic advantage and disadvantage'.[13] Binding war to ethical principles is not just valuable instrumentally, however; it is also inherently important precisely because all wars are a human tragedy. A widely used tool for ethical assessment is the centuries-old and constantly debated legitimization framework known as the just war tradition. This framework is comprised of two strands: *jus ad bellum* (the justice of going to war) and *jus in bello* (the just conduct of war). Just war theory within Western philosophical traditions traces its origins to the fourth century when, after Christianity became the official religion of the Roman Empire, Christian ethics on violence shifted from strict pacifism to a belief in the right or duty to fight for a just cause. A series of moral thinkers and legal theorists developed just war doctrine over the centuries, including Augustine (AD 354–430), Thomas Aquinas (1225–74) and Hugo Grotius (1583–1645). Today, secularized notions of just war are influential components of international laws, such as the 1949 Geneva Conventions (*jus in bello*) and certain provisions of the 1945 United Nations (UN) Charter (*jus ad bellum*).

Although adherence to rules is commonly held out as having the potential (to some extent at least) to redeem war morally, the just war tradition may rightly be subjected to criticism. Some welcome the principles within this tradition as providing a pragmatic framework for civilizing the inevitable human tendency to war, whereas others deride these as merely a sophisticated litany of excuses for departing from a pacifist ethics. Tony Burke, for example, has argued that the 'formal rigidity of just war theory, which allows it to tolerate the killing of innocents provided it is done within its rules, fetishizes procedure over complexity and "intention" over effects'.[14] And Jeff McMahan has lamented that 'as soon as conditions arise to which the word "war" can be applied, our scruples vanish and killing people no longer seems a horrifying crime but becomes instead a glorious achievement'.[15] A response to the latter observation might be that, through adherence to just war principles, 'our scruples' engage (rather than 'vanish') by prohibiting our *deliberate* killing of certain *kinds* of people (non-combatants) and by leading us to pursue by violent means only causes that are just.

From its earliest years, air-based violence specifically has been often advocated as a mode of restrained warfare that could reduce the overall duration and suffering of war. In the United States, for example, Brigadier General William Mitchell argued in 1925 that using an independent air force to attack an enemy nation's industrial and economic works would benefit not only his own country but also the enemy nation. According to Mitchell, the benefits of airpower would be the avoidance of costly land battles (such as those seen in World War I), the shortening of wars by attacks on the heart of the enemy nation instead of its military forces, and ultimately the saving of much blood and treasure on both sides. In other words, airpower was supposed to give rise to a new and more humane type of warfare.[16] The world war that followed demonstrated, unfortunately, that any form of warfare can be exercised in an unrestrained fashion if the political will to do so is present. When British Air Chief Marshal Arthur Harris took over Bomber Command on 14 February 1942, the British Government ordered: 'the primary object of your operations should now be focussed on the morale of the enemy civil population and in particular of the industrial workers.'[17] Accordingly, Harris directed the strategic bombing of German cities until the end of World War II in Europe. There was a sense afterwards that 'what he had done was ugly', and Michael Walzer reports that there seemed to have been 'a conscious decision not to celebrate the exploits of Bomber Command or to honor its leader'.[18] It was at the end of this conflict in the Pacific theatre, however, that the potential horror and inhumanity of airpower reached its zenith, when the US bomber Enola Gay dropped an atomic bomb on the Japanese city of Hiroshima.

As a form of airpower, armed drones tend to be considered not in terms of awesome destructive power but rather in terms of precise application of minimal force. And whereas the crews of World War II bomber aircraft suffered heavy casualties, a key *raison d'être* of the drone is to remove its operator from physical risk. Given the newness of drone technology, there is no vast record of empirical data to which just war analysis can be directed. Nevertheless, it is not only possible but also important to offer ethical assessments – albeit ones that are sometimes necessarily speculative – before particular military technologies have been used or are used extensively. New forms of warfare challenge us to rethink traditional ethical principles that govern and restrain the use of force, but equally the enduring normative power of such principles challenges us to look for what is good and bad about a given technological innovation. A caveat to this is that, for the ethics of war to apply, there must first be war. Although the character of war – how, by whom and for what purpose it is waged – can and does change, the nature of war is immutable. War, to be war, must be a contest. For the Prussian major-general Carl von Clausewitz (author of the seminal work *On War*) it was 'the element of the thing itself' that 'War is nothing but a duel on an extensive scale', and he likened it to a match between 'two wrestlers' each of whom 'strives by physical force to compel the other to submit to his will'.[19] Arguably, if killing occurs in circumstances that cannot plausibly be characterized as a contest, such killing is not in the nature of war. It follows that a non-war cannot be just in the sense of being able to occupy the unique moral space for permissible killing that war provides. Because drone technology enables risk-free killing, it arguably poses a fundamental challenge to the traditional notion of war as something morally distinguishable from other forms of violence, and it also challenges the professional virtue of the warrior as a courageous risk-taker. The ideas and information provided in this book are focused on this dual challenge.

Armed drones and the ethics of war

Physical risk (and the avoidance thereof) is central to the next chapter, which situates America's use of armed drones in a political and strategic context. Whereas in past wars fought for great purposes there was an implied willingness to accept a large number of casualties, there is today arguably a preference in the West for so-called 'post-heroic' forms of warfare characterized by reduced risk to both the wielders and the victims of force. This is the background for understanding how and why the United States came to use armed drones, why such use (including by other countries) is likely to increase and develop in the future, and why it is important now and in the long term for judgement and decision-making on this issue to be guided by an awareness of ethical principles.

Chapter 3 offers an ethical assessment of the effect that the availability of drone technology has on political decisions to use force. A fundamental principle in just war thinking is that, as war inevitably brings much death and destruction, the burden falls on those who favour the use of force to explain why it is morally justified. The chapter discusses armed drones in the light of six criteria (each related to the others) for justly resorting to force (*jus ad bellum*): just cause, proportionate cause, right authority, right intention, reasonable prospect of success, and last resort.[20] The overarching question is whether the availability of remotely controlled drones (as distinct from inhabited aircraft) lowers the threshold for deciding to go to war. It may be, for example, that this technology causes decision-makers to feel less anxious when contemplating the use of force to solve political problems, since the traditional countervailing moral considerations as regards one's own side (deaths, injuries, grieving families) no longer apply.

The fourth chapter considers the moral permissibility of armed drones as a particular mode of conducting warfare. The focus is on Pakistan where the US Government has used drones most extensively, in a large-scale campaign of air strikes that is simultaneously conspicuous and shrouded in official secrecy. The analysis in this case study details uncertainties regarding the ethical soundness of these strikes and highlights the consequent need for greater official transparency. Available evidence is assessed in the light of three interrelated criteria for the just conduct of war (*jus in bello*): that the use of force is necessary and beneficial to the achievement of a legitimate military objective; that it discriminates between combatants and non-combatants; and that the anticipated harm (including unintended non-combatant deaths) is proportional to the expected military benefit. The murky picture that emerges is an inadequate foundation for determining finally whether US drone strikes in Pakistan constitute a just or an unjust use of force. Arguably, however, the very persistence of doubt on this point undermines international norms on the use of force and the reputation of the United States as a champion thereof.

The relationship between *jus ad bellum* and *jus in bello* principles is central to the discussion in Chapter 5. The use of armed drones sets up a circumstance of radical asymmetry in the use of force where, from the perspective of the stronger side, the risks that usually accompany the conduct of war are not as great an impediment to resorting to war. In an uncontested airspace, and with drone operators in a remote location experiencing no physical risk, force can be applied with apparent impunity. This potentially poses ethical difficulties, first, if it affects an enemy's ability to exercise an inherent right of self-defence and, second, if it constitutes the systemic transferral of risk from combatants to non-combatants. The chapter explores ways of surmounting these difficulties, including by abandoning the traditional notion that combatants on each side of a conflict are morally equal in terms of their licence to kill and their liability to be killed. Further to this notion, in Chapter 6 the focus shifts from war to warriors, and attention turns to the status of a drone operator as a moral agent. At issue is whether a drone operator's purpose and actions are genuinely warlike and thus whether they are consistent with the warrior ethos that sustains the military profession. If the peculiar characteristic of war is that it is a potentially lethal contest in which one combatant using force against another does so in a relationship of mutual risk, the risk-free use of armed drones as a mode of killing challenges traditional notions of what it means to be a warrior. It is nevertheless important to note that, although physical risk is not a realistic prospect for a US-based drone operator, there may still be psychological risks associated with conducting drone strikes.

If physical limitations and risks are what is driving pilots out of aircraft cockpits and into ground-based control stations, psychological risks and mental limitations might be reasons to reduce human control of drones even further or to remove it altogether. Chapter 7 speculates on a hypothetical future of robotic war in which drones are no longer remote-controlled but self-controlled. Although the technology for applying artificial intelligence to achieve military objectives is today in its infancy, there is a strong desire in sections of the US military to pursue with vigour the eventual deployment of lethal autonomous weapon systems that can operate independently in the absence of communication links. From an ethical perspective, however, there are profound problems associated with designing and deploying a machine that can decide for itself to kill a human being. An argument in favour of autonomy is that an armed drone could be programmed to do a better job than humans of avoiding wartime atrocities, but a counterargument is that war (and the ethics of war) is necessarily and inescapably a human affair. Although it might seem fanciful at first to contemplate 'post-human war', the seeds of this idea have been planted already. In the United States and elsewhere in the West, a potent political appetite to reduce risks to human life manifests in a contemporary preference for wars that are post-heroic.

2 Post-heroic war and armed drones

In the past, when wars in the West were fought in a heroic effort to achieve grand purposes, governments and citizens were apparently willing to accept large numbers of casualties. Today, by contrast, there tends to be a preference for 'post-heroic' forms of warfare characterized by reduced physical risk to the wielders of violence and possibly to the victims too. New military technologies afford greater capacity for stand-off and accuracy in the use of force, and the possibilities of airpower are especially attractive. Such is the background for this chapter's discussion of some key technical aspects of armed drones, and of how and why the United States has come to use this technology. Such use (including by other countries) is likely to increase and develop in the future, and this is an important reason for decision-making on this issue to be guided by ethical principles.

Heroic and post-heroic war

Some wars are 'heroic'. The term is not complimentary in the way it might be if used to describe an individual (a 'hero'), but rather it refers to the collective undertaking of an enterprise of killing and dying on a large scale and for a great purpose. In Europe, periods of 'total' war from the eleventh century onwards included the religious wars of 1500–1648, the revolutionary wars of 1789–1815, and the national and ideological wars of 1914–89.[1] Interspersed between these periods were various limited, non-heroic wars fought for lesser purposes and on smaller scales. In the period following the 1648 Peace of Westphalia that ended the brutal Thirty Years War in Europe, armies that had hitherto largely consisted of mercenaries hired on an *ad hoc* basis began to be replaced by professional standing armies. The notion of restraint in the conduct and scale of war – spectacularly defied by rampaging mercenaries – became linked to this development because 'professional armies, representing investment over many years, were very costly and most certainly were too expensive to lose'.[2] Later, however, a combination of industrialism, nationalism and revolutionary fervour in Europe saw vast, professional armies delivering and suffering death on a grand scale. In terms of the sheer quantity of humanity and collective human effort involved, the archetype of heroic war dates from the reign of the French emperor Napoleon

Bonaparte. Michael Ignatieff has written that, whereas war in Europe prior to the French Revolution might have resembled merely 'a tournament between aristocracies', Napoleonic war was by contrast 'democratic' in the sense of being population-based: 'with the whole of the population to draw upon, Napoleon could afford to be profligate with the lives of his soldiers.'[3] The emperor's enemies suffered large losses too, of course, and in the three decades between the Revolution and the final defeat of Napoleon in 1815, as many as three million soldiers and one million civilians lost their lives.[4] Far from seeking to isolate society from war, Revolutionary France sought to render its military effectiveness 'dependent upon the level of popular commitment to the struggle'[5] against the monarchies of Europe, as reflected in the exhortation from *La Marseillaise*: '*Aux armes, citoyens!*'

Harnessing whole societies to a heroic war effort – making a country's capacity to wage war so closely dependent on its domestic productive capacity – precipitated a blurring of the distinction between soldiers and civilians, and this legacy of the nineteenth-century Industrial Revolution achieved extreme manifestation in the two world-wide wars of the century that followed. Christopher Coker has observed that, from the early twentieth century onwards, the heroic effort of the 'virtuous state' in Europe was one of endurance. In fighting against a British, German or Russian enemy, 'The citizen was told he would have to endure long-term sacrifice if the next generation was to escape a worse fate in the future.... The present was the moment in which the future was being secured.'[6] Beyond Europe, heroic war was pursued by the United States too, and Coker has written of 'America's historic mission to rid the world of tyrants', be they 'eighteenth-century [British] kings or twentieth-century German gauleiters' or 'Soviet commissars'.[7] From 1945 onwards, and especially after the American nuclear monopoly was broken, the use of nuclear weapons was a reason to avoid escalation to conflicts as large as the two world wars. At the same time, however, the two Cold War superpowers locked in ideological struggle (the democratic United States against the communist Soviet Union) each threatened the other with maximum damage for the grand cause of national survival which, according to the logic of mutual assured destruction, was to be achieved through national suicide. In his 1961 Inaugural Address, US President John F. Kennedy declared:

> Let every nation know, whether it wishes us well or ill, that we shall pay any price, bear any burden, meet any hardship, support any friend, oppose any foe, in order to assure the survival and the success of liberty.[8]

During and after America's war in Vietnam, however, it became politically more difficult to express such heroic sentiments and to expend heroic efforts. According to Coker, 139,000 young American men refused to be drafted to serve in the Vietnam War mainly because 'historical metaphors such as manifest destiny which had mobilised the nation in the past had begun to lose their imaginative appeal'.[9] Between 1961 and 1975 the United States was nevertheless able to endure 47,364 combat deaths in Vietnam. But by the following decade, the American polity's strong aversion to US casualties had set in, and the deaths of 243 Marines from a truck bomb in Beirut in late 1983 precipitated a rapid abandonment of US operations in Lebanon.[10]

The degree of aversion to casualties is not determined simply by the anticipated or recorded number thereof. Rather, as Richard Betts has argued, the Vietnam War revealed that US public support is undermined by 'casualties in an *inconclusive* war, casualties that the public sees as being suffered indefinitely, for no clear, good, or achievable purpose'.[11] It follows that, in circumstances where political leaders' and the public's attitudes towards a given war differ, a government beholden to its citizens might try to garner more political room to manoeuvre by promising and pursuing casualty rates lower than those experienced in the heroic wars of yore. By 1993 it had been recognised in a US Army Field Manual that: 'The American people expect decisive victory and abhor unnecessary casualties. They prefer quick resolution of conflicts and reserve the right to reconsider their support should any of these conditions not be met.'[12] The turning point for the United States had come just prior to the entry of this and similar statements into military doctrine. In the 1991 Gulf War, for the first time,

> casualty minimization became from the start an independent operational objective; both the formulation of war aims and the conduct of military operations were governed by dread among the... leadership that too many American lives lost would implode public and congressional support for the war.[13]

If, as Mark Clegg has argued, the protection of one's own forces goes to 'the moral component of a nation's fighting power' and serves to reinforce 'national will',[14] this new way of war amounted to a stark reversal of the high-casualty Napoleonic model. No longer heroic, America's wars began to be characterized instead as 'post-heroic'.

The term 'post-heroic war' can be traced to a 1995 article in *Foreign Affairs* magazine by the military historian Edward Luttwak. A higher tolerance for casualties, Luttwak argued, was 'congruent with the demography of pre-industrial and early industrial societies, whereby families had many children and losing some to disease was entirely normal'.[15] For families to lose a child in combat, although tragic, 'was therefore fundamentally less unacceptable than for today's [American] families' with fewer children, each of whom 'is expected to survive into adulthood and embodies a great part of the family's emotional economy'.[16] At the end of the Cold War, birth rates in all the most advanced countries were falling sharply, and parents were far more reluctant to 'sacrifice their male offspring'.[17] Populations in the United States and many other Western countries continue to age, so it is reasonable today to anticipate a future in which a smaller and decreasing number of young people are able (even if willing) to be recruited for military service and deployed to risk their lives in combat. Beyond demographics, the very notion of post-heroic war reflects a fundamental shift in the relationship between the military profession and the civilian society it serves. Over the course of the twentieth century, which eventually saw the ending of conscription in the West, there grew a greater gulf between military and civilian values. Ignatieff's observation in his 2000 book *Virtual War* was that, because 'peace has become a settled expectation of civilian populations', martial sacrifice and death in combat were 'extreme destinies ... increasingly implausible to cultures raised to count on a full adult life'.[18] In the living of that life, there is now less of the 'passive stoicism in the face of great danger'[19] that might have been required of people living in the twentieth and earlier centuries, and a drastic decline in tolerance for combat deaths is arguably to be expected of a society that 'no longer accepts with a fatalistic shrug the notion of accidents and bad luck'.[20] Life in general, perhaps, has become less heroic, and in war specifically the value of the individual has increased commensurate with what Coker sees as 'disillusionment with the great utopian projects of the past'.[21] Indeed, according to Yee-Kuang Heng, 'a negative, if not dystopian, outlook'[22] is instead the characteristic of a society for which war is not the pursuit of noble causes but rather the mere management of risks.

The risks to be managed in post-heroic war include those experienced by individuals as well as by states and entire populations. In both dimensions, military technology has been and remains an important mediating factor. Since at least the time of World War II, which was ended in the Pacific by using newly invented atomic bombs, the American way of war has been characterized by reliance on advanced technology. Airpower in particular – as wielded by the most technology-focused of services, the US Air Force (USAF) – has played a critical role in the shift from heroic to post-heroic war. For Tom Mahnken, US use of airpower throughout the 1990s 'seemed uniquely suited to the types of conflicts in which the United States was involved – wars for limited aims fought with partial means for marginal interests'.[23] And Eliot Cohen has observed that 'air power is an unusually seductive form of military strength, in part because, like modern courtship, it appears to offer gratification without commitment'.[24] With today's military lexicon including such terms as 'coercive diplomacy' and 'precision strikes', airpower is often lauded for being conducive to uses of force that are deliberately restrained in a strategic and/or tactical sense. Consistent with an aversion to strategic risk, the idea is that airpower is a restrained mode of problem-solving that precludes resort to what might be called 'full-scale war' involving the panoply of military capabilities. In addition, airpower is especially well suited to prevailing political appetites if applied in parts of the world where air space is uncontested or poorly contested. The tactical risk to pilots in such circumstances is certainly much less, and the use of 'precision' air-to-surface munitions can be seen as a way of reducing the risks also to other participants and bystanders in a conflict. Chapter 4 discusses problems with the term 'precision' in the context of discrimination between combatants and non-combatants, but for now it is worth noting that the promise of precision cuts two ways in connecting tactical consequences to strategic purposes. On the one hand, because it raises expectations of destroying military targets *without* so-called 'collateral damage', the availability of precision technology might lower leaders' reluctance to use force. On the other hand, if or when those expectations are dashed by the incurring of *any* collateral damage, the consequent loss of public support (at home and abroad) might increase reluctance to use force.

An exemplar of air-powered post-heroic warfare was the 1999 campaign by NATO member states (Operation Allied Force) against Serbia in its southern province of Kosovo. During the campaign, the Serbs' SA-13 anti-aircraft missile – a low-altitude, short-range system – could be evaded simply by flying at a sufficient height,[25] and commanders were so determined not to lose any NATO pilots that they ordered bomber aircraft to remain above 15,000 feet (and thus well beyond the range of retaliation). According to the Kosovo After Action Review presented before the US Senate Armed Services Committee in October 1999, Operation Allied Force was 'an overwhelming success' because

> We forced [President] Milosevic to withdraw from Kosovo, degraded his ability to wage military operations, and rescued and resettled over one million refugees. We accomplished this by prosecuting the most precise and lowest-collateral-damage air campaign in history – with no US or allied combat casualties in 78 days of around-the-clock operations and over 38,000 combat sorties.[26]

In the aftermath of such a result, it is unsurprising that a 2000 report by the Armed Services Committee stated that 'the American people are coming to expect that military operations are casualty-free'.[27] Such expectation did not, however, extend to casualties that might be experienced by enemies of the United States.

The following year, the American people themselves suffered casualties in spectacular fashion, and the armed response that followed continues to this day. In New York City, on the day after the attacks of 11 September 2001, Americans gathered outside the ruined World Trade Center and held placards, some of which read 'We need heroes – Now'.[28] In the week that followed, US President George W. Bush declared: 'I have faith in our military. And we have a job to do... we will rid the world of evil doers.'[29] Military recruitment soared, and the United States soon afterwards used massive force (across the full spectrum of its military capabilities) to overthrow despotic regimes in Afghanistan and Iraq. To rid the world of 'evil doers' seemed a grand purpose indeed, and perhaps Bush's words would have resonated strongly in the bygone era of heroic war. In his 2009 book *Virtuous War*, James Der Derian observed that 'The rhetoric of the [Bush] White House favors and clearly intends to mobilize the moral clarity, nostalgic sentimentality, and uncontested dominance reminiscent of the last great empires against the ambiguities, complexities, and messiness of the current world disorder'.[30] Nevertheless, despite Bush espousing 'noble meta-narratives of democracy and human rights', the impression of others might have been that

'America exuded not optimism but fear' given that the post-war goal in Afghanistan and Iraq was merely to prevent those places from providing safe haven for terrorists.[31] Such a purpose is less grand by far than ridding the world of evil doers, and yet it was still one for which the American people were apparently willing to spill much American blood for a lengthy period. As of the end of 2012, US military casualties in Afghanistan (Operation Enduring Freedom) were, according to official statistics: 2,153 fatalities and 18,116 wounded in action. And in Iraq (Operation Iraqi Freedom), the United States suffered 4,409 military fatalities and 31,925 personnel wounded in action.[32] Moreover, the combined economic cost to the United States of the wars in Afghanistan and Iraq has been estimated to be nearly US$4 trillion.[33] Perhaps it was premature, therefore, for Sir Charles Guthrie, who directed the British contribution to the 1999 Kosovo campaign, to declare shortly afterwards that 'western society is not very well adjusted to the prospect of fighting. It involves risks to people's lives when they have become used to the idea of not having to die for their beliefs.'[34] Although Coker insists that the casualties of the US-led War on Terror 'number far fewer than those of an average-size Napoleonic battle',[35] the human and economic costs of the former must seem large, and the effort a heroic one, to twenty-first-century civilian Westerners who have grown accustomed to peace. Even if the War on Terror began as a heroic one, it nevertheless may be that such a war could not long withstand the post-heroic impulse to reduce risks to American personnel. By 2010 this concern appeared to have extended even to the 'deaths' of virtual American soldiers: military bases across the country banned the sale of a new version of the video game *Medal of Honor* in which a player could pretend to be a Taliban fighter and shoot US troops in Afghanistan.[36] US ground forces have since withdrawn from Iraq and (as at the time of writing) are preparing to withdraw from Afghanistan. Elsewhere, however, the War on Terror continues to be conducted from the air, albeit increasingly without Americans being *in* the air.

The rise of armed drones

In his 1989 book *The Rise of American Airpower*, Michael Sherry observed that the aeroplane was never viewed solely as a weapon but also as the instrument of 'a whole new dimension in human activity ... uniquely capable of ... transforming man's sense of time and space, transcending geography, ... releasing humankind from its biological limits'.[37] Historically, however, military uses of aircraft have generally not seen humans released from the physical requirement of onboard control. Piloting an aircraft has usually meant being present therein, and that presence has sometimes entailed a high degree of physical risk. The world's first aerial bombardment occurred in November 1911, during the Italian-Turkish War over Libya, when the Italian army pilot Giolio Gavotti threw four bombs out of his cockpit onto a camp of enemy troops to the east of Tripoli.[38] Although aircraft enabled the Italians to hold the 'high ground' there, opposing combatants on the ground and in the air still fought in a relationship of mutual risk: on

25 August 1912 Petro Manzini became the first aeroplane pilot killed in war, not as a result of enemy fire but in a flying accident.[39] In Europe during World War II, airspace was fiercely contested, and bomber crews generally had the highest casualty rates among combatants in the Allied forces. In the British Bomber Command, for example, only 24 out of every 100 men survived.[40] Even during NATO's 1999 Kosovo campaign, commonly cited as an example of the risk-free use of airpower, the alliance suffered human losses when two US Apache helicopters crashed during training in Albania; one crash was due to human error and the other was due to technical failure.[41] Thus it seems that a true and complete surmounting of what Sherry calls humankind's 'biological limits' is to use aircraft in a way that does not endanger the user.

Starting in the 1950s, aircraft carrying cameras and/or other sensors to gather intelligence increasingly became uninhabited and controlled by operators situated on the ground. These early drones, stingless (unarmed) like their male honeybee namesake, had a limited range, could only stay in the air for short periods, and were prone to communications and control problems.[42] During the Vietnam War, for example, US drones took photographs of less than half of their planned reconnaissance targets, mainly due to navigation errors.[43] Gradually, due to technological advances, the military utility of drones increased as they became more durable and reliable. An early version of the Predator made its debut in the Balkan wars of the 1990s, gathering information for US military commanders on refugee flows and Serb air defences.[44] The use of drones for information-gathering spared pilots from the physical risks associated with such activity, but inhabited aircraft were at this time still the dominant means of exercising air power. Pilots, then as now, were precious, and in 1995 the USAF flew 500 manned missions over five days to rescue Captain Scott O'Grady after his F-16 fighter jet was brought down over Bosnia.[45] Not only was the use of inhabited aircraft in that theatre of conflict risky, it was also expensive. Two years previously, a study by military aviation firm Lockheed Martin had found that

> Tomahawk cruise missiles, used extensively in the 1991 Gulf War, offered only a partial solution to the need to strike targets without risk of pilot loss or capture ... since a $1.4 million airframe is thrown away every time a cruise missile flies.[46]

A better solution, predicted by Lockheed Martin employee Armand Chaput in the year after the O'Grady episode, was that the 'unmanned tactical aircraft' would end up one day as a delivery weapon for the United States because 'we continue to get involved in wars in which loss of life is not an acceptable alternative'.[47] A similar allusion to post-heroic war was contained in a recent United Kingdom (UK) document on British military doctrine which stated: 'the capture and exploitation of downed aircrew by an enemy may have a considerable effect on the morale of one's own forces and, particularly in today's wars-of-choice, may affect the support given to the campaign by a nation's domestic population.'[48]

Just as the pilots of early forms of aircraft (used mainly for surveillance) started dropping grenades out of their open cockpits, so too the original RQ-1 Predator (R for 'reconnaissance') was transformed into the MQ-1 Predator (M for 'multipurpose'). This drone became a 'hunter-killer' following the test-firing in February 2001 of mounted AGM-114 Hellfire anti-tank missiles that are normally fired from attack helicopters.[49] Equipped with two of these 100-pound air-to-surface munitions, today's Predators can strike at a range approaching 5 miles. The US Army uses a version of the Predator (known as the Gray Eagle) which has a few more reconnaissance and strike capabilities, and the MQ-9 Reaper – faster, larger and with greater payload capacity – was the first drone purpose-built to be armed (see Table 2.1).

At present, drones almost always fly for hours at a time in a benign air environment where the enemies of the United States have little or no air-defence capability. However, research and development is under way into combat drones – featuring greater payload and speed as well as stealth capabilities – that are 'designed to carry air-to-air weapons and other systems that may allow them to undertake air superiority missions'.[50] One example is the prototype Avenger, a jet-powered drone manufactured by General Atomics Aeronautical Systems (which also manufactures the Predator and the Reaper). Faster than its turboprop-powered predecessors, the Avenger would be better able to prevail in air combat, especially if equipped with air-to-air missiles (such as the AIM-9 Sidewinders used on the Reaper).[51]

Since 1911, inhabited aircraft have provided valuable military capabilities, but drone technology increasingly promises and delivers comparable capabilities at a lower cost. A single drone system consists of four aircraft, a ground station, a satellite link, and a maintenance crew at the launch site on a local base, but the system is nonetheless considerably less expensive than a single inhabited fighter jet. A Predator system costs US$20 million and a Reaper system US$53 million.[52] By comparison, a F-22 fighter costs about US$150 million.[53] Cost issues aside, there is also the matter of pilot vulnerability. The central idea behind an air force – inhabited (or 'manned') flight – had begun to be questioned following World War II when long-range guided missiles were developed,[54] and now a point has been reached where the US military's next inhabited combat aircraft (the F-35 Joint Strike Fighter) is predicted to be its last.[55] Thereafter, drone operators will be expected to take on every type of mission currently flown by the pilots of inhabited aircraft. The trend towards greater reliance on drones faces some resistance within the USAF, not least because combat pilots continue to dominate that service's leadership. Nevertheless, the momentum has already shifted, and since 2009 the Air Force has been training more drone operators than fighter pilots.[56] The drone inventory of the Defense Department as a whole has grown rapidly, from 167 in 2002 to nearly 7,500 in 2010,[57] and inhabited aircraft made up 69 per cent of all US military aircraft at the end of 2011 (compared to 95 per cent in 2005).[58] The number of drones is expected to increase by a further 35 per cent in the decade to 2020, and the bulk of planned spending is for the more expensive large- and medium-sized drones designed to conduct

Table 2.1 US armed drones

System (no. of vehicles)	Length (ft)	Wingspan (ft)	Gross weight (lbs)	Endurance (hrs)	Maximum altitude (ft)	Payload capacity (lbs)	Hellfire missiles
MQ-1A/B Predator (161)	27	55	2,250	24+	25,000	450	2
MQ-1C Gray Eagle (26)	28	56	3,200	40	25,000	800	4
MQ-9 Reaper (54)	36	66	10,500	24	50,000	3,750	16 (or a mix of 500-pound and small diameter bombs)

Data sourced from Jeremiah Gertler, *US Unmanned Aerial Systems*, Washington, DC: Congressional Research Service, 3 January 2012, pp. 8, 31, 33–5.

reconnaissance missions and/or attack ground targets.[59] Around 730 of these will be purchased, and money will also be spent improving drones already in service. All told, the US Congressional Budget Office has estimated the cost at around US$36.9 billion over ten years,[60] including over US$13 billion on Reapers (an extra 288) and 'next-generation' Reapers alone.[61]

The United States clearly anticipates a future need to increase the scale and intensity of its drone use. More evidence of this is that competition is under way among US defence contractors to develop 'unmanned blimps' capable of hovering at an altitude of 70,000 feet for months at a time while carrying a 4,000-pound payload (including weapons).[62] In addition, the US Navy hopes by 2018 to be able to deploy Unmanned, Carrier-Launched Airborne Surveillance and Strike aircraft,[63] perhaps to counter the long-range 'carrier killer' missile that China is reportedly developing. With an operational range three times greater than the Navy's existing fighter jets, a sea-based drone of this kind would allow a US carrier group to stay further away from China's coast and Chinese land-based missiles.[64] For the time being, however, the United States is heavily occupied using Predators and Reapers against adversaries that are vastly weaker. US drones target individuals inside territories where the United States engages openly in armed conflict (Afghanistan, Iraq and Libya) as well as in territories where it does not (Pakistan, Somalia and Yemen). Correspondingly, drones are used in two different ways: the military predominantly employs them for surveillance and air-support to assist American troops conducting various ground-based missions in combat zones, whereas the CIA uses drones to strike individuals deemed to be terrorists in areas far removed from what would traditionally be perceived as a battlefield.[65]

Military use of armed drones in open warfare has been of longest duration in Afghanistan, and the war that began there in late 2001 was the first in which drones are known to have been used as weapons platforms.[66] In the Third Afghan War of 1919, the British secured victory after 'three bombs dropped on Kabul finally persuaded the Emir to concede defeat'.[67] By contrast, modern-day US forces operating beyond Kabul have found that airpower is far from decisive. The main challenges in the US military's initial air campaign were Afghanistan's large area, uneven terrain, low target density, and long distance from the nearest US bases in the region. Inhabited aircraft could spend little time over their Afghan targets because they had to fly sorties from aircraft carriers in the Arabian Sea, from the Indian Ocean island of Diego Garcia, or even from bases in the US mainland.[68] These physical challenges were soon overcome in large measure by effecting a separation of aircraft and pilot. Predators (and later Reapers) came to be assembled, maintained, armed, launched and landed in-theatre, but their surveillance and strike functions remained under the control of drone crews seated in ground-control stations at Creech Air Force Base, Nevada (31 miles from Las Vegas). In what became a wide-ranging counterinsurgency in which the efforts of ground troops spread thin over a large area were of primary importance, a combination of inhabited and uninhabited aircraft provided support in the form of surveillance and strike capabilities. Similarly, in

Iraq from 2003 to 2012, armed drones and other military aircraft supported what was in essence a ground-based campaign, although drones were used earlier to help enforce no-fly zones over southern Iraq.[69] In Libya in 2011, the United States again used armed drones to support ground forces, but this time these were the only aircraft used and the ground forces were those of Libyan rebels seeking the overthrow of President Muammar Gaddafi.[70]

The use of armed drones in Afghanistan, Iraq and Libya was openly acknowledged as assisting the pursuit of US military goals in terms of things happening on the ground. Covert uses of drones are of particular interest, however, because these have entailed their use in a stand-alone capacity. In such circumstances, it is easier to discern the operational effects and ethical implications of armed drones in and of themselves. A peculiar characteristic of America's secret drone strike campaigns, moreover, has been the lethal participation of intelligence professionals rather than military ones. In early November 2002 the CIA carried out what appeared to be its first drone-based 'targeted killing'[71] in Yemen. Anonymous sources from within the US Government revealed that six suspected Al Qaeda members died when the vehicle they were travelling in (on a road 100 miles east of Yemen's capital city, Sana'a) was hit by a missile fired from a CIA Predator. According to Yemeni sources, those killed included Ali Qaed Senyan al-Harthi, a man the US Government had linked to the October 2000 attack on the warship USS *Cole* off the coast of Aden in which 17 American sailors lost their lives.[72] In a television interview on 5 November 2002, US Deputy Defense Secretary Paul Wolfowitz effectively acknowledged US responsibility for the Yemen drone strike: 'it's a very successful tactical operation.... And one hopes each time you get a success like that, [you] not only have gotten rid of somebody dangerous, but [you] have imposed changes in their tactics and operations and procedures.'[73] On the same day, Swedish Foreign Minister Anna Lindh called the strike 'a summary execution that violates human rights',[74] and political disagreement over the military benefits and ethical downsides of covert drone strikes has persisted ever since. Not until nearly nine years later did another CIA drone strike occur inside Yemen,[75] but by September 2011 the reported belief of US intelligence officials was that members of Al Qaeda inside Yemen were posing a greater threat than members inside Pakistan.[76] In June of that year, drone strikes had been extended to Somalia,[77] with US drones operating there and in Yemen flying from bases in Djibouti, Ethiopia and the Seychelles.[78] The territory in which the United States has conducted drone strikes most extensively and most conspicuously is Pakistan, and the scale and nature of this CIA campaign are described in detail in Chapter 4. For now, it is worth noting that, in contrast to the apparent acquiescence of Yemeni and Somali leaders, Pakistani politicians have regularly and loudly denounced the US Government's use of armed drones as a violation of their country's sovereignty.[79]

Political objections aside, in all the places where the United States has deployed armed drones, these aircraft have remained unmolested in the sense of enjoying air superiority. However, in other circumstances and in the future, air superiority might first need to be won by drones themselves. Here it is worth noting that, prior to the 2003 US-led invasion of Iraq, Predators enforcing a no-fly zone fired air-to-air Stinger missiles at Iraqi MiG fighters,[80] and in November 2012, Iranian jets fired their 30-millimetre cannons at a Predator conducting surveillance over the Persian Gulf.[81] Beyond such challenges posed by inhabited enemy aircraft, the United States also faces the prospect of one day confronting (at home or abroad) an armed, non-American drone. Besides the United States, the only countries known to have used armed drones are Britain (in Afghanistan) and Israel (against Hezbollah in Lebanon and against Hamas in Gaza).[82] However, just as there is pressure for the relevant technology to proliferate vertically, so too it is likely to proliferate horizontally as its apparent operational advantages become more widely attractive. In a 2010 report, for example, the US Defense Security Service warned that American drone technology had become a prime target for foreign spies.[83] With or without unauthorized access to US blueprints, there are states that are probably pursuing their own capacity to deploy armed drones, while some of America's allies (Australia, Germany, Italy and Turkey) appear to be interested in formal agreements to acquire such a capacity from the United States.[84] Already, dozens of other states – including states that the United States would regard as potential adversaries – use unarmed drones for surveillance purposes, and many of these have started in-country development programmes for armed versions because US exports thereof are restricted.[85] A rapid increase in drone research and development in China, for example, was described by the US Defense Science Board in 2012 as 'a worrisome trend'.[86] Worldwide, the number of different drone programmes was recently estimated to be 680 (there were 195 in 2005), and one prediction is that global expenditure on such programmes will be at double 2011 levels by 2020.[87] Such a situation can plausibly be described as an arms race; a global race to build more drones to higher levels of technical sophistication.

Conclusion

In the United States, the rise of armed drones continues a trend away from heroic war and towards post-heroic war. In large measure, it is being driven by a desire both to manage strategic risks as much as possible from the air and to avoid exposing America's tactical users of force to physical risk. Demographic changes and prevailing societal sensibilities inside the United States are such that, in a post-heroic age, the life of every American (warriors included) is more precious and less dispensable. The War on Terror that began in 2001 might for a time have been heroic in nature – involving two large-scale military commitments and costing thousands of US combat deaths – but Americans' intolerance of human and economic costs is resurging in what is increasingly regarded as a war of choice rather than necessity. As ground troops depart the field, the option of fighting more from the air holds greater appeal, especially if those who control the aircraft are not at physical risk. It will probably not be long, however, before the numerical and technical superiority of America's armed drones comes to be challenged by other actors, and there are signs that the US Government sees the wisdom and virtue of championing normative limitations on the use of armed drones. In April 2012 the White House's counterterrorism adviser, John Brennan, described those within the Obama Administration as 'very mindful that, as our nation uses this technology, we are establishing precedents that other nations may follow', and he warned that 'not all of those nations ... share our interests or the premium we put on protecting human life, including innocent civilians'.[88] Such remarks invite ethical consideration of the use of armed drones, and specifically whether it could generate an unjust increase in the incidence and/or lethality of armed conflict. Accordingly, the next chapter begins by assessing armed drones in the light of just war principles governing the resort to force.

3 Drones and the war threshold

As more armed drones become available to more states, the degree of political willingness and the number of perceived opportunities to use them are likely to increase. From an ethical perspective, the challenge posed by more frequent drone use is to guard against any associated increase in the number of unjust decisions to resort to force at all. In 2011 a UK Ministry of Defence Joint Doctrine Note warned

> It is essential that, before unmanned systems become ubiquitous (if it is not already too late), we... ensure that, by removing some of the horror, or at least keeping it at a distance, we do not risk losing our controlling humanity and make war more likely.[1]

The Note's author could well have recalled an observation made during the US Civil War by the Confederate general Robert E. Lee at the 1862 Battle of Fredericksburg: 'It is well that war is so terrible, or we would grow too fond of it.'[2] Lee's words should not be taken to imply that war *ought* to be as terrible as possible, but rather they point to a causal link between the horrors of war and a reluctance to experience same. Just as psychologists might argue that human motivations and behaviour are partly a factor of weighing incentives and disincentives, so economists might argue that demand for a product (war) increases as the price (terribleness) goes down.[3] If so, it is a plausible proposition that, in circumstances where the physical risks to one's own forces are greatly reduced (or nil), there is less (or no) reason to hesitate before waging war. Political leaders, having less cause to contemplate the prospect of deaths, injuries and grieving families, might accordingly feel less anxious about using force to solve political problems. And citizens, if not called upon to spill their own blood for a cause, might feel less inclined to 'dissuade leaders from foreign misadventures and ill-planned aggression'.[4] Moreover, if violent solutions to political problems come at little cost (in terms of physical risk and political opprobrium) there is perhaps less reason to be rigorous in the pursuit of non-violent solutions. For the would-be user of force, the difference between the two options (violence and non-violence) would not be so great, and indeed the latter might be dismissed as insufficiently decisive or overly time-consuming.

The prospect of increased availability of armed drones warrants contemplation of a future in which the resort to force is less constrained by the expectation of loss, and this sits uneasily with ethical principles that have traditionally set a high threshold for going to war. Within the just war tradition, the justice of going to war (*jus ad bellum*) is determined according to whether such action has a just and proportionate cause, whether it is properly authorized and motivated by right intention, whether there is a reasonable prospect of success, and whether war is a last resort. Although these principles can be traced to early Christian thought in the late Roman Empire, they resonate in other religious traditions including Islam, the faith of many of those targeted in US drone strikes. Key religious texts pertaining to Shari'a (Islamic law) state that, for a war to be just, 'there must be a legitimate authority, a just cause, and right intention', and a commander 'must consider issues of proportionality and reasonable hope of success'.[5] A *jus ad bellum* assessment of the use of armed drones by reference to Islamic ethics is beyond the scope of this book, but it suffices to note that the principles discussed in this chapter are commonly understood across many cultures.

Just cause

The default ethical position in the just war tradition is that war is wrong. This fundamental principle is manifested in Article 2(4) of the UN Charter which provides that all states 'shall refrain in their international relations from the threat or use of force'.[6] A state seeking to resort to armed force has the onus of proving that the justice of its cause outweighs the inevitable calamity that war would bring. The cause of a state seeking to wage war must also, in order for it to be just, appeal to something of greater moral importance than mere self-interest. A desire to exact revenge, greed for more territory or resources, or simple aggression can all be motivating forces for going to war, but none of these qualifies as a just cause. Contemporary international norms and practices indicate that only two justifications for using force have the potential to pass muster from an ethical perspective: the first is self-defence, and the second is military intervention to prevent or mitigate a large-scale, deliberately caused humanitarian disaster.

Regarding the just cause of self-defence, a restrictive view (based on strict adherence to the wording of Article 51 of the UN Charter) is that the right of self-defence may only be invoked and acted upon 'if an armed attack occurs'.[7] A more permissive view (based on customary international law) is that the right of self-defence may also be exercised against a real and imminent threat when the necessity of that self-defence is 'instant, overwhelming, and leaving no choice of means and no moment of deliberation'.[8] The most permissive view contemplates the use of force even when a threat is not imminent and where uncertainty remains as to the time and place of an enemy's attack. It currently has no foundation under international law, although the need to establish a new norm of 'preventive war' is hotly debated.[9] Prior to the War on Terror, in 1981, Israeli aircraft attacked Iraq's Osirak nuclear facility because of Israel's concern that

Iraq would use the reactor to produce highly enriched uranium for nuclear weapons. Although Israel claimed it was exercising its right of self-defence, the attack attracted widespread international condemnation because Israel could not readily establish that the threat to its security was sufficiently imminent. Following the attacks of 11 September 2001 in the United States, political and intellectual pressure began to be exerted to change notions of what constitutes an 'imminent' threat. The Administration of President George W. Bush argued that the concept of self-defence needed to be expanded to include pre-emptive use of force in order to meet what it saw as the changed circumstances and dynamics of international security. Its 2002 *National Security Strategy* stated:

> We must adapt the concept of imminent threat to the capabilities of today's adversaries.... As was demonstrated by the losses on September 11, 2001, mass civilian casualties is the specific objective of terrorists and these losses would be exponentially more severe if terrorists acquired and used weapons of mass destruction.... To forestall or prevent such hostile acts by our adversaries, the United States will, if necessary, act pre-emptively.[10]

It remains the case, however, that the view of self-defence subscribed to most widely by states is the restrictive view. Reasoning from the position that self-defence is reactive rather than proactive, one could argue that the United States has a just cause for using force, including via armed drones, in Afghanistan on the grounds of self-defence. Indeed, a US State Department lawyer argued in 2010:

> as a matter of international law, the United States is in an armed conflict with al-Qaeda, as well as the Taliban and associated forces, in response to the horrific 9/11 attacks, and may use force consistent with its inherent right to self-defense under international law.[11]

By contrast, it is less easy to characterize US drone strikes (or any other use of force) in Iraq as being essentially defensive. This is because the Iraq War as a whole was one started pre-emptively by the United States rather than in response to an armed attack against it by Iraq. Likewise, drone strikes in Pakistan, Yemen and Somalia (countries with which the United States is not at war) appear rather more pre-emptive than defensive and thus they arguably lack a just cause. Alternatively, if pre-emptive use of force is to be regarded as legitimate, it may be that some individuals are more legitimate targets than others for the purposes of forceful self-defence. For example, regarding drone strikes carried out in Yemen and Somalia, there is debate within the US Government about the scope of its fight against Islamist militants. On the one hand, there is a view (taken by the US State Department) that the United States may only target those few high-level militant leaders who are personally linked to plots to attack the United States. On the other hand, the US Defense Department reportedly insists that force may also be used against the thousands of low-level militants whose political concerns are local.[12] The narrow view is more easily defensible because individuals who are actively plotting to attack the United States more obviously attract (pre-emptive) defensive action than do individuals who merely happen to possess an antipathy towards Americans in a general sense.

In the context of the 2011 civil war in Libya, although US use of armed drones there was not for self-defence, there was nevertheless arguably a just cause in the form of humanitarian intervention. There is a widespread and long-prevailing attitude that military action of this kind violates the fundamental principle of state sovereignty which underpins international stability. However, an emerging and strengthening view in the international community is that intervention is acceptable if civilians are faced with the threat of serious and irreparable harm in the form of genocide, war crimes, ethnic cleansing and crimes against humanity.[13] By the middle of March 2011, Gaddafi's government forces had been about to attack the rebel-held city of Benghazi and, as threatened, to clear its population of one million people 'house by house'.[14] Under such circumstances, the prevention or mitigation of such a humanitarian disaster was a just cause for the use of force. In anticipation of this imminent attack, the UN Security Council (UNSC) authorized the use of 'all necessary measures ... to protect civilians and civilian populated areas under threat of attack ... while *excluding a foreign occupation force* of any form on any part of Libyan territory'.[15] The latter qualification meant airpower (rather than ground troops) was the military instrument of choice, and the United States (a minor contributor compared to European states in the NATO alliance) chose to restrict itself to the use of armed drones.

Right authority and last resort

Determinations regarding proper authorization to wage war relate to the just cause invoked, be it self-defence or humanitarian intervention. The latter requires UNSC authorization, although NATO's 1999 Kosovo intervention might have initiated the emergence of a norm that regional security organizations too may sanction the resort to force. Thus the *jus ad bellum* criterion of right authority appears to have been satisfied (at the international level) when the United States used drones in Libya. At the domestic level, however, establishing right authority for drone strikes is arguably more problematic. If the just cause invoked is self-defence, the defending state has an inherent right to use force (no international authority is required), and the US use of drones in territories other than Libya could be said to be sanctioned by the 2001 Authorization for the Use of Military Force (AUMF). This was and remains Congress's authorization for America's president to exercise the country's right to self-defence and to 'use all necessary and appropriate force' in order to prevent future acts of terrorism against the United States. Two salient features of such authorization are, first, that it grants the president sweeping power to determine who counts as the enemy and, second, that it does not impose geographical limitations of any kind.[16] The idea, presumably, is that nationality and territoriality are meaningless in a global battlefield where terrorist threats transcend international borders. This view was reflected in a 2011 speech by counterterrorism adviser John Brennan at Harvard Law School:

> The United States does not view our authority to use military force against Al Qaeda as being restricted solely to 'hot' battlefields like Afghanistan. Because we are engaged in an armed conflict with Al Qaeda, the United States takes the legal position that – in accordance with international law – we have the authority to take action against Al Qaeda and its associated forces without doing a separate self-defense analysis each time.[17]

That Congress has not revoked or curtailed the AUMF signifies that it is still formally applicable. However, as more time passes and as more events intervene, it is becoming more difficult to maintain that the anti-US violence of America's enemies is a continuation of the same threat that manifested on 11 September 2001. Rather, it could be violence that has an essentially new and different origin. If, for example, the United States was to be still waging a War on Terror in 2019, it is conceivable that a drone strike conducted as part of that war could be directed against an 18-year-old individual. Yet many observers would find it extremely difficult, intuitively, to understand why such an attack (on someone born after 11 September 2001) could plausibly be a defensive response to '9/11'. If it could not be so characterized, such an attack would seem to require new and separate authorization.

For the time being, neither the US Congress nor a large enough segment of the American population seems inclined to demand specific authorization for drone strikes in the War on Terror. Arguably, any reluctance or indifference on this matter is attributable to the fact that US drone strikes do not endanger US lives, but this itself appears to have precipitated the beginnings of a shift in the kind and degree of authorization bestowed on the resort to force. The broader context for this shift is that, in an age of post-heroic war, there is increasing estrangement in the relationship between the military and civilians in a democratic society. In 2002 Paul Kahn warned

> Riskless warfare... may take the destructive power of war outside of the boundaries of democratic legitimacy, because we are far more willing to delegate the power to use force without risk to the [US] president than we are a power to commit the nation to the sacrifice of its citizens.[18]

Nine years later, the promise that US deployment of drones to Libya would be casualty-free fed into an argument that the usual rules for congressional authorization did not apply. The White House instead argued in June 2011 that Congress did not need to authorize US military operations in Libya extending beyond the 60 days already authorized at the President's discretion because

> US operations do not involve sustained fighting or active exchanges of fire with hostile forces, nor do they involve the presence of US ground troops,

US casualties or a serious threat thereof, or any significant chance of escalation into a conflict characterized by those factors.[19]

The 60-day rule in question originated in the 1973 War Powers Resolution which Congress passed towards the end of the Vietnam War, and it is worth noting that the scope of that war was expanded to include American B-52 bombers flying at high altitude to strike targets in Cambodia 'in secret, half a world away from Washington and with little or no risk to American lives'.[20]

At least two conclusions could be drawn from any acceptance of the Obama Administration's assertion regarding the Libya situation: first, that the standard of authority to wage war had been lowered; or second, that authority was unnecessary for something that did not really count as 'war' in the first place. Relevant to the latter possibility, to be explored further in Chapters 5 and 6, the view of Martin van Creveld is that 'War does not begin when some people kill others; instead, it starts at the point where they themselves risk being killed in return'.[21] If one assumes, for the sake of argument, that risk-free warfare is not an insurmountable paradox, it nevertheless raises questions about the relationship between combatant risk and right authority. For example, if drone operators experience no physical risk, why should other US citizens spare a thought for their safety? Why should they care about a politically motivated enterprise of killing when it is not their family and friends who are dying? And why, if US citizens are untouched and unaffected by drone strikes, should the US Government be required to obtain special permission from those citizens to use force in this way?

Whether due to civil–military disengagement or some other cause, any lowering or removal of the authorization standard for using force is also relevant to the *jus ad bellum* principle requiring war to be a last resort. The abstract notion of 'last' is supposed to have the effect of retarding the process of going to war by compelling would-be users of force to expend genuine effort to avoid it. Recourse to violent action must only occur after every other reasonable, nonviolent way of achieving a political aim has proven to be (or reasonably appears to be) unavailable or ineffective. An example of this principle is the statement in the Obama Administration's National Security Strategy (2010) that '[w]hile the use of force is sometimes necessary, we will exhaust other options before war whenever we can'.[22] Subsequent to the 1999 US-led NATO intervention in Kosovo, the USAF reported:

> The air war over Serbia offered airmen a glimpse of the future, one in which political leaders turned *quickly* to the choice of aerospace power to secure the Alliance's security interests without resorting to more costly and hazardous alternatives that would have exposed more men and materiel to the ravages of war.[23]

The resort to airpower might be quick, but it is difficult to draw an ethical line between 'quick' and 'too quick'. Lowering the threshold for political decisions to use force is not necessarily a bad thing; if the cause for war is just, why not hasten in its pursuit? However, if such lowering and hastening is the result of civilian disengagement from the war-making process (because imaginations are not excited at the prospect of physical risk and personal sacrifice), doubts might arise as to whether there is sufficient civilian authorization for the use of force. As Ignatieff wrote after the Kosovo intervention, 'If war becomes unreal to the citizens of modern democracies, will they care enough to restrain and control the violence exercised in their name?'[24] Even when, in the case of drone use, a nation's government claims (in respect of the 2011 Libya campaign) that there is no 'significant chance of escalation', such a risk remains inherently difficult to gauge and perhaps impossible to eliminate. A state that would wage war in the name of its citizens, thus potentially exposing those at home to the dangers of escalation and blowback, arguably requires their express consent to such an undertaking. If so, the lack of a blessing from Congress for the US use of drones in Libya in 2011 constitutes a deficit of right authority.

Proportionate cause and right intention

A decision to use armed drones – for a just cause, properly authorized, and as a last resort – should also be proportionate to the harm anticipated, and it should be motivated by right intention. For *jus ad bellum* purposes, the principle of proportionality requires that a just cause be also grave enough to warrant going so far as to wage war, with all the death and destruction that that entails. To respond to an insulting remark from a foreign ambassador by invading his or her country, for example, would be an overreaction; resorting to war would become the greater of two evils. To use a real example, the US-led expulsion of Iraqi forces from Kuwait in 1991 was proportionate to the injury (invasion) suffered by that country, but for Kuwait's defenders to have then gone on and engaged in a wholesale invasion of Iraq itself would have been disproportionate. In general terms, proportionality is supposed to prompt a weighing of costs and benefits. Would-be users of force must anticipate that the benefits of their success outweigh the costs of pursuing it, and even a war fought for a just cause is made morally wrong if the damage it will cause is excessive.[25] To the extent that drones facilitate the restrained application of force, and where their use does not amount to an overreaction, this is consistent with the principle of proportionality. Daniel Brunstetter and Megan Braun have characterized the use of drones as 'a coercive measure short of full-scale war' which, to the extent it successfully counteracts perceived threats, is a response more proportional than resorting to troop deployments or intensive bombing campaigns.[26] However, the trouble with seeking to distinguish (for proportionality purposes) 'large-scale' from 'small-scale' uses of force is, first, that such a distinction might well be meaningless from the perspective of those at the receiving end. Second, and more importantly, by ostensibly raising the threshold for resorting only to what a would-be user of force would regard as large-scale measures, such a move might effectively operate to lower the threshold for resorting to violence on any other scale. Thus there is potential for tension, regarding *jus ad bellum*, between the principles of proportionality and last resort. If armed drones are seen (in the eyes of their users) as perpetrating merely 'small-scale' acts of violence to which the principle of last resort applies differently or not at all, this might 'encourage countries to act on just cause with an ease that is potentially worrisome'.[27]

Even if the resort to proportional violence is overly swift, a determination to eschew large-scale and intense uses of force could nevertheless have merit in terms of right intention. This *jus ad bellum* principle is of central importance to just war thinking because it can and should influence decisions about the manner in which force is used (*jus in bello*) as well as about shaping the just peace that ought to follow the termination of hostilities (*jus post bellum*). As Gray insists, war is not a self-validating occurrence, but rather 'warfare always should be waged with as much regard to the character of the subsequent peace as immediate military necessity allows'.[28] In the application of airpower specifically, it was the conviction of Giulio Douhet that repeated bombardment from the air was likely to be decisive in war because 'A people who are bombed to-day as they were bombed yesterday, and who know they will be bombed again tomorrow and see no end to their martyrdom, are bound to call for peace at length'.[29] His thesis was disproven in World War II during which both German and Allied bomber aircraft were deliberately used to target civilians. The intention was that those terrorized civilians would pressure their governments to surrender, but the reverse occurred; terror from the skies only stiffened the resolve of citizens and governments alike on both sides to keep fighting. More than 60 years later, the use of armed drones is airpower applied in a way that is radically different. To the extent that drone strikes generate effects on a smaller scale and are consistent with the *jus in bello* principles of necessity, discrimination and proportionality (to be discussed in the next chapter), their use might signify a just desire to bring about a good post-war peace – a peace not haunted by excessive physical damage and aggravated popular resentment against an overzealous intervener.

Alternatively, choosing drone-based war – deliberately waged from on high and from afar – might signify a lack of prior commitment (right intention) to stay on after the fighting is concluded and see that a good peace is established. In their 1992 book *The Imperial Temptation*, Robert Tucker and David Hendrickson observed that the American formula for going to war involved casualty minimization and short engagements. The 'peculiar vice' of this formula, they argued, is that

> it enables us to go to war with far greater precipitancy than we otherwise might while simultaneously allowing us to walk away from the ruin we create without feeling a consummate sense of responsibility. It creates an anarchy and calls it peace. In the name of order it wreaks havoc. It allows us to assume an imperial role without discharging the classic duties of imperial rule.[30]

Following through on the resort to force by sticking around to nurture the post-war peace can entail immense risks, as the US experience in Afghanistan and Iraq has shown, and it grates against the post-heroic impulse to safeguard the lives of deployed US personnel. Far more comfortable, perhaps, are the less risky campaigns which involve drones alone (Libya, Pakistan, Somalia and Yemen). And yet, when contemplating right intention, one criticism might be that the deployment of uninhabited aircraft (in an uncontested or poorly contested air space especially) reflects a desire to use force in the pursuit only of causes that are not worth dying for. This factor (real or perceived) might in turn militate against satisfying the ethical requirement that the use of force should have a reasonable prospect of success.

Reasonable prospect of success

It is an important principle within the just war tradition that, because death and destruction inevitably result from war, there should be a reasonable chance that a would-be user of force will be victorious and bring about a better peace than what currently exists. To wage war in the knowledge that the damage caused is likely to be in vain is unjust. This principle thus serves as an important prudential constraint upon war making and is, according to Tony Coady, 'a dampener to the unbalancing effects of enthusiasm, outraged feelings, and triumphalist fervour that often precede the decision to go to war'.[31] Regarding the limited and precise application of force using drones, a dilemma arises regarding the wisdom and virtue of restraint. Is the use of armed drones likely to be interpreted by adversaries as a sign of strength: the restraint of the powerful deciding not to be as heavy-handed as they could? Or is it a sign of weakness: the restraint of risk-averse people who would rather not place themselves in harm's way? Is the remote-controlled, risk-free application of airpower a foretaste of worse things to come and thus dissuasive of enemy action, or is it indicative of a reluctance to use force at all and thus an encouragement for an enemy to continue? Where there is doubt on such questions, a campaign of drone strikes is vulnerable to strategic failure.

Niccolò Machiavelli wrote:

> Men ought either to be well treated or crushed, because they can avenge themselves of lighter injuries, of more serious ones they cannot; therefore the injury that is done to a man ought to be of such a kind that one does not stand in fear of revenge.[32]

In its use of armed drones in the Middle East and Central Asia, the US Government exhibits an intention not so much to crush its enemies but rather merely to decapitate them (i.e. to deprive them of leaders). In 2009 the then-director of the CIA, Leon Panetta, stated that drone strikes in Pakistan, for example, are 'the only game in town in terms of confronting or trying to disrupt the al Qaeda leadership'.[33] A vital strategic and *jus ad bellum* question is whether this one 'game' has a reasonable prospect of success. Based on 'the conventional wisdom... that removing key leaders can greatly weaken a terrorist organization', targeted killings continue to be described as an effective strategy.[34] A major problem, however, is the paucity of empirical evidence that would validate this claim. The logic of decapitation strikes leading to strategic success appears to assume that the United States is dealing with a meritocratic system in which enemy leaders are individuals with the greatest talent rather than, for example, the strongest ideological commitment. If this is not the case, decapitation might in fact induce the emergence of more skilful (and thus more dangerous) leaders.[35] Beyond such speculation about the inner workings of targeted organizations, findings based on analysis of limited empirical data have been mixed. A study by Jenna Jordan, published in 2009, adds weight to the notion that drone strikes are ineffective or even counterproductive. Jordan's research on 298 occurrences of leadership decapitation against 96 organizations globally from 1945 to 2004 led her to conclude, contrary to conventional wisdom, that

> decapitation is not a productive counterterrorism strategy. It is actually less effective than not targeting a group's leadership. While decapitation is still successful against certain types of groups, in many cases, organizations that have not had their leaders removed have a higher rate of collapse. Decapitation is actually counterproductive against large, old, and religious groups.[36]

Decapitated organizations 31–40 years old are less likely to fall apart than groups under 10 years of age, 'the utility of decapitation is negative' where a group has more than 500 members,[37] and religious groups that have undergone decapitation 'are 16 per cent less likely to fall apart than those that did not'.[38] If one were to consider the insurgent Pakistani Taliban (a large, umbrella organization established in December 2007) against whose leaders the CIA has directed drone strikes, Jordan's findings would suggest the organization's relative youth makes it more vulnerable to decapitations. On the other hand, the Pakistani Taliban's religious ideology and large membership might serve to make it less vulnerable.[39] This uncertainty is compounded by a pair of studies published in 2012 which concluded that killing or capturing the leaders of militant organizations can reduce the effectiveness of those organizations or even cause them to disintegrate. The first study, an analysis of 118 decapitation attempts from a sample of 90 counterinsurgency campaigns, concluded that 'leadership decapitation (1) increases the chances of war termination; (2) increases the probability of government victory; (3) reduces the intensity of militant violence; and (4) reduces the frequency of insurgent attacks'.[40] Killing insurgent leaders was found to be of more likely effectiveness than capturing them,[41] and the removal of leaders made the defeat of an insurgency around 25 to 30 per cent more likely.[42] The second study, analysing the effects of leadership decapitation on the survival rate of 207 terrorist groups from 1970 to 2008, found 'Strategies and tactics aimed at removing terrorist leaders may have negative consequences in the short term, but they increase the mortality rates of the groups they lead'.[43] Two important caveats on all three sets of findings are, first, that they are not restricted to drone strikes and, second, that they illustrate only a relationship of correlation (as distinct from causation) between decapitation and organization survival. It is no straightforward matter, therefore, to establish on this basis that, for *jus ad bellum* purposes, a campaign of drone strikes against militant leaders has a reasonable prospect of success.

Setting aside the contribution of US drones to the 2011 defeat of Gaddafi in Libya, the success of which was mostly attributable to European aircraft and rebel ground forces,[44] the US Government appears to be counting on remote-control airpower to subdue, eliminate and eventually defeat its enemies in the War on Terror. It would be a mistake, however, for it not to consider human factors in war alongside technological ones. When it comes to destroying objects, weapons technology can be readily assessed in linear terms of cause and effect. By contrast, in the realm of societal attitudes affecting the collective will to fight, predicting immediate effects and the longer-term prospects of success is more difficult. War, far from being merely 'a laboratory exercise in applied technology',[45] is driven by human passions, and enemy behaviour is not controlled as easily as is a guided missile. During World War II, against the political expectation of forced surrender according to which strategic bombing was justified, British attacks on German cities instead made the survivors 'hate their attackers more and thus encourage[d] support for the Nazi leadership as the only recourse they had'.[46] Anti-civilian air bombardment thus probably served to prolong rather than shorten the war in Europe, and Germans who felt confirmed in their role as victims were emboldened.[47] In the case of US use of armed drones, it might not be enough to hear assurances from one's far-away enemy that harm to non-combatants is 'collateral' rather than deliberate. What might matter more is the fact that non-combatants in targeted territories experience physical risk while America's remote-control killers experience none. Popular outrage based on perceptions of unfairness weighs against the putative ability of armed drones to achieve strategic success, and that in turn poses an ethical challenge at the level of *jus ad bellum*. If it were to emerge that drone strikes cause enemies of the United States to redouble rather than give up their efforts to fight back, this would militate against the overall wisdom and legitimacy of a drone campaign.

Even if the idea and actuality of risk-free killing cause outrage, this does not necessarily condemn such use of force to failure. For example, NATO's 1999 Kosovo campaign could stand as evidence that success can be achieved through the exclusive use of airpower in circumstances where one side's combatants experience far less physical risk than the other's. Nevertheless, although the United States and its allies were there able to declare a military victory, it is worth recalling that the relevant success to be achieved was a humanitarian one. Ultimately, the ethnic cleansing of Kosovar Albanians at the hands of Serbs was stopped, but the air campaign was arguably conducted in such a way as to be sometimes inconsistent with achieving a humanitarian end. For example, in the NATO bombing of Serb forces, there appeared to be a systemic trade-off between altitude of aircraft and accuracy of target identification when it came to the release of munitions. There was also, in Jeffrey Record's observation, 'a bizarre disconnect between political ends and military means in which an exclusive and initially timid application of air-power provoked an acceleration of the very Serbian ethnic cleansing of Kosovo that formed NATO's immediate causus [*sic*] belli'.[48] NATO had gone to war in the first place to stop the cleansing, but this effort was hindered in large measure by the effort to prevent Allied casualties. It is therefore in the broadest conceptualization of the Kosovo campaign – as a study in casualty-avoidance – that the seeds of its potential failure are most apparent. This is the lesson of greatest relevance to the use of drones when contemplating the *jus ad bellum* success criterion.

The 1999 intervention was, according to Ignatieff, 'the kind of war a nation fights when it wants to, not when it must, when values rather than survival are on the line; when commitment is intense but also shallow'.[49] Had success in Kosovo required escalation of NATO efforts to include the deployment of ground troops, the whole enterprise would likely have foundered on a strong aversion to seeing friendly casualties in a non-necessary war. Crucially, the very circumstance (casualty aversion) that necessitated the placing of strict limits on where, how and by whom force could be used was what also precluded escalation. In a contemporaneous RAND study, Daniel Byman and his co-authors highlighted the dilemma as follows:

> Because the public and allies often see air strikes as a low-risk, low-commitment measure, air power will be called on when US public or allied commitment is weak – a situation that will make coercion far harder. The prospects of escalation will be difficult in such circumstances.
> [...]
> [A]ir power's very strengths with regard to domestic support and coalition dynamics could become weaknesses, if they lead air power to be used in situations that lower its credibility. Such use of air power may damage its credibility in future contexts and make coercion even harder.[50]

In its use of armed drones, the United States might justly be seeking to coerce its enemies into giving up their struggle, and it is a plausible proposition that high-technology weaponry could be so awe-inspiring as to be ultimately overwhelming. However, using force in this way is arguably less likely to achieve long-term success if it signals timidity rather than determination. A wise and patient enemy will be cognizant that a post-heroic war is a style of war in which success for those waging it becomes a less reasonable prospect once the cost of pursuing it exceeds domestic political expectations. Perhaps, by an enemy simply waiting out a succession of drone strikes or learning to live with them, actual defeat will be indefinitely postponed. On this point, Coker's likening of air-only campaigns to siege warfare is apt: 'Such operations are extensive, but they are attrition, and likely to remain inconclusive. All that air power can do is contain a problem, not solve it.'[51]

In Afghanistan, by contrast, US airpower (drones included) has supported what is primarily a ground-based effort to solve security problems through a strategy of counterinsurgency (COIN). It is beyond the scope of this book to examine factors relevant to a reasonable prospect of success for COIN generally, but drones warrant particular consideration inasmuch as they are a means of force protection and risk avoidance. To this extent, drone strikes in Afghanistan have a post-heroic flavour comparable to that of NATO's Kosovo campaign. However, their ability to contribute to overall success is questionable given that they are emblematic of a seemingly intractable dilemma for US COIN commanders: counterinsurgents must avoid risk in order to satisfy concerned American citizens at home, but they must share risk with the local Afghan people in order to gain their respect, trust and support.[52] In 2010 a US air commander in Afghanistan, Major General Stephen P. Mueller, told the *New York Times* that the steady bird's-eye view provided by drones 'means that our ground forces can get out and about amongst the population and into smaller units than you would typically think about'.[53] The idea is that, by helping to create a safer environment for US troops, drones give a COIN campaign time to unfold. Missile strikes from drones would reportedly occur when troops were caught in fire fights or when patrolling drones came across a person who appeared to be planting an improvised explosive device.[54] Although it is clear from this that US ground troops in Afghanistan experience some physical risk, that risk is attenuated by the hovering presence of drones, and the drone operators themselves experience no physical risk at all. Thus, the use of armed drones appears to conflict with what the former US commander in Afghanistan, General Stanley McChrystal, saw as a strategic imperative: to 'share risk, at least equally, with the people'.[55] The contradiction inherent in prioritization of force protection, sometimes to the point of superseding the declared objective of a war,[56] is a phenomenon that extends far beyond the use of drones. In the context of contemplating risk and reasonable prospect of success, however, this particular issue serves to illustrate what is perhaps a more general incompatibility as between COIN and post-heroic war.

A final point worth making in this *jus ad bellum* assessment of armed drones is that the reasonableness of prospective success will be determined by the scope of the just cause to be violently pursued. If the cause invoked is boundless, success is necessarily inconceivable. A campaign of drone strikes undertaken as part of the War on Terror could not succeed if, for example, its objective was 'to defeat evil'. When accepting the 2009 Nobel Peace Prize, President Obama said: 'Evil does exist in the world',[57] and political leaders in the United States may indeed find that maintaining a good-versus-evil dichotomy supports the production of legitimacy and the maintenance of morale. However, there is danger in regarding such rhetoric as constituting an ethical framework for war. Any timeframe for defeating evil could only be an open-ended one, and the objective itself is best characterized as unattainable. In a war against evil, using armed drones and/or other technologies, weighing military means against strategic ends is virtually meaningless when ends are seemingly infinite. As such, it could have no place in the just war tradition because that tradition is all about limits. In the face of evil, and because of the supreme moral importance of defeating it, would-be users of force might distort just war principles to the point of obsolescence. As Christian Henderson has warned, the standard of 'necessity' to deal with evil adversaries could see decision-makers dispense with the requirement of prior or imminent attack, and non-violent measures in general could be bypassed due to a blanket moral predetermination that they are inadequate or of no use at all.[58] There would, in effect, be no prohibition on resorting to the use of force. With this in mind, the government secrecy surrounding US drone strikes in Pakistan, Somalia and Yemen is troubling. Absent an official explanation of precisely what a drone-based war is intended to achieve and whether that aim is achievable, it is difficult to judge whether such a war has a reasonable prospect of success. If such a war is of a kind to be unending, it is almost certainly unjust. The just war tradition compels users of force to contemplate the ending of wars, and ethical restraints on the resort to and use of force are given meaning by the imagining of lives being lived in a subsequent peace. The war threshold, once crossed, should not be a point of no return.

Conclusion

The use of uninhabited aircraft, especially in a non-contested or poorly contested airspace, is action well suited to the prevailing political appetite for postheroic war. However, mere ability is not to be equated with moral permission; it is fallacious to assume that 'can' implies 'should'. As the availability of armed drones increases in the United States and elsewhere, and as the number of perceived opportunities to use them grows, there is an ethical imperative to consider the impact this technology has on political decisions to resort to the use of force. The plausible danger discussed in this chapter is that drone technology will enable an increase in the overall quantum of force being used in the world inasmuch as force – even if described as small-scale and precise – could be resorted to more easily and quickly. From a *jus ad bellum* perspective, such an increase would be unjust if force was resorted to without a just cause. The recent record of drone use has included the US Government's interventions in Libya for humanitarian purposes and in Afghanistan for self-defence purposes, but elsewhere its pre-emptive use of armed drones is less easy to justify. In the War on Terror, if the degree and manner of drone use exceeds what is required for self-defence, the United States might emerge as an actor more sinning than sinned against. Moreover, by asserting a right to strike preemptively against those suspected of planning attacks, the United States is running the risk of creating a dangerous international norm. It is worth contemplating, therefore, the grounds upon which the United States could credibly object if, for example, China sent drones into Kazakhstan to strike Uighur Muslims it accuses of plotting terrorism. Similarly, what principled objection could there be to India using drones to hit terrorism suspects in the disputed territory of Kashmir, or to Russia using drones in former Soviet states like Georgia?[59] Any objection could only be one that is founded on an ethical presumption against the use of force in international affairs, and yet the United

States has recently challenged that presumption by exhibiting remarkably little reluctance to use violence.

When it comes to the *jus ad bellum* requirement for right authority, a UNSC blessing is required where drones are used for humanitarian purposes (as they arguably were in Libya in 2011). However, in matters ostensibly related to the exercise of a state's inherent right of self-defence, the standard of authorization at the domestic level might be changing with the post-heroic times. If the risk-free nature of drone-based killing sees citizens disengaging from the wars waged in their name by their governments, it is worth asking whether such use of force has right authority and whether it is truly a last resort. At the same time, if drone technology enables minor uses of force in response to minor threats, and if this is done with the intention of forestalling the emergence of major threats, this would appear to satisfy ethical requirements that force be resorted to in a proportionate fashion and with a desire to achieve a better post-war peace. As for whether success is a reasonable prospect, recent empirical analyses leave room for doubt about whether the use of drones to decapitate enemy organizations would be effective in the long term. Expanding the range of targets to include lower-level enemies might work better, but in this approach there is also greater potential to generate non-combatant casualties. If success in the War on Terror requires more than that – if it requires the defeat of evil – it is surely unattainable. To pursue it regardless would make for an unjust endeavour overall, and along the way there could be a strong temptation to distort or ignore ethical principles governing the conduct of hostilities. As the *New York Times* editorialized in May 2012, 'The United States cannot be in a perpetual war on terror that allows lethal force against anyone, anywhere, for any perceived threat. That power [for a President] is too great, and too easily abused.'[60] It is some cause for comfort, however, that when John Brennan stated in 2010 that the US Government 'will take the fight' to extremists 'wherever they plot and train in Afghanistan, Pakistan, Yemen, Somalia and beyond', he acknowledged that 'an action that eliminates a single terrorist but causes civilian casualties can, in fact, inflame local populations and create far more problems – a tactical success but a strategic failure'.[61] Clearly, the likelihood that drone strikes will bring strategic success for the US Government is closely connected to the manner in which these strikes are conducted, and so the discussion now turns from *jus ad bellum* to *jus in bello*.

4 Conducting drone warfare
The case of Pakistan

Building upon the previous chapter's discussion of *jus ad bellum* issues, this chapter examines whether or how the use of armed drones satisfies the requirements for justice in the conduct of war (*jus in bello*). The possibility to be considered is that drone technology, as well as unjustly increasing the frequency of war, will also unjustly increase war's harmfulness to its human victims. The analysis focuses on Pakistan where the US Government has used drones most extensively, albeit in an undeclared and unacknowledged campaign, notwithstanding that this very secrecy is a critical factor perpetuating uncertainties regarding the ethical soundness of drone strikes. It is widely reported that individuals in Pakistan are targeted by CIA drone operators in cooperation with the Pakistani Government,[1] although the US Government will not confirm such reports.[2] However, it is a poorly kept secret when anonymous US intelligence officials are regularly and routinely quoted in the media. Moreover, only the United States has both the capability and the motivation to deploy Predators and Reapers in that part of the world. The CIA has reportedly been operating drones out of at least one Pakistani airbase 200 miles south-west of Quetta in Baluchistan, with Pakistani military support and with Pakistani informants and intelligence officers helping to select targets.[3] One unofficial tally indicates that the Agency carried out one drone strike in Pakistan in 2004 and another in 2005, three strikes in 2006, and five in 2007. The drone programme then escalated sharply: from 35 strikes in 2008 (mostly in the second half of the year), to 54 in 2009, to 117 in 2010. The following year saw 64 drone strikes, and in 2012 there were 46.[4]

Acknowledging the lack of official US Government transparency on exactly how and how many CIA drone strikes have been conducted in Pakistan, this chapter assesses available evidence in the light of three *jus in bello* requirements. In the conduct of war, the use of force should: (1) be necessary and beneficial to the achievement of a legitimate military objective; (2) discriminate between combatants and non-combatants; and (3) be anticipated to generate a level of harm (including unintended harm to non-combatants) that is proportional to the expected military benefit. Here it is again worth noting the parallels to principles within Shari'a (Islamic law). Ethical reasoning in that tradition requires war to be 'conducted with honor'; it consistently affirms that non-combatants among the enemy 'are not to be the direct and intentional target of attack', and it prohibits 'weapons that might cause disproportionate harm'.[5] Some activities in war are, by any reasonable standard, unethical because they are obviously unnecessary (e.g. bombing what you know to be a graveyard full of dead enemies), disproportionate (e.g. bombing the site of a building for ten hours even though you know the building itself was completely destroyed in the first ten seconds), and/or indiscriminate (e.g. bombing a school building that you know contains only small children). But it is in the grey areas of differing interpretations (related to one's state of knowledge based on intelligence or observation) that the real debate about adherence to ethical principles takes place. The murky picture that emerges from Pakistan is an inadequate foundation for determining finally whether US drone strikes there are conducted justly or unjustly. However, the very persistence of doubt on this point arguably undermines international norms on the use of force and the reputation of the United States as a champion thereof. It behoves the US Government therefore to explain publicly why CIA drone strikes are beneficial, discriminate and proportionate.

Ethics and counterinsurgency

As at the time of writing, the US Government has an immediate strategic interest in Pakistan because of that country's close connection to the ongoing US-led war in neighbouring Afghanistan. Pakistan's north-western tribal areas are used as bases by insurgent Taliban and Al Qaeda militants to launch attacks against Afghan Government and allied forces (as well as against civilian targets) across the border. The US Government also has a strategic interest in countering an insurgency that threatens the political stability of Pakistan itself. A descent into disorder in this nuclear-armed state would likely generate consequences detrimental to other states in south and central Asia, with flow-on negative outcomes for the United States in terms of power balance in the region. The American strategy in Pakistan may be characterized as counterinsurgency (COIN) incorporating counterterrorism. The US Government is concerned to assist in defeating an organized movement which aims to destabilize and delegitimize the Pakistani Government, and which also engages in cross-border cooperation with insurgents who aim to achieve such ends in Afghanistan. Hidden among and assisting the insurgents in Pakistan are members of the Al Qaeda movement,[6] so the US Government is concerned also to use force against these individuals as a defensive response to the attacks of 11 September 2001 in the United States. As President Obama remarked in 2009, a strategic goal of the United States is 'To disrupt, dismantle and defeat Al Qaeda in Pakistan and Afghanistan, and to prevent their return to either country in the future'.[7]

According to Edward Luttwak, American COIN efforts are doomed to failure. His reasoning is that, due to the US Government's 'principled and inevitable refusal to out-terrorize the insurgents', a tranquil occupation of conquered territory is impossible.[8] Luttwak scorns the application by a territory's occupiers of 'specialized counterinsurgency methods or tactics' because he sees the only requirement for success as being a simple willingness to ensure that, for the local people, 'fear of reprisals [by the occupiers] outweighs the desire to help the insurgents or their threats'.[9] Beyond the imposition of curfews and other restrictions that are merely 'inconvenient', he argues, US armed forces have no capacity to 'inflict collective punishments'.[10] Such a view, which Luttwak advances partly by drawing comparisons to the practices of ancient Roman legions, is sharply at odds with contemporary COIN doctrine, as well as being quite obviously incompatible with just war thinking. Adherence to the conventions of civilized warfare is important for its own sake, and it is an important component of any strategic contest in which the so-called 'hearts and minds' of the local population are the prize. Walzer has argued, for example, that 'one of the things most of us want, even in war, is to act or to seem to act morally',[11] and Gray has observed that 'it does not pay strategically to be ethically challenged'.[12] Although moral virtue does not guarantee success, a paucity thereof can undermine a political project that requires the threat or use of organized violence.[13] The common notion here is a plausible one: that strategy and ethics are necessarily interdependent. From a *jus in bello* perspective specifically, and relevant to the issue of armed drones, the manner and means of applying force can affect the likelihood of overall success in a war and the prospects for a better peace thereafter.

In a 2009 book, Australian army officer Mark O'Neill emphasized the importance to COIN of 'rectitude' and 'acting morally with integrity and justice'.[14] Remarking that insurgents and their supporters make decisions 'influenced by their hearts as well as their heads', he argued that counterinsurgents lacking rectitude will struggle to get others 'to accept whatever is morally ambivalent about their position or deeds'.[15] As an example of 'what not to do', from the Second Boer War (1899–1902) in southern Africa, he cited 'The cruel conditions that incarcerated civilians endured in concentration camps [which] worked against British claims of moral legitimacy and provided a powerful motivation for many Boers to keep fighting'.[16] The most comprehensive statement of contemporary COIN doctrine for US forces is set out in a 2006 joint Army/Marine Corps Field Manual. The chapter on 'Leadership and Ethics' notes that American soldiers and marines are held 'to the highest standards of moral and ethical conduct'.[17] These standards, derived from the centuries-old just war tradition, include the principles of necessity, discrimination and proportionality. Such principles are victim-oriented rather than weapon-specific, and they apply regardless of whether force is used by land, sea or air. In the context of drone strikes in Pakistan, however, no published manual exists to confirm that non-military (CIA) officers are ethically bound in like fashion. Perhaps, in practice, they are. But persistent uncertainty and suspicion on this point problematizes the rendering of an ethical judgement on what CIA drone operators do and how they do it. In the meantime, even if they too are secretly held to 'the highest standards of moral and ethical conduct', any harm to non-combatants generated by drone strikes is liable to be perceived and portrayed as deliberate and unjust.

When winged aircraft were for the first time used for military purpose, in the skies over Libya in 1911, the Italian army enjoyed complete control of the air but, due to technical limitations, many things did not go according to plan. Most of the five-pound Cipelli grenades, thrown from the cockpit, missed their targets and some hit non-combatants. This, according to van Creveld, 'not only proved counterproductive, helping drive people into the [Libyan] insurgents' arms, but led to lively condemnations in the international press'.[18] Even more relevant for present purposes are observations on airpower by a British officer who in 1923 wrote:

> In Waziristan [in the north-west of modern-day Pakistan] the demoralizing effect of the airplane was disappointing, on account of the difficulty of killing the enemy.... [In] small war operations, the limitations which to us appear to be the most permanent are: the transitory influence of aircraft attack, due mainly to the shortness of time the aeroplane can remain in the air; its lack of power to occupy a disturbed district;... and the danger of indiscriminate slaughter of friend and foe, of women and children as well as armed men. Such slaughter is an action which does not harmonize with British traditions, and which ethically has again and again been proved to be unsound.[19]

Further to the issue of ethical soundness, and in line with *jus in bello* requirements, the US COIN Field Manual states: 'The principles of discrimination in the use of force and proportionality in actions are important to counterinsurgents for practical reasons as well as for their ethical and moral implications.'[20] One of the most effective ways for insurgents to undermine political support is 'to portray their opposition as untrustworthy or illegitimate', and this works 'especially well when insurgents can portray their opposition as unethical by the opposition's own standards'.[21] In the context of drone strikes, the ethical standard that applies to US conduct in Pakistan is embodied in international humanitarian law, according to which a targeted killing

> must be militarily necessary, the use of force must be proportionate so that any anticipated military advantage is considered in light of the expected harm to civilians in the vicinity, and everything feasible must be done to prevent mistakes and minimize harm to civilians.[22]

Some analysts in government and academia have sought to establish that different standards apply if the armed conflict is between a state and alleged terrorists. Most famously, on the issue of torturing prisoners, former White House Counsel Alberto Gonzales wrote in 2002: 'the nature of the new war [on terrorism]... renders obsolete Geneva's [the 1949 third Geneva Convention on the Treatment of Prisoners of War] strict limitations on questioning of enemy prisoners.'[23] The expression of such views has not, however, led to the emergence of a new international norm on engaging in torture in the course of war, and it remains the case that using force against prisoners is generally condemned as being indiscriminate and disproportionate. Jean Bethke Elshtain, although she has argued that the overall justification for waging war (*jus ad bellum*) against terrorists needs to be recast in terms of the struggle of good against evil, nevertheless warns against stooping to the savage, indiscriminate standards of violence (*jus in bello*) employed by terrorists themselves.[24] To do so would not only be ethically objectionable but also counterproductive, and so the traditional standard quoted above continues to apply.

This standard clearly incorporates requirements of discrimination and proportionality in the use of force, but the notion of what is 'militarily necessary' is less clear. Walzer has observed that the doctrine of military necessity tends to be invoked in a way that 'justifies not only whatever is necessary to win the war, but also whatever is necessary to reduce the risks of losing, or simply to reduce losses or the likelihood of losses in the course of war'.[25] Rather than actually being about necessity, Walzer regards the term 'military necessity' as a 'hyperbolical' way of speaking about probability and risk:

> Even if one grants the right of states and armies and individual soldiers to reduce their risks, a particular course of action would be *necessary* to that end only if no other course improved the odds of battle at all. But there will always be a range of tactical and strategic options that conceivably could improve the odds.[26]

A definition of military necessity can be traced back to the US Civil War and the US Government's General Orders No. 100 (1863), better known as the Lieber Code (after its author, Francis Lieber). Article 48 of the Code defined the term as 'those measures which are *indispensable* for securing the ends of the war, and which are lawful according to the modern law and usages of war'.[27] More recently, the US Army's 2005 Field Manual on the Law of Land Warfare has referred to 'military necessity' as '[t]hat principle which justifies those measures not forbidden by international law which are *indispensable* for securing the complete submission of the enemy as soon as possible'.[28] In practice, for the reasons outlined by Walzer, indispensability is neither a realistic nor a useful criterion for assessment. However, for a particular mode of using force to be plausibly characterized as militarily necessary, it is reasonable to require that it must at least be more *beneficial* than costly in terms of achieving a legitimate military objective.

Necessity

The principle of necessity is inextricably linked to the other two *jus in bello* principles considered later in this chapter. For example, the deliberate targeting of non-combatants who pose no threat (a violation of the discrimination principle) is unnecessary. And in any cost–benefit calculation related to the proportionality principle, the achievement of unnecessary objectives cannot be weighed against anticipated damage (including harm to non-combatants). In Pakistan, if one assumes that the overall legitimate military objective to be achieved is self-defence, there must be a discernible defensive benefit to be derived from any and all US drone strikes there. Targeting an enemy in this way might indeed hold great strategic appeal if, as Avery Plaw suggests, 'It allows states to seize the initiative against terrorist groups and to attack them at their weakest rather than trying to defend against them when they are at their strongest'.[29] The continued presence and use of armed drones has reportedly 'cast a pall of fear' over areas in Pakistan where Al Qaeda and Taliban militants once moved freely, forcing them to abandon satellite phones and large gatherings, to move around more stealthily and quickly, and to communicate by courier.[30] In the words of Leon Panetta, 'the most aggressive operation that CIA has been involved in' has resulted in Al Qaeda 'having a very difficult time putting together any kind of command and control... they are scrambling'.[31]

Another purported benefit of drone strikes, discussed previously in the context of the *jus ad bellum* principle of reasonable prospect of success, is the supposedly disruptive effect of targeting insurgent and terrorist leaders. On hearing reports that Pakistani Taliban leader Hakimullah Mehsud had died in a drone attack in January 2010, for example, the director of the Center for Research and Security Studies in Islamabad declared: 'If he's gone, it's a fatal blow.... At one point, the Taliban had a lot of momentum and a charismatic leader. Now they've been uprooted and lost all credibility.'[32] The Taliban has since endured, and it might well be too soon to judge the effectiveness of CIA drone strikes. However, just as uncertainty persists with respect to long-term success in a *jus ad bellum* sense, so too there is reason to doubt whether the immediate benefits of drone strikes outweigh the costs. If they are counterproductive, drone strikes are worse than useless, in which case they cannot for *jus in bello* purposes be characterized as necessary. When Panetta stated in 2009 that US drone strikes in Pakistan are 'the only game in town in terms of confronting or trying to disrupt the al Qaeda leadership',[33] the implied message seemed to be: 'We (the US Government) should do something rather than nothing. This (drone strikes) is the only thing we can do. Therefore, we should do it.' But there are dangers in the logical fallacy that 'can' implies 'should'. At the nexus of technology, ethics and strategy, as John Kaag and Whitley Kaufman have observed, 'the very ease of striking a target becomes the rationale for doing so; the technology determines what counts as a legitimate military target rather than vice versa'.[34] Even if the US Government is using armed drones in Pakistan in the *bona fide* hope that this will be strategically effective, there is a critical need also to consider the possibility that drone use will turn out to be worse than ineffective. On this point, the benefit or detriment derived from killing leaders by using drones specifically is usefully judged in the context of the vexed issue of so-called 'collateral damage'.

From a COIN perspective, drone strikes are beneficial if they assist in winning over a local population, and yet the widespread perception of drone strikes as being insufficiently discriminate militates against such an outcome. Although the US Government has always implied that there is a tacit understanding between it and the Pakistani Government, the latter has consistently and publicly argued that drone attacks are a hindrance rather than a help because they fuel popular anger and boost support for anti-government militants. In 2010, for example, a Pakistani foreign ministry spokesman described US drone strikes in the north-west of his country as having 'neither justification nor understanding', adding that the drone campaign was 'not serving the larger strategic interests, especially in the context of our efforts to win hearts and minds, which is part and parcel of our strategy against militants and terrorists'.[35] Regarding the prize of 'hearts and minds', so often mentioned in discussions of COIN in Pakistan and elsewhere, public opinion is a crucial factor when assessing the relative benefits and costs of using armed drones. In a survey report based on face-to-face interviews in Pakistan conducted over two weeks in April 2010, the Washington-based Pew Research Center found little support for US drone strikes against extremist leaders. Just over one-third of Pakistanis (35 per cent) had heard about the strikes, and nearly all (93 per cent) of these respondents said they are a bad thing. Most (56 per cent) said drones are not necessary to defend Pakistan from extremist groups, while 32 per cent said they are. And 90 percent said they thought drone strikes kill too many innocent people.[36] A more recent survey found that only 17 per cent of Pakistanis supported US drone strikes against leaders of extremist groups, and 74 per cent considered the United States to be an enemy.[37]

The caveat on such survey results is that it is difficult to obtain independent and reliable assessments of the impact and popularity of drone strikes in those areas of Pakistan where they mostly occur. The tribal regions (including North and South Waziristan) bordering Afghanistan are virtually inaccessible to foreign journalists, and the people living there are probably often scared to speak out. Another survey, conducted by the Ariana Institute in Islamabad, found that around 80 per cent of people interviewed in Pakistan's tribal regions felt that the targeting in drone strikes was accurate. But Khadim Hussain, director of the Institute, has said that research about whether or not Waziris resented the drone strikes has proved inconclusive.[38] Neither the Pew surveys nor the Ariana survey provide a solid foundation for arguing that CIA drone strikes either mostly assist or mostly undermine the COIN objective of winning over the local population. However, an official body count issued by the US Government, revealing the balance of combatant and non-combatant deaths resulting from drone strikes, might provide a more reliable indication of whether Pakistanis' perceptions are justified or overblown. Unless or until such information is made public, it is difficult for those outside the US Government to make a plausible determination on whether the effects of drone strikes are more beneficial than costly. In the meantime, the very existence of doubt on this point is itself costly to US interests because it allows local concern over allegedly excessive rates of non-combatant casualties to persist. Greater transparency in this regard on the part of the US Government would need to be accompanied by an official explanation of who qualifies as a non-combatant in the first place. Further to this point, the discussion now turns to whether, as required by the just war tradition and the US Government's own ethical standards for COIN, the use of armed drones in Pakistan is discriminate.

Discrimination

According to the principle of discrimination, only combatants may be deliberately targeted; non-combatants ought to be immune from attack. In international humanitarian law this principle is manifested in, for example, Article 51(2) of the 1977 Additional Protocol (I) to the 1949 Geneva Conventions which provides: 'The civilian population as such, as well as individual civilians, shall not be the object of attack.'[39] Historically, the application of force from the air has shown a tendency to be less rather than more discriminate, and this problem reached its zenith on 6 August 1945 when the US bomber aircraft Enola Gay dropped an atomic device on the Japanese city of Hiroshima. Earlier, in 1932, former British prime minister Stanley Baldwin had alluded to the deliberate targeting of civilians when he said: 'I think it is well also for *the man in the street* to realise that there is no power on earth that can prevent him from being bombed. Whatever people may tell him, the bomber will always get through.'[40] During the world war that followed this prediction, the months-long Blitz carried out by German bombers killed 43,000 British civilians and destroyed or damaged a million London houses.[41] The same city suffered the use, from 1944 onwards, of technological precursors to uninhabited aircraft: German V-1 and V-2 rockets. These weapons, described by Theodor Adorno as 'Hitler's robot bombs', were of a kind to operate 'with total blindness' and thus to generate indiscriminate effects.[42] A plan (never implemented) to counter the rockets, advocated by US General Henry Arnold, was no less indiscriminate: 'to fly 500 unmanned, radar-controlled, fully loaded B-17 bombers and crash them into enemy cities'.[43] Over the decades since Baldwin insisted that 'the bomber will always get through', the norm against indiscriminate uses of force has strengthened as powerful states have acquired the technological wherewithal to be more precise. As Alex Bellamy has observed, 'the advent of PGM [precision guided munition] warfare has significantly increased societal expectation about the minimization of non-combatant casualties'.[44] Thus the killing of non-combatants, while tragic in itself, is also bad for business politically and strategically. So when Panetta described drone strikes as 'the only game in town', he also offered the assurance that they are 'very precise' and 'very limited in terms of collateral damage'.[45] Similarly, in a live internet forum in January 2012, President Obama said 'drones have not caused a huge number of civilian casualties.... For the most part they have been very precise precision strikes against Al Qaeda and their affiliates.'[46] Such statements notwithstanding, the actual balance of combatant and non-combatant casualties resulting from drone strikes is far from clear, as is the US Government's ethical basis for assigning people to either of these categories. This lack of transparency makes a *jus in bello* assessment more difficult, but also makes it important to attempt one nonetheless.

It must be acknowledged that, in contrast to the crude rockets used during World War II, modern-day drones like the Predator and Reaper are not *inherently* indiscriminate. That is, US drone strikes are not indiscriminate attacks in the sense of being attacks 'which employ a method or means of combat the effects of which cannot be limited ... [and] are of a nature to strike military objectives and civilians or civilian objects without distinction'.[47] Drones may therefore be contrasted with so-called 'weapons of mass destruction': biological weapons that cause disease contagion, chemical weapons that distribute a toxic agent over a wide area; and nuclear weapons that generate a huge blast radius and radioactive fallout. Because the lethal substance and form of such weaponry (micro-organisms, gases and radiation respectively) cannot easily be contained, possession and use thereof are prohibited or (in the case of nuclear weapons) restricted by law. It is rather in the nature of an armed drone that, like many so-called 'conventional' weapons, it can be used discriminately or indiscriminately depending on the intentions of the user. A rifle, for example, could be used to shoot an innocent child as easily as an enemy soldier,[48] or indeed it could be used (notwithstanding its design characteristics) to stir a bucket of paint. Even so, in the case of a drone operator intending to use a Hellfire missile against a legitimate target (an enemy combatant), he or she could still end up killing a non-combatant.

In Pakistan (and in all other places where the US Government uses armed drones) the enemy wears no uniform, so discrimination between combatants and non-combatants can only occur on the basis of received intelligence or interpretation of someone's observed actions (such as firing a weapon). Across the border in Afghanistan, the USAF has already experienced the drawbacks of poor intelligence and misinterpreting actions. The circumstances of the October 2001 bombing by US aircraft of a Red Cross warehouse in Kabul were that 'the warehouse was attacked with "stand-off" weapons launched from a high altitude and/or from a distance, meaning that the pilot was unable to verify the target visually'.[49] Likewise, the June 2002 bombing of a wedding party was a conspicuous example of target misidentification. On the basis of erroneous information, US aircraft were dispatched to strike what they believed to be a Taliban headquarters. When shots were fired in the air, as commonly occurs at Afghan weddings, the American pilots overhead apparently mistook this for anti-aircraft fire and responded with lethal force to defend themselves.[50] During NATO's 1999 Kosovo campaign, the Serbs' use of camouflage, decoys and other techniques to foil NATO air strikes was all the more effective because high-altitude hampered their opponents' visual ability to identify targets.[51] On one occasion, NATO pilots flying at 15,000 feet bombed a convoy of buses carrying refugees because they mistakenly believed these were Serbian tanks.[52] Arguably, such mistakes are less likely to occur when drones are used instead of inhabited aircraft.

In circumstances where an on-board pilot has to eyeball a target on the ground and accordingly release a missile or bomb, the altitude at which he or she is flying is an important factor determining the level of risk not only to the pilot above but also to non-combatants below. A common criticism of bombing from a high altitude and with the naked eye has been that it necessarily involves transferring risk towards the very people who ought to be least touched by war. For example, Walzer's position is that commanders should be prepared to place combatants in harm's way in order to reduce the risks to enemy non-combatants.[53] Bellamy asks: 'What level of risk should [pilots] accept in order to increase the chances of distinguishing between combatants and non-combatants?'[54] And Martin Cook, referring to the high-altitude bombing conducted in Kosovo, has observed: 'one cannot help but note that the precision would have been higher still had the aircraft operated at lower altitudes (and greater risk).'[55] The common assumption here is that discrimination is enhanced by physical proximity; by taking on more risk, the users of force can better avoid causing non-combatant deaths. However, the real enabler of discriminate application of force is accurate visual identification. Drones are technically capable of achieving this, notwithstanding the fact that they fly at high altitude and their ground-based operators assume no physical risk. In other words, drone technology breaks the traditional nexus between the visual and the physical when it comes to discrimination; the proximity of the operator need not be a factor as regards target identification and strike accuracy. Because camera-equipped drones can hover undetected over an area for long periods of time while relaying imagery back to base, they are a means of obtaining a superior picture of what usually happens (and of any unusual happenings) in that area. If from one minute to the next the situation suddenly changes, a planned strike can be rapidly aborted or redirected. This is a much stronger basis for applying force in a discriminate manner to persons more readily identifiable as either combatants or non-combatants. Errors of fact are still possible: for example, viewed from directly overhead, a child playing with toys by the side of the road could be mistaken for a man burying an improvised explosive device. Nevertheless, a drone operator with more time and opportunity to watch what is going on might generally be better able to wield force discriminately than is the on-board pilot of a fast-moving aircraft.

Another consideration, regarding drone operators themselves, is that being physically absent might be conducive to discrimination. Peter Singer acknowledges the argument that removal of risk allows decisions to be made in a more deliberate manner, and that uninhabited systems also remove anger and emotion: 'A remote operator isn't in the midst of combat and isn't watching his buddies die around him as his adrenaline spikes; he can take his time and act deliberately in ways that can lessen the likelihood of civilians being killed.'[56] Similarly, Bradley Strawser observes: 'Once fear for their own safety is not a pressing concern, one would assume the operator would be more capable, not less, of behaving justly.'[57] A contrary view, expressed by Philip Alston, is that the safety felt by drone operators will induce them to consider what they do as merely a game, with dangerous consequences for the targets therein.[58] On this point it is worth noting that the control units for some smaller drones (albeit unarmed) do indeed resemble Playstation and Gameboy consoles,[59] and that the control station for a Predator or Reaper does not differ markedly from a flight simulator unit used for training purposes. Moreover, a trainer of Predator operators told the *Boston Globe* in 2005: 'We have to impress upon them that they are not just shooting electrons. They're killing people.'[60] These and other issues related to drone operators' state of mind are explored in greater depth in Chapter 6. Suffice to say at present that the argument advanced by Singer and Strawser is a plausible one: a combination of technical (visual identification) and psychological (physical separation) factors could make armed drones a mode of warfare ethically superior to other forms of ranged weaponry (inhabited aircraft, missiles, artillery, etc.), at least in theory.

In practice, the empirical picture is murky. This is due to a dearth of reliable data on combatant and non-combatant casualties resulting from drone strikes. In Pakistan, where the United States has engaged in drone strikes most extensively, unofficial assessments of the casualty impact have relied largely on sketchy reports in the local and international media. It is difficult to know the ratio of combatants to non-combatants killed, not least because in many cases there has been no positive identification of bodies. According to records maintained by the *Long War Journal* since 2006, at the time of writing there had been 2,480 'leaders and operatives from Taliban, Al Qaeda, and allied extremist groups' killed, and 153 'civilians' killed.[61] This indicates that around 5.8 per cent of those killed by drones are non-combatants. However, according to the New America Foundation's data, 337 drone strikes since 2004 had caused a total of between 1,953 and 3,279 deaths, including between 427 and 630 non-'militant' deaths.[62] This indicates a much higher overall proportion (around 18–23 per cent) of non-combatant deaths; a figure more likely to be regarded as excessive. In a rare empirical analysis published in November 2010, researchers at the University of Massachusetts Dartmouth argued that CIA drone strikes in Pakistan 'have not only been impressively accurate, but they have achieved and maintained a greater proportionality than either ground operations in the area or targeting campaigns elsewhere'.[63] Matthew Fricker and his colleagues compiled and analysed a database of Pakistani and US newspaper reports of drone strikes. They found that, as of 19 June 2010, only 68 (or 4.95 per cent) out of the total 1,372 killed in drone strikes could clearly be identified as civilians. Another 1,098 (or 80 per cent) were reported to be 'suspected militants', and the status of the remaining 206 (or 15 per cent) was 'unknown'.[64] The researchers stressed that 'even if every single "unknown" is assumed to in fact be a civilian, the vast majority of fatalities would remain suspected militants rather than civilians – indeed, by more than a 4:1 ratio'.[65] Leaving 'unknowns' aside, they found a ratio of approximately 16.5 suspected militant fatalities for each civilian death. This, the authors observed, appeared to be a better ratio of suspected militant to civilian fatalities than that of ground-based operations undertaken in the area by Pakistani and US troops.[66]

These figures are presented in such a way as to indicate that the effects of drone strikes are highly discriminate as between combatants and non-combatants, or at least more so than the effects of non-drone operations. However, there is still plenty of room for doubt. First, the authors of the study acknowledged 'the limited and sometimes contradictory reports emanating from the inaccessible tribal areas'.[67] Second, the proportion of 'unknown' victims (15 per cent) is large. And third, it is not known on what grounds, reasonable or otherwise, and by whom, a given person is deemed to be a 'suspected' militant. If the suspicions underlying this designation are unfounded or politically motivated, the ratio of militants to civilians killed remains open to question. A lower rate of non-combatant casualties resulting from drone strikes would make them more ethically acceptable; demonstrating a close alignment of intended and actual outcomes. But a higher rate would blur the practical and ethical distinctions the report's authors seek to draw between drone and non-drone operations. Figures emanating from the US Government itself (via anonymous officials cited in media reports) suggest that CIA drone strikes have been much more discriminate, but inconsistent accounts do little to inspire confidence. For example, in April 2011, US officials were reported as claiming that 'about 30' Pakistani civilians had died in drone strikes between August 2009 and August 2010. But a year later, a senior Obama Administration official claimed that the total number over that period was in the 'single digits'.[68] The confusion is compounded by uncertainty over who the US Government counts as a non-combatant in the first place and why. In May 2012, several White House officials were reported as claiming that President Obama had embraced a method of counting casualties that 'in effect counts all military-age males in a strike zone as combatants... unless there is explicit intelligence posthumously proving them innocent'.[69] Such a counting method, and the physical difficulty of gathering evidence of a target's identity following a drone strike, might well explain US Government claims of extremely small numbers of non-combatant deaths.

From a human rights perspective, according to David Rodin, a given individual has 'the right not to be attacked or exposed to excessive risks, and this right can be alienated or lost only on the basis of some relevant feature of the person him or herself'.[70] In the above example (assuming it is true), maleness and location appear to be regarded as relevant features, but this is to take a *status* approach to who counts as a combatant. The principle of discrimination ought rather to operate to legitimize targeting based on combatant-like *behaviour* rather than enemy-like identity. The latter approach has been an unfortunate feature on both sides of the ongoing Israel–Palestine confrontation. A status approach was taken in 2008, for example, when the Israel Defense Forces (IDF) viewed all policemen in Gaza as legitimate targets who 'could be attacked without regard to what they were doing at the time or the threat they posed'.[71] More broadly, as Burke has observed:

> Groups such as Hamas or Islamic Jihad justify targeting Israeli civilians with suicide bombers with the argument that, by voting for politicians who sanction the killing and dispossession of Palestinians, individual Jews have become indistinguishable from the Israeli state; similarly the Israel Defense Forces (IDF) feel that they are justified in conducting operations that kill innocents or amount to collective punishment because many Palestinians appear to support the suicide attacks.[72]

This is not discrimination between combatants and non-combatants, but rather it is discrimination based merely on who is 'the enemy' (in the broadest sense) and who is not. The US Government, by contrast, does not use drones against an to be reliable? Is the targeted person a combatant or a non-combatant? If killing the targeted person is likely to kill non-combatants also, is the number of non-combatants endangered so high that, because the harms outweigh the benefits, the attack is illegitimate? The latter question relates to the principle of proportionality – to be discussed in the next section of this chapter – but such discussion is usefully preceded by some detailed consideration of the accuracy and destructiveness of 'precise' munitions.

In September 2012, during a visit to Washington, Yemeni President Abed Rabbo Mansour Hadi said US drone strikes 'pinpoint the target and have zero margin of error'.[87] His was a political proposition rather than a mathematical one. The accuracy of bombing is measured using a standard index known as the 'circular error probable' (CEP). This equates to 'the radius of the circle [centred on an aim point] within which 50 per cent of the bombs that are released from an aircraft ultimately fall'.[88] In a typical World War II bombing mission involving 1,500 aircraft delivering 9,000 unguided bombs, only 4,500 of those bombs would have fallen within 1,000 metres of the aim point (with the remainder falling further away), so the CEP of such an attack would have been 1,000 metres.[89] After US aircraft joined the Allied bombing campaign in Europe in August 1942, American bombardiers supposed their Norden bombsights to be devices affording 'precision' even though 'bombs regularly fell at least a quarter mile from the target'.[90] Where a target is located in an urban area (such as a German city), a high CEP brings a high risk of injury to non-combatants. But because the same target could today be 'attacked by one aircraft delivering just one guided bomb with a CEP of 10 metres or less' the expected risk or level of non-combatant injury would be very low by historical standards.[91] Even so, the fact that the CEP index has as its benchmark 50 per cent means, as Zehfuss has argued, that 'precision' weapons are inherently imprecise: 'A certain level of imprecision is indeed part of the definition of precision.'[92] The putative CEP precision of a given weapon is expected to be achieved on average only every other time it is used. In the other 50 per cent of cases, a weapon with a CEP radius of 10 metres will land more than 10 metres away from the aimed-for target.[93] Yet in an urban area especially, a margin of even just a few metres could mean the difference between life and death, and that is so even before the blast radius of a precisely placed weapon is taken into account. Even assuming that a munition's point of impact is extremely close to where its user wanted it to be (i.e. at the exact location of a legitimate military target), the blast generated by that munition exploding is anything but pinpoint when contemplating non-combatants in the vicinity. Data from the early stage of the current war in Afghanistan indicate that 500-pound Paveway II bombs, for example, had a 'lethal [to 50 per cent of exposed persons] blast range' of about 20 metres,[94] and in general the 'recommended safe distance' (for unprotected troops) from the impact point of 500-pound bombs is 500 metres.[95]

In June 2000, when James Der Derian interviewed US general Wesley Clark (the former commander of NATO's 1999 Kosovo campaign), he asked: 'Do you think air power, in particular, the use of precision munitions, is fundamentally more or less ethical than other forms of warfare?' Clark's answer included the statement: 'We always try to use the most discriminate weapon, we always try to use the smallest weapon. It's always preferable to use a BB-gun rather than tear a hole in you, if that's what it takes.'[96] When drone strikes are carried out using a Predator, the weapon is a 100-pound Hellfire missile, and the larger Reaper can also carry 500-pound bombs which have a greater blast range. Thus it is difficult to characterize armed drones as 'the most discriminate weapon', and their use arguably entails a higher degree of risk to non-combatants than would the use of less destructive weaponry. For example, there is no large-scale blast effect from a bullet fired at an enemy combatant from the rifle of a soldier, although there is still a risk that a bullet so fired will miss or pass through the intended target and hit a non-combatant. In the context of a large-scale deployment of ground-based troops, there would be a cumulative risk to non-combatants associated with the use of so many rifles and bullets. The question that then should arise is: would the latter risk to non-combatants be greater or smaller overall than the risk associated with the use of armed drones? However, in line with the US appetite for post-heroic war, the question tends rather to be: which mode of force would entail the least risk (if any) to US personnel? The problem of systemic risk transfer is discussed further in Chapter 5, but for now it is a plausible proposition that Hellfire missiles in Pakistan are merely 'the most discriminate weapon' *available* in circumstances where the American users thereof are not on the ground and not experiencing physical risk.

Proportionality

In addition to the *jus in bello* requirement that damage anticipated from a drone strike should not be deliberately directed towards non-combatants, the principle of proportionality requires that such damage should not outweigh the benefit to be gained by inflicting it. The principle features in the US COIN Field Manual,[97] and it underpins rules of international law such as Article 57(2)(iii) of the 1977 Additional Protocol (I) to the 1949 Geneva Conventions, which prohibits attacks 'which may be expected to cause incidental loss of civilian life, injury to civilians, damage to civilian objects, or a combination thereof, which would be excessive in relation to the concrete and direct military advantage anticipated'.[98] Proportionality, a principle inextricably linked to necessity and discrimination considerations, is perhaps the most difficult to apply for *jus in bello* assessment purposes. One challenge is that, in advance of an attack using an armed drone or some other platform, gauging proportionality (by weighing anticipated costs and benefits) is an exercise in predictive consequentialism. And yet, as Rodin has observed, the 'consequentialist mode of assessment seems most appropriate in retrospect when it is of least use (for we want ethics to function as a guide for future action)'.[99] Another challenge is potentially more emotive: inevitably, because humans are involved (willingly or not) in war, the value of human life ends up being weighed against something that appears more abstract and ephemeral – military benefit. Rebecca Barber insists that there can be no balancing formula because 'the considerations being weighed on each side – the value of human life on the one hand, the value of a military objective on the other – are in many respects simply not amenable to comparison'.[100] And in the specific context of killing 'high-value targets' using drones, Noel Sharkey has posed the question: 'What could the metric be for assigning value to an alleged Al Qaeda leader relative to the value of non-combatants, particularly children who could not be accused of willingly contributing to insurgent activity?'[101] On the one hand, it cannot reasonably be claimed that a single human life is always so valuable as to outweigh the importance of achieving any military objective whatsoever. On the other hand, the proportionality condition surely 'forbids killing thousands of civilians as a side effect of achieving some trivial military goal'.[102] Between these extremes are the 'hard cases' and, in a given instance of the use of force, reasonable minds will differ on whether the principle of proportionality has been upheld. For the purposes of a *jus in bello* assessment of US drone strikes, the making of proportionality judgements is complicated by the aforementioned uncertainties surrounding the military benefits and human costs of US drone strikes. Add to this the uncertainty over who counts as a non-combatant in the first place, and the task is made all the more difficult.

In May 2012 a *New York Times* investigation, involving interviews with dozens of current and former officials within the Obama Administration, revealed that the president had been personally involved in drone strike decisions at weekly counterterrorism meetings in the White House Situation Room. The journalists found that 'When a rare opportunity for a drone strike at a top terrorist arises – but his [the terrorist's] family is with him – it is the president who has reserved to himself the final moral calculation'.[103] Without explanation by the US Government, one can only speculate as to the existence of some kind of decision-making algorithm to guide proportionality calculations. In an attempt to kill a high-level enemy (like Pakistani Taliban commander Baitullah Mehsud), is it worth carrying out an attack in circumstances where there is a high risk of harm to, say, up to ten non-combatants? If the enemy combatant is only mid-level, however, could an attack proceed only if there is a high risk of harm to five or fewer non-combatants? And if the enemy is only a low-level combatant, would a high risk of harm to just one non-combatant be enough to preclude an attack? Presumably, the calculation of proportionality would differ also in circumstances of only moderate or low risk of harm to a particular number of non-combatants. Another relevant factor when weighing the relative value of anticipated harms and benefits might be the drone operator's level of confidence that the right person is in the crosshairs. Given that DNA analysis of bodies has sometimes revealed that the intended target was not present at the time and place of some drone strikes, it has been suggested that 'the target value must be weighted by a probability of presence/absence'.[104] Following the 2011 killing of Osama Bin Laden by US Navy SEALs in Pakistan, President Obama reportedly said:

> Even though I thought it was only 50–50 that Bin Laden was there, I thought it was worth us taking a shot. And I said to myself that if we have a good

chance of not completely defeating but badly disabling Al Qaeda, then it was worth both the political risks as well as the risks to our men.[105]

The reference to 'political risks' might have included any moral opprobrium surrounding the killing of any nearby non-combatants, although it is not clear from the president's statement what value he assigned to those lives in his calculations. As for the risks to 'our men', had this not been a factor (because a drone operator was the one 'taking a shot'), it seems possible that a missile strike would have been carried out even if there had been less than a 50–50 likelihood that Bin Laden was present at the target site.

Even if proportionality calculations are made in the Situation Room in the way described, there remains the problem of whether leadership decapitations are really as militarily beneficial as the US Government seems to think. If the benefit is only slight, the permissible degree of expected but unintended harm to non-combatants would need to be much reduced, possibly to the point of not allowing any such harm at all. However, the US Government appears rather to have extended the rationale for leadership decapitations to embrace a wider range of targets. In 2008, as part of a dramatic expansion of the Pakistan drone campaign, the CIA was reportedly authorized to attack not only high-value individuals whose names are on an approved list ('personality' strikes) but also suspected militants of lower value whose names are not known.[106] The expanded authority for the latter ('signature' strikes), granted by President George W. Bush and maintained by the Obama Administration, permits the CIA to rely on so-called pattern-of-life analysis, using evidence about individuals and locations collected by surveillance cameras on drones and from other sources. In the words of one senior US official (speaking anonymously): 'We might not always have their names but... these are people whose actions over time have made it obvious that they are a threat.'[107]

The transformation of the US drone programme in Pakistan – from a narrow effort aimed at killing Al Qaeda and Taliban leaders into a large-scale campaign of air strikes against whichever militants are deemed to pose a threat to the United States – explains the sharp increase in the reported number of drone strikes and consequent deaths from the middle of 2008. However, whereas proportionality is about adjusting forceful means to take account of strategic ends, this more closely resembles a case of ends being adjusted to the means. Equipped with the means to kill enemies by using drones that are capable of transcending time and space, the US Government's initially narrow goals have arguably been redefined in order to fit the available technology. Yet at what point does the careful selection of targets – in increasing numbers and over a long period of time – become attrition rather than decapitation? And if this *is* a war of attrition in which, as an anonymous US official said in September 2011, drone strikes in Pakistan are causing Al Qaeda to be 'losing people faster than they can put them in',[108] does it end only once Al Qaeda's membership is reduced to zero? If so, given that membership replenishment occurs beyond Pakistan too, such an enterprise could be virtually unending and thus highly unlikely to succeed. If the US

Government's cause is more modest – to respond to the attacks of 11 September 2001 and defend pre-emptively against further attacks – it is difficult to see how it measurably furthers that objective to kill individuals who are engaged in localized insurgent activities but are not actively planning to attack the United States. However, even if there is a slight benefit in carrying out such killings, it is worth asking whether it outweighs the cost of causing harm (albeit unintended) to even one Pakistani non-combatant. Added to this immediate human cost might be a cumulative strategic cost over the medium to long term as more non-combatant deaths (even if they are unintended) generate 'increased hostility among the civilian population, thereby fueling and prolonging the hostilities'.[109] Such an outcome militates against the CIA's drone programme in Pakistan having a reasonable prospect of success, thus underlining again the important relationship that sometimes exists between *jus in bello* and *jus ad bellum* considerations.

Conclusion: a call for transparency

From a *jus in bello* perspective, any drone-driven increase in the lethality of armed conflict is unjust to the extent that more non-combatants are being deliberately killed (a crime of which no evidence has emerged to date) or unintentionally killed to an anticipated degree that is excessive in relation to what is militarily necessary. Drone technology, incorporating powerful target identification capabilities, has the theoretical capacity to enable adherence to the spirit of discrimination and proportionality principles that is greater than what is achievable using other platforms. In practice, however, reported statistics differ markedly on the ratio of combatant to non-combatant deaths resulting from drone strikes, and ethical judgement is made more difficult when there is uncertainty over what kinds of people get counted as non-combatants in the first place. On the latter point, what little evidence is available suggests that the US Government is taking a broad (perhaps overly broad) view of who is targetable. Weighing against the putative military benefit of disrupting militant activities is the immediate human cost of drone strikes measured in innocent lives lost, and there is also a strategic cost imposed by a persistent and widespread perception among Pakistanis that armed drones are insufficiently discriminate. The justness (or otherwise) of the balance of benefits and costs is at present hard to gauge, and the ethical picture that emerges from this chapter's analysis is a murky one. It does not amount to an adequate foundation for determining finally whether US drone strikes in Pakistan constitute a just or an unjust use of force. Arguably, however, the very persistence of doubt on this point undermines US strategic objectives in Pakistan, as well as international norms governing the use of force and the reputation of the United States as a champion of those norms. For so long as the US Government eschews transparency, it is in a weak position to argue for restraint in the use of drones by other states. Such restraint is potentially important for all people everywhere, but Americans especially are likely to sense its importance more as US dominance of drone technology is eroded over time.

In 2010, US State Department lawyer Harold Koh appeared, in an oblique fashion, to be addressing public concerns over CIA drone strikes when he stated:

> In US operations against al-Qaeda and its associated forces – including lethal operations conducted with the use of unmanned aerial vehicles – great care is taken to adhere to these principles in both planning and execution, to ensure that only legitimate objectives are targeted and that collateral damage is kept to a minimum... the principles of distinction and proportionality that the United States applies are not just recited at meetings. They are implemented rigorously throughout the planning and execution of lethal operations to ensure that such operations are conducted in accordance with all applicable law.[110]

Two years later, President Obama himself offered the parsimonious assurance that 'this thing is kept on a very tight leash'.[111] Unfortunately, however, it is not easy to accept such statements at face value, and they still leave room for insurgents in Pakistan to 'portray their [US] opposition as unethical by the opposition's own standards'.[112] Adherence to the principles Koh referred to must be demonstrated rather than asserted, not least because of recent controversy surrounding the US Government's attitude to torture. As one editorial in the *New York Times* put it: 'After the abuses under President Bush, the world is not going to accept a simple "trust us" from the White House.'[113] In a media appearance in October 2012, on the eve of a presidential election, Obama described putting in place a legal architecture to govern drone strikes as something 'we've got to do'.[114] The obvious and disturbing conclusion to be drawn from this is that drones strikes had hitherto been carried out in the absence of a legal architecture. While ever this absence persists, the ethical soundness or otherwise of CIA drone strikes in Pakistan is a matter for speculation, and those who oppose US policy may be quick to assume and proclaim the worst. If an official claim is made without reference to relevant and reliable data, it is reasonable to be cautious in responding to that claim. In mid-2009, for example, Pakistani military officials claimed that their air force, using F-16 fighter jets, had improved its ability to strike precisely at insurgent targets in the north of Pakistan. The putative consequence of increased precision using inhabited aircraft was a reduction in non-combatant casualties and a higher degree of discrimination and therefore an ethically superior mode of applying force had been achieved. However, US officials were reportedly sceptical about this claim at the time: 'We don't have access to battle-damage assessment or the information on the actual strike execution, so we cannot make a qualitative comparison of what the intended effect was versus the actual effect.'[115] By exactly the same reasoning, scepticism could be directed to claims emanating from the US Government that US drone strikes in Pakistan are 'very precise' and 'very limited in terms of collateral damage',[116] and that 'the principles of distinction and proportionality that the United States applies ... are implemented rigorously'.[117]

However much the US Government might intend to use force in ways that are ethically sound, professing good intentions does not obviate the need to demonstrate good consequences. Accountability, if it is to be meaningful, requires that there be an accounting. Those who profess a concern to use force justly can show their sincerity by inquiring into and reporting on the effects of their violent actions, and by implementing measures to prevent and punish any effects that are unjust. From John Brennan's 2011 statement that 'the US Government has not found credible evidence of collateral deaths',[118] it is not clear how hard the US Government has been looking, although it is clearly in its interests to 'find' that only a small proportion of the total number of deaths resulting from drone strikes have been non-combatants. More transparency is required for there to be a reliable tally. As for the importance of denying any state what Alston has described as 'a virtual and impermissible license to kill', transparency is also required regarding 'the procedural and other safeguards in place to ensure that [targeted] killings are lawful and justified, and the accountability mechanisms that ensure wrongful killings are investigated, prosecuted and punished'.[119] Responding to a demand for greater transparency and remedying an apparent 'accountability vacuum' on CIA drone strikes need not entail full disclosure, and indeed Alston accepts that 'States may have tactical or security reasons not to disclose criteria for selecting specific targets (e.g. public release of intelligence source information could cause harm to the source)'.[120] The US Government might also, and with good reason, be reluctant to reveal when and where drone strikes may be authorized, as this would assist potential targets in avoiding attack. At a minimum, however, greater US transparency should entail releasing information on the kinds of people against whom drone strikes can be authorized and why, the number of combatant and non-combatant deaths resulting from each drone strike, and how the conduct of individual CIA drone operators is overseen and regulated.

The latter information is particularly important, and the US Government arguably has a higher onus of public reassurance, given that CIA officers (rather than military personnel) are the ones doing the killing. The very existence, let alone the content, of ethical standards to guide CIA use of force is a mystery. By contrast, the US military has published 'established frameworks for promoting accountability, including institutionalized procedures for applying humanitarian law standards and investigating possible violations'.[121] In 2003 a US Army colonel observed that, whereas the US Department of Defense 'is legally bound to execute its military operations in accordance with the laws of armed conflict', the CIA 'is under no similar requirement'.[122] Even if this officer's observation was incorrect, or the situation has changed since it was made, it would be reassuring if the US Government were to confirm that the CIA applies the same standards as the US military. Such a demonstration would serve the strategic interests of the United States in Pakistan by helping to dispel damaging popular perceptions that CIA drone strikes are unjust. It would also provide reassurance of US adherence to its own ethical standards for COIN and to international norms of restraint in war.

5 Radical asymmetry and the moral equality of combatants

Although there are important connections between individual *jus ad bellum* and *jus in bello* principles, each set of principles taken as a whole is conventionally assumed to be independent of the other. Consequently, 'a state can be justified in its resort to war but violate the *in bello* conditions in how it fights, or initiate war unjustly but use only tactics that are morally allowed'.[1] The first part of this chapter explores whether or how that strict separation is sustainable when armed drones are used in circumstances of radical asymmetry. In an uncontested airspace, and with drone operators in a remote location experiencing no physical risk, force can be applied with apparent impunity. This potentially poses ethical difficulties if it affects an enemy's ability to exercise an inherent right of self-defence, and if it constitutes the systemic transferral of risk from combatants to non-combatants. The second part of the chapter then assesses possibilities for surmounting these difficulties, including by abandoning the traditional notion that combatants on each side of a conflict are morally equal in terms of their licence to kill and their liability to be killed. The moral equality of combatants – a principle that fundamentally supports the distinction between *jus ad bellum* and *jus in bello* – makes it possible and desirable for a combatant to fight justly in a war that is or might be unjust. But if this principle were abandoned, it would need to be somehow established that US drone operators are morally superior because they (and not their enemies) are pursuing a just cause. As 'just combatants', US personnel would not be morally liable to be killed by their unjust opponents, so there would be no problem with the former experiencing no physical risk in the course of a radically asymmetric encounter.

The problem of radical asymmetry

On a chessboard, two opposing sides engage in a perfectly symmetrical contest. Each side has clear and distinguishable uniforms (black or white), the battlefield is physically bounded (64 equal-sized squares), and there are immutable rules on how the contest is commenced, conducted and terminated. Not only is the game of chess a completely fair fight between 'combatants' (the chess pieces), therefore, it is also a fight in which there is never any participation by non-combatants. In exploring the ethics of asymmetric war, Rodin has argued that 'when conflict diverges too drastically from the assumption implicit in the chessboard image of war we experience serious difficulties in interpreting and applying standard judgments of just war theory'.[2] This is not to suggest that war *ought* to be symmetrical. The use of force by opponents in war should be necessary, discriminate and proportionate, but there is no ethical requirement for war to be 'fair' in the sense of being evenly balanced. Indeed, according to Rodin, it would be 'an improper importation from the trivial and inappropriate morality of games' to insist upon and attempt to achieve 'a "fair" fight between the two sides, in the sense of a rough equality of capabilities, symmetrically and reciprocally deployed'.[3] Rather, his argument is that it might be more difficult to achieve and to discern justice in war when there is a vast power disparity between the stronger and the weaker side.

From its earliest days, airpower technology has been held to confer on its users an overwhelming advantage in war. For example, in his seminal work *Il diminio dell-aria* (*The Command of the Air*), first published in 1921, Italian major-general Giulio Douhet argued that airpower is 'a weapon superlatively adapted to offensive purposes, because it strikes suddenly and gives the enemy no time to parry the blow'.[4] More recently, and relevant to the notion of strikingly mismatched opponents, modern US airpower has been likened not to Goliath but rather to David:

> Since biblical times at the latest, Western culture has placed a premium on the worth of the individual. One dimension of this has always been the effort to preserve life in war by developing the ability to deliver projectiles with maximum accuracy from a maximum distance – precision and standoff. David was able to sling his stone at Goliath accurately from a standoff distance that kept him out of the giant's reach. Nowhere is this phenomenon more pronounced than it is in the United States.[5]

Regarding the use of armed drones specifically – controlled from far away and flying unseen at a high altitude – an alternative 'biblical' characterization is that the United States possesses 'a godlike power to call down destruction from the skies' upon its enemies.[6] Godlike or not, the wielding of such power occasions fresh consideration of just war principles, especially if it challenges traditional understandings of the nature of war itself.

War-as-contest

The term 'asymmetry' can refer to any imbalance in the strength that each side in a conflict can bring to bear against the other. All wars may and should be regarded as asymmetric in the sense that perfect equality of strength at a given time and place is both highly unlikely to occur and practically impossible to verify. *Radical* asymmetry, however, is an imbalance so obvious and so profound that one side is apparently unable to apply – in a just fashion, at least – any strength at all against the other. Such a relationship places stress on a longstanding assumption by warriors and ethicists alike that war is essentially a contest. For the reasons described above, war does not need to be a *fair* (evenly balanced) fight, but arguably it needs to be a *fight*. Where there is no contest *per se* going on, there is no war. And where there is no war, so defined, there is only unidirectional politically motivated violence. Although it is a well-known Clausewitzian aphorism that war is the continuation of politics by other means, Clausewitz also offered the more fundamental observation that 'War is always the shock of two hostile bodies in collision, not the action of a living power upon an inanimate mass, because an absolute state of endurance would not be making War'.[7] For present purposes, the question that arises is whether the United States places itself and its combatants in such a state through the radically asymmetric application of force using armed drones. If it does, it may be that this technology is not merely transforming the character of war (as so many other technologies have done in the past) but rather enabling a form of violence so fundamentally different in nature that it does not count as war. The *mutual* experiencing of physical risk is surely elemental to any violent contest, whereas a one-sided experience of risk is merely (to use Clausewitz's words) 'the action of a living power upon an inanimate mass'.

From an ethical perspective, the problem with a 'non-war' is that it cannot be a just war. The unidirectional application of force might be consistent with acting justly if the purpose is law enforcement, although a later section of this chapter will discuss problems with characterizing drone strikes as such. Alternatively, if a drone 'war' is still contestable by those against whom it is waged, it is an ethical problem if they are only able (albeit not permitted) to participate in an unjust fashion (for example, by deliberately targeting non-combatants). If it is the case that one side's use of armed drones places the other side in a position where it is unable to strike back, or at least to strike back justly, a problem arises in respect of a state's and/or individual's right to self-defence. Arguably, depriving an entity of the ability to exercise this inherent and inalienable *jus ad bellum* right presents a fundamental challenge to the just war tradition. Suzy Killmister has observed, for example, that 'remote weaponry can create situations in which the targeted state has all moral options for retaliation closed off, forcing it to either surrender or transgress civilian immunity'.[8] There are two alternative problems with such situations.

One option is to accept that the superior military technology of the stronger side engenders a superior moral claim, such that those targeted by remote weaponry are morally obliged to surrender. For Rodin, however, what is 'morally troubling' about this and other asymmetric uses of force is that 'the weak party is required by the rules of war to give up something that… has real moral importance in itself – the effective pursuit of just war [self-defence] aims'.[9] He goes on to argue that

> if (as the just war theory assumes) war is a morally appropriate remedy to redress certain kinds of injustice, then fairness ought to dictate that it be a remedy open to the weak as well as the strong. Indeed, it is precisely the

weak who have most need of the protection provided by the norm of self-defence. An interpretation of the right of self-defence that effectively denied recourse to the weak while ensuring it for the strong would be a perverse interpretation indeed.[10]

Further to this *jus ad bellum* concern, Jai Galliott argues that asymmetry in war might reach such a level – 'a radical imbalance in the level of life-threatening risk incurred between warring parties' – as to render the superior side in violation of the principle of proportionate cause.[11] In circumstances of extreme disparity in technological competence, that is, 'it seems that the harm that the technologically superior state hopes to thwart will in many cases be so insignificant that it would present problems for the proportionality calculus' of harms caused versus harms avoided by going to war.[12] In other words, the benefit derived from the stronger party going to war would not outweigh the harms thus generated.

The prospect of harm is relevant for *jus in bello* purposes also when assessing the dangerousness or otherwise of individuals. If one were to assume that the 'weak' side on the receiving end of US drone strikes were completely deprived of any ability to retaliate, all individuals on that side would be 'innocent' and unable to be targeted. In the context of war (as distinct from law enforcement), the term 'innocence' is not used to convey a judgement on the moral status (non-culpability) of an individual. Rather, it is understood by reference to its Latin etymology: to be innocent is to be not *nocentes* ('not harming'). A non-combatant is innocent, therefore, not in the sense of being free from moral blameworthiness, but in the sense of posing no threat. On this point, and relevant to the use of armed drones, Zehfuss has argued that 'the use of weapons that put combatants out of their enemies' range invalidates one of the most common arguments for the permissibility of targeting enemy combatants, namely that they are in the business of harming the combatants doing the targeting'.[13] If circumstances are such that 'enemy combatants [and non-combatants] are equally unable to inflict harm',[14] she argues, immunity and protection from attack should be available to both. For present purposes, it is unnecessary to delve too far into such a proposition because US drone strikes can and do attract at least a scintilla of retaliation. Enemies of the United States are able to strike back, albeit in a manner contrary to *jus in bello* principles. Ground-based drone operators who release missiles against targets in the Middle East and Central Asia might themselves be virtually untouchable in their secure bases deep inside the American homeland, but ordinary (non-combatant) Americans can be and have been targeted in deliberately indiscriminate (terrorist) attacks.[15]

This leads to the second option for responding to Killmister's idea that remote weaponry creates 'situations' in which moral opportunities for retaliation are closed off. That option is, first, to acknowledge that, although a genuine war-as-contest *is* going on, the technologically weaker side is practically capable only of participating using unjust (e.g. indiscriminate) methods. And second, it requires an acceptance that, in order for the weaker side to retain any semblance of an ability to strike back in self-defence, the stronger side's non-combatants cannot (as a matter of principle) be immune from attack. The overall dilemma, therefore, is that 'remote weaponry has the consequence of rendering just war theory either an ally of the powerful, or obsolete'.[16] On the one hand, no US government is likely to accept that, for the sake of fairness, radically asymmetric uses of force should be contingent on a willingness to expose American civilians as legitimate targets. And on the other hand, no enemy of the United States is likely to submit humbly to the notion that 'might is right' when it comes to justice in war. If ethical principles are to retain any purchase on war-as-contest, it seems that the traditional notion of 'combat between combatants' must continue to be realized even in the face of technological change. When it comes to the use of armed drones, however, the elimination of physical risk to the drone operator appears to preclude any (just) contest. First, it is (or is likely to be perceived as) an exercise in the systematic transfer of risk from US personnel to non-combatants in targeted territories. And second, the repeated spectacle of non-combatants deaths (combined with the enemy's inability to strike back directly at those Americans doing the killing) is likely to induce unjust behaviour in the form of terrorism. Both eventualities occasion concern from a *jus in bello* perspective.

Drones and risk transfer

Non-combatants within the strike range of a drone-launched missile are at risk of being killed unintentionally – as 'collateral' when an enemy combatant is struck, as a result of technical malfunction, or because of an intelligence-based targeting error – and also, in theory at least, as a result of a drone operator's deliberate decision to violate the discrimination principle. US Government officials comment openly or anonymously on the first of these risks, but official opacity prevents outside scrutiny of whether or how often the other possibilities become realties. Whatever the precise cause of harm, and taking the example of Pakistan as discussed in the previous chapter, the number of non-combatant deaths resulting from the CIA's use of armed drones there might be large or it might be small (depending on which unofficial body count is regarded as more reliable). For the purposes of this chapter, however, what matters most is that a US drone operator cannot be killed while carrying out a missile strike. As such, it is plain to all observers that the immediate experience of physical risk is one-sided.

Consistent with the American appetite for post-heroic war, there has long been a concern to reduce as far as possible the exposure to risk of US personnel. Arguably, the practical consequence of such risk 'reduction' has often rather been the transferral of risk to others. In a report to Congress on the 1991 Gulf War, the US Defense Department declared that munitions and delivery systems were chosen to reduce collateral damage 'to the degree possible and consistent with *allowable risk* to aircraft and aircrews'.[17] Military personnel deployed to use force in the Gulf were required to 'exercise reasonable precautions to minimize incidental or collateral injury to the civilian population or damage to civilian objects, consistent with mission accomplishments and *allowable risk* to the attacking forces'.[18] Such language is clearly informed by the *jus in bello* principles of necessity, discrimination and proportionality. Most significant, however, is the way in which the lives of US personnel are apparently weighed in the balance, not only against the importance of overall victory, but also against the lives of local non-combatants caught up in the conflict. As the level of 'allowable risk' to US personnel gets lower, the importance of protecting them increases. From a strategic perspective, force protection can become an objective so all-consuming as to distort or jeopardize mission accomplishment. This presents a potential problem from an ethical perspective too, in terms of the *jus ad bellum* requirement for a reasonable prospect of success. Moreover, there is a *jus in bello* dimension to force protection if it manifests in methods and means of stand-off warfare that effectively transfer risk from friendly combatants to 'enemy' non-combatants. Such use of force sits uneasily with the principle of discrimination, especially if the lives of combatants are accorded the highest value in any proportionality calculation.

Militarily and morally, it is necessary and desirable for commanders to be concerned for the safety of their soldiers, sailors and airmen. Human rights law requires states to expend effort protecting the right to life of all those in their jurisdiction, and even if citizen-soldiers voluntarily assume the risk of being killed, 'that does not mean that no regard should be paid to their safety, even in conflict'.[19] It remains the case, nevertheless, that combatants 'are legitimate targets of military force and their deaths are an expected consequence of war'.[20] History shows that non-combatant deaths can be expected too, but these are not morally acceptable as a matter of course. That the death in war of a non-combatant is a greater tragedy than the death of a combatant (the life of the former being more valuable) is a view confirmed by the *jus in bello* prohibition on deliberately targeting non-combatants, and it fits with Paul Christopher's observation that 'risking one's life is part of what it means to be a soldier'.[21] Indeed, it is probably on the basis that soldiers' lives weigh less in the moral balance than civilians' lives that Walzer has argued 'even if the target is very important, and the number of innocent people threatened relatively small, [users of force] must risk soldiers *before* they kill civilians'.[22] In practice, however, non-combatant status by no means always trumps combatant status when the value of lives is being weighed. As Thomas Hurka has observed, although the relative value of combatants' lives is reduced by their 'voluntary assumption of risk', there is a tendency to value more highly the lives of 'our' combatants because of a 'special relationship of co-nationality'.[23]

In the Afghanistan War that began in late 2001, it may be that the United States 'displayed national partiality', as Bellamy has claimed, 'by prioritizing the safety of its military personnel over that of Afghan non-combatants'.[24] US commanders there 'chose not to deploy significant numbers of ground forces or forward air controllers to identify and verify targets, presumably because of the attendant risks of doing so', with the result that some targeting 'relied on unverified intelligence provided by Afghan sources that often proved unreliable'.[25]

Two years previously, as part of NATO's Kosovo intervention, US pilots had been involved in similar targeting errors. Although those high-altitude bombers themselves suffered no combat casualties, approximately 500 Yugoslav civilians were reportedly killed as a result of that bombing campaign.[26] The problem in both these situations was not that individual pilots violated the discrimination principle by deliberately targeting non-combatants. Rather, it was that force was used in a way that consistently reflected a valuing of the lives of US combatants above the lives of non-combatants in enemy territory. As such, any non-discrimination was not immediate and tactical in nature but instead systematic and strategic. It is a characteristic of what Martin Shaw calls 'risk-transfer militarism' that '[b]ombing is undertaken in the firm knowledge that it will increase the risk to civilians compared with other possible means, military as well as non-military'.[27] Indeed, airpower features prominently when strong powers like the United States choose to 'use tactics and weapons designed to shelter their own troops from harm, but which impose avoidable risks upon enemy non-combatants'.[28] And just as it is safer for a user of force to operate far above the place where the enemy stands, so it is safer still not to be there at all.

Armed drones, controlled remotely from as far away as the other side of the world, open up a new dimension of risk-transfer. An individual drone operator can be punctilious in upholding the discrimination principle, and a drone campaign has the potential – from one airstrike to the next – to be one less harmful to non-combatants than other uses of force. Nevertheless, it is a deliberate and systematic feature of drone use that a drone operator experiences no physical risk while at the same time endangering non-combatants. That danger – be it the result of imperfect targeting intelligence, mechanical malfunction, or simply being too close to an exploding Hellfire missile – is not something from which a non-combatant can be removed like a pilot can be removed from a cockpit. That the US Government repeatedly issues assurances that drone strikes are 'precise' does not necessarily alleviate concern, because 'precision' munitions (being inherently *imprecise* according to the CEP index) are a double-edged sword in a political sense. Precision technology carries the promise of *fewer* non-combatants deaths than would likely result from using other technologies. Yet, by 'talking up' its technological proficiency, the United States arguably causes others to be surprised or suspicious when *any* non-combatant deaths occur as a result of its violent actions. As Mahnken has warned: 'The ability of weapons to destroy targets reliably and accurately has fostered the notion that war is a bloodless and error-free undertaking. In such an environment, targeting errors ... are likely to be perceived as deliberate acts.'[29] This brings the discussion to the second major problem with radical asymmetry: that it induces the weak to use force unjustly in response to what they perceive (rightly or wrongly) as injustice perpetrated by the powerful. America's enemies – feeling deprived of their ability to exercise self-defence by (justly) attacking an 'available' US combatant, being disinclined to surrender in the face of adversity, and casting about for someone against whom to retaliate – instead turn to softer (non-combatant) targets inside the United States.

Asymmetric jus in bello

Faisal Shahzad, the Pakistani-born American who attempted in 2010 to detonate a bomb in New York's Times Square, reportedly said: 'US drone strikes don't see children, they don't see anybody. They kill women, children; they kill everybody.'[30] His expressed attitude and attempted action resonate strongly with a statement made by Osama Bin Laden in a 1998 television interview:

> American history does not distinguish between civilians and military.... The only way for us to fend off these assaults is to use similar means.... We do not differentiate between those dressed in military uniforms and civilians; they are all targets in this fatwa.[31]

Evident in the statements of both men is a cruel and perverse notion of reciprocal justice in war. Each wrongly assumes, first, that actual outcomes (non-combatant deaths) are necessarily the same as intended outcomes. Neither logic nor evidence supports such an assumption. Second, Shahzad and Bin Laden seem to insist that (allegedly) bad behaviour by those on one side of a conflict generates moral permission for those on the other side to behave in the very manner that they deplore. Such reciprocity might be intuitively appealing according to a crude, 'eye for an eye' notion of righteous revenge. However, even in circumstances of radical asymmetry, combatants on the weaker side are arguably not entitled to attack non-combatants on the stronger side in order, according to some notion of fairness, to restore balance. And yet, at the same time, it is reasonable to insist that for a war-as-contest to *be* a contest, someone on the other side must somehow be 'in the fight'.

Unfortunately for the United States, the Al Qaeda vision of reciprocally indiscriminate war looks likely to remain somewhat plausible to many observers and would-be victims of US violence, and it will probably continue to have political purchase in the context of post-heroic war. Even if the intentions of each and every US drone operator are purely informed by respect for *jus in bello* principles, the wider spectacle of systemic risk-transfer that a drone programme generates plays right into the hands of enemies who derive benefit from portraying Americans as cowardly killers who endanger others while avoiding danger themselves. This predicament might not, however, be inescapable. The US Government is likely neither to change minds nor save lives simply by pointing out to would-be terrorists that their ethical argument for indiscriminate violence is flawed. Therefore it seems to be important, or at least worth a try, for the United States to be more proactive, perhaps by changing the way in which it characterizes and/or conducts its drone strikes.

One option might be for the US Government to characterize drone strikes not as acts of war but as actions taken only for the purpose of law enforcement. By taking the traditional expectation of war-as-contest off the table, this could circumvent any 'fairness' objection to radical asymmetry. Since the War on Terror began, US Government rhetoric has often contained mixed messages as regards which moral paradigm applies, with the result that American use of force has variously taken on the appearance of war, law enforcement, both and neither. Former president George W. Bush told the US Congress that, on 11 September 2001, 'enemies of freedom committed an act of war against our country' and he promised that 'whether we bring our enemies to justice, or bring justice to our enemies, justice will be done'.[32] Such language exhibits a curious and perhaps convenient mix of war and law enforcement motivations. According to Burke, the first response (bringing enemies to justice) 'implies using legal processes and neutral/universal standards of judgment', whereas the second (bringing justice to enemies) 'suggests the use of extra-legal means' such as 'killing at a distance on the basis of minimal evidence or suspect intelligence'.[33] In the War on Terror thus far, America's leaders have arguably wanted to have it both ways; to be able to use force more freely because it is warlike, and also to present the United States as the morally superior dispenser of justice to lowly criminals. As such, this has been a peculiar war because it amounts to 'an armed conflict where state forces have the privilege to use force against those who lack such privilege – a situation that normally prevails in peacetime, under the law enforcement paradigm'.[34] There is an apparent reluctance to acknowledge America's enemies ('terrorists') as warriors, and yet it is only warriors who may be directly subjected to warlike use of force. Criminals, by contrast, attract a law enforcement response that does not necessarily (but might) include violent measures.

In his 2010 report as the UN Special Rapporteur on Extrajudicial, Summary or Arbitrary Executions, Philip Alston lamented that 'In the legitimate struggle against terrorism, too many criminal acts have been re-characterised so as to justify addressing them within the framework of the law of armed conflict'.[35] At the same time, in the case of the United States, the language and moral gravitas of the law enforcement paradigm ('crime and punishment') continue to be borrowed for political purposes, without acceptance of all the responsibilities that normally come with it. One example of this is the way in which the 'guilt' of a suspected terrorist is not formally determined in a court of law, but based on intelligence.[36] If state action against terrorists is based on the notion of criminal culpability (as distinct from dangerousness in war), such framing should trigger the application of peacetime human rights norms including the right to a fair trial and protection against the arbitrary taking of life and liberty.[37] In September 2011, however, the US Government appeared to walk along both sides of the street when it killed one of its own citizens. Was this law enforcement or an act of war? Anwar al-Awlaki, born in New Mexico, was a Muslim cleric and Al Qaeda propagandist who had eluded US and Yemeni intelligence officials for the previous two years. He had allegedly been involved in a number of plots to attack the United States, but this allegation was not brought to trial and no US court handed down a sentence. Rather, 'law enforcement' occurred when a CIA drone fired Hellfire missiles that hit the car in which al-Awlaki and three others were travelling as they drove through a remote part of north-eastern Yemen.[38]

As much as removing US drone strikes from the war paradigm appears to offer an escape from the problem of radical asymmetry, the al-Awlaki case suggests that such removal seems unlikely to occur. In circumstances where arrest, trial and sentencing are deemed to be infeasible, the US Government is likely to favour maintaining a useful ambiguity as between war and law enforcement. In any event, to recharacterize the use of armed drones as an exclusively law enforcement endeavour would be highly implausible. First, technology designed for remote-control killing simply does not lend itself to a criminal justice purpose. In a law enforcement paradigm, where the peacetime rules governing state violence apply, human rights considerations dictate that 'a targeted killing in the sense of an intentional, premeditated and deliberate killing by law enforcement officials cannot be legal because, unlike in armed conflict, it is never permissible for killing to be the *sole objective* of an operation'.[39] Second, even if the United States is tempted to characterize its own use of force via drones as an example not of war but of something more like policing, people on the ground in targeted territories are likely to retain the perspective that drone strikes look and feel like war. A better option, therefore, might be for the United States to resolve the paradigmatic ambiguity of its drone programme by instead characterizing it as exclusively warlike. Any 'fairness' objection to the problem of radical asymmetry would instead be addressed by the United States holding itself to a higher standard of matching *jus in bello* intentions to actual consequences. By thus raising the standard of justice in war (rather than lowering it, as Osama Bin Laden preferred), any associated reduction of harm to non-combatants might in turn reduce the grievance (and the motivation to use indiscriminate violence) felt by America's enemies in the War on Terror.

In the context of asymmetry more generally, Rodin has argued in favour of requiring the strong to 'take exceptionally rigorous steps to ensure that they do not harm non-combatants or expose them to risks of incidental harm in the course of military operations'.[40] One example of this, he suggests, is to 'require certainty or near-certainty as to the status of a proposed target through clear, unambiguous and reliable evidence'[41] before an attack is authorized. Here, there is a consistency with Walzer's notion of 'double intention' according to which two things are ethically necessary. First, that the good (killing an enemy combatant) be achieved, and second, that the foreseeable evil (harm to non-combatants) be reduced as far as possible: 'aware of the evil involved, [the user of force] seeks to minimize it, *accepting costs to himself*.'[42] The cost to the United States, when conducting drone strikes in radically asymmetric circumstances, might be to afford the lives of non-combatants a much higher value relative not only to the immediate military value of targeted combatants but also to the value of the mission as a whole. The effect would be to forego any strike which placed a certain number of non-combatants at a certain level of risk. Whatever number and level the US Government currently uses as a benchmark (assuming it has one) for the purpose of proportionality calculations would have to be lowered, thus lowering the relative importance of killing combatants and of pursuing the overall cause. In effect, America's asymmetric drone war would be conducted in such a way that the safety of non-combatants was as high a priority as the safety of US drone operators themselves. If, under a stricter *jus in bello* standard, a local non-combatant's life was worth the same as a US-based drone operator's life, effort would be needed to ensure that each was exposed to the same level of risk. And because a drone operator experiences no physical risk, it follows that a US drone strike would need to carry zero risk of harm to non-combatants too (assuming they are correctly and plausibly identified as such). The application of force according to such a strict standard would likely be painstakingly difficult, and even more so if the possibility of certain technical malfunctions (such as the accidental release of a missile) was factored in. In practice, the process of targeting might become so careful as to resemble closely the judicial tasks of weighing evidence, rendering a verdict, and imposing a punishment that fits the crime (and affects nobody but the convicted criminal). The relative freedom that the paradigm of war (as distinct from law enforcement) provides to use force would be severely curtailed, and thus a drone war might become so inconvenient as to be not worth pursuing at all.

Such a prospect could well prove highly unattractive to the US Government, so it remains to consider a third way in which it might get around the problem of radical asymmetry when it comes to drone strikes. This involves focusing not on *jus in bello* dimensions but rather on what provides moral cause for war in the first place (*jus ad bellum*). For Rodin, 'it is reasonable that the laws of war place higher *jus in bello* demands on the strong', because 'strong states are more likely to engage in unjust "wars of choice", wars which the strong, moreover, possess the overwhelming capability to win'.[43] However, if it could be established that the United States uses armed drones for a just and necessary cause, an argument could be made that its technological strength is a moral asset and that imposing stricter *jus in bello* restrictions on itself is morally undesirable. Accordingly, the second part of this chapter assesses the notion that the problem of radical asymmetry is resolved by the strong side (in this case the United States) having a superior *jus ad bellum* claim. Such a notion necessarily brings with it the assumption that US drone operators are morally superior combatants rather than merely the moral equals of combatants on the weaker side.

The moral equality of combatants

In philosophical debates among ethicists, there are 'collectivists' who argue that killing in war is a function of a relationship between collectives (e.g. states) not persons, and there are 'individualists' who argue that the rules governing killing in war are the same as the rules governing defensive killing between individuals.[44] The collectivist position is the orthodox one, and it is best represented in the influential work of Michael Walzer, but it has recently come under challenge by individualists like Jeff McMahan.[45] The collectivist position insists upon the distinction between *jus ad bellum* and *jus in bello*: 'We draw a line between the war itself, for which soldiers are not responsible, and the conduct of the war, for which they are responsible.'[46] This distinction is reflected in Shakespeare's play *Henry V* when, on the eve of the Battle of Agincourt, an English soldier (John Bates) declares: 'we know enough if we know we are the King's subjects: if his cause be wrong, our obedience to the King wipes the crime of it out of us.'[47] Bates was also in a position identical and morally equal to that of any French soldier in service to the French king, irrespective of the justice of that king's cause. The principle of the moral equality of combatants, as applicable today as it was in Shakespeare's time, stems from 'the belief that it would be unfair to hold that combatants act wrongly simply in virtue of their leaders' wrongful decision to wage an unjust war'.[48] Such combatants still 'act wrongly' if they fail to uphold *jus in bello* principles, however, and so their moral equality is dependent on having the same commitment as their enemies to use force in a just manner. In any event, the *jus ad bellum* context of the fight in which they find themselves is generally held to be irrelevant. Moreover, it can be argued that issues like just cause and right authority *ought* not to affect combatants' equal moral status if, for reasons of duress or inadequate information, combatants on either or both sides of a conflict are incapable of acting on the basis of independent moral determination. By taking up arms for a cause (just or not) and thus posing a threat (via the institution they serve) to other human beings, combatants weaken or to an extent give up their right to life. In particular, the life of a combatant is partially and temporarily devalued in relation to the life of a non-combatant who has *not* taken up arms. This notion of (relatively) diminished life-value vitally supports, first, the moral equality of combatants who thereby possess an equal right to engage in a potentially life-depriving way towards each other. Second, and at the same time, it supports the principle of discrimination whereby non-combatants (whose right to life is undiminished) may not be intentionally targeted. The moral equality of combatants therefore appears to be integral to the way in which *jus in bello* principles are conventionally supposed to civilize the conduct of wars, be they just or unjust.

The work of McMahan, which presents a serious challenge to this collectivist orthodoxy, is highly relevant to an ethical assessment of radically asymmetric drone warfare and of the moral status of drone operators. In his 2009 book *Killing in War*, McMahan rejects the notion that war is a distinct moral universe. Rather, he argues that the justifications for killing people in war are no different from those that apply in other contexts, such as individual self-defence. This amounts to a radical critique of the just war tradition, of the traditional distinction between *jus ad bellum* and *jus in bello*, and of the presumed moral equality of combatants. McMahan prefers the morality of conflict that applies in contexts other than war and which is 'almost invariably asymmetric: those who are in the right may be permitted to use force and violence but those who are in the wrong are not'.[49] An example is a robber who is clearly 'in the wrong' when he leaps out and mugs a pedestrian on the street. The robber does not have permission to use force for this purpose, whereas the pedestrian is right to do so in order to resist the violence wrongly visited upon her. When it comes to war itself, McMahan's contention is that, if it is wrong to fight in an unjust war (one that lacks a just cause), there is moral inequality as between what he calls 'just combatants' and 'unjust combatants'.[50] The overall injustice of an unjust combatant's cause renders unjust every act to further it. Unjust combatants breach the discrimination principle because just combatants are not legitimate targets, and they breach the proportionality principle because, being without a just cause, there is no 'good' to be achieved as could be weighed against any harm anticipated.[51] For present purposes, the critical question is whether the operators of armed US drones – flying over Afghanistan, Iraq, Pakistan, Yemen, Libya, Somalia or elsewhere – are 'in the right'. If so, they (as just combatants) are permitted to use force against an enemy (an unjust combatant), but that enemy cannot justly harm them. That a drone operator should kill for a just cause while experiencing no physical risk thus seems entirely proper. However, if a drone operator is 'in the wrong', it seems entirely improper that they (as unjust combatants) should be able to use force while rendering themselves physically immune to legitimate attack.

The fact that, in Pakistan for example, the operators of US armed drones engage in a form of killing that entails no physical risk to themselves does, at first, appear to suggest that they are using force in pursuit of a cause not worth dying for. According to John Stuart Mill, a regime of freedom 'requires men and women who value freedom enough to risk their lives in its defense',[52] and Walzer has argued that 'There must be purposes that are worth dying for, outcomes for which soldiers' lives are not too high a price'.[53] Ignatieff, for whom the 1999 NATO campaign in Kosovo was a war waged with impunity, has raised the question: 'if impunity is required before values are defended, what exactly are values worth?'[54] It does not necessarily follow, however, that America's cause is unjust because the specific means (remote-control killing) chosen to pursue it involves no shedding of American blood (Anwar al-Awlaki aside). An alternative explanation might be that the cause in pursuit of which drones are used is of such moral importance that the deaths of US personnel would be an impermissible setback. In other words, by staying alive, a drone operator is able to contribute further to the victory that is so morally urgent. Conversely, if the United States used force in a slightly less asymmetric fashion – for example, by deploying inhabited aircraft rather than drones – and if more just combatants were killed as a result, those deaths would weaken America's ability to achieve its just cause.

The issue of whether the US operators are using force in pursuit of a just cause was explored in Chapter 3, but for present purposes it is important to emphasize that a rejection of the moral equality of combatants necessarily involves privileging *jus ad bellum* over *jus in bello*. If what matters most morally is not what combatants *do* but rather what they do it *for*, everything seems to ride upon the existence of a just cause. To adopt McMahan's reasoning could indeed be a way to establish the permissibility of radically asymmetric uses of armed drones, but history shows that a 'just cause' – claims of which are frequently and notoriously contested – can be a fragile moral foundation for violent action. Even if one takes the view that 'most wars are unjust', it is no straightforward matter to identify exactly which wars are unjust and which are not. Learned and reasonable minds will differ and, in any event, 'all belligerents profess the justice of their cause'.[55] From a legal perspective, Michael Schmitt has asked: 'How does one reliably identify an [unjust] aggressor within a body of [*jus ad bellum*] law that is at the same time sparse and highly malleable?'[56] And Colin Gray too has raised the spectre of uncertainty by describing the 'principles, niceties, and nuances' of just war theory as having the characteristics of 'porousness and wide scope for self-interested interpretation'.[57]

As the United States uses armed drones to wage war in a post-heroic, radically asymmetric fashion, it could well be doing so for a just (self-defence or humanitarian) cause. However, there are reasons to hesitate before making that assumption about powerful states in general. When contemplating asymmetry, as Rodin has warned, there is a need to be generally mindful that

> The temptations of recourse to unjust war are greater for the strong than for the weak. Because they are rich, the strong can more easily absorb the material costs of war. Because their defences are strong, there is little risk that they will be forced to fight on their own soil, with all the hardship and devastation this entails. Because the strong have professional [non-conscript] armies, their broader society is substantially insulated from the experience of war.[58]

As a strong state, the United States invaded Iraq in 2003, but uncertainty persists over whether that war was just and thus whether (according to McMahan's formulation) the American invaders were just combatants. In *Killing in War*, McMahan at one point argues that a 'preventive war' is a type of 'offensive or aggressive war' that is 'potentially just'.[59] But he elsewhere portrays the Iraq War specifically as an unjust endeavour in which American soldiers participated only after becoming 'victims of positive deception... by the Bush administration that Iraq possessed weapons of mass destruction'.[60] Acknowledging 'epistemic limitation', McMahan observes: 'Combatants usually act in ignorance of a great many factual matters that are relevant to the determination of whether the war in which they have been commanded to fight is just.'[61] For example, if 'war erupts suddenly', combatants 'may simply have no opportunity for gathering relevant information and engaging in careful deliberation'.[62] Nevertheless, in such circumstances, it remains unclear exactly *who* deliberates and determines – and who is *competent* to determine in a timely fashion – whether a war (and a combatant therein) is objectively just or unjust. Objectivity is difficult and perhaps impossible in war; even decades or centuries after a conflict, military historians (with extensive access to declassified action reports and government documents) debate 'what the war was really about' and 'what really went on'. In any event, judgements in hindsight are of limited worth because ethics ought to guide future action. For these reasons, and because of the uncertainty that seems endemic to all wars everywhere, the traditional, 'just-in-case' approach of assuming moral equality between combatants seems fairer and more prudent.

The notion of such equality also serves as an important check on users of force who might otherwise become overly preoccupied with the *jus ad bellum* dimensions of war. By granting to combatants on both sides of a conflict the ability to fight justly (*jus in bello*) in a war that might or might not be just, and by expecting of them equally a commitment to do so, there is hopefully less likelihood of cruel means being subordinated to supposedly noble ends. The United States and other Western democracies are not automatically made morally superior by their own determination that 'we're the good guys' and, for Coady, such conviction is 'a powerful recipe for folly at the least and self-righteous vice at the worst'.[63] A particular concern might be that the rights and lives of the 'bad guys' are too readily devalued, with the result that the manner of violently engaging them is allowed to be more cruel than it would otherwise be. Relevant to this point, Gray has warned:

> Liberal values do not provide protection against the horrors of warfare, indeed quite the reverse can be the case. If the cause is held to be sufficiently sacred, means and methods may obey no rule save that of an expediency equated with a necessity that should tolerate no compromise.[64]

Such a prospect is all the more worrisome if Burke is correct in his view that America's 'disregard for international law is built upon a particularly claustrophobic idea of moral community; a bifurcated moral universe that casts the United States and its allies as virtuous and its enemies as ineradicably threatening and evil'.[65] If the charge of US combatants is to attempt nevertheless to eradicate such evil, the danger then is that even the cruellest military means may appear justified.

Before the outbreak of World War II, the German philosopher Carl Schmitt warned that describing a military adversary in stark moral or criminal terms works to justify violent actions against that enemy.[66] Soon afterwards, participants on both sides of that war ended up using force in a manner at odds with *jus in bello* principles, on the grounds perhaps that 'nothing can be allowed to hinder the pursuit of Good and the elimination of Evil'.[67] Such conduct was arguably seen as justifiable in light of the perceived and overriding moral importance of victory. In Europe, for example, the Allies argued that deliberate attacks on civilian populations with the purpose of destroying popular morale would prevent a Nazi victory, with the result that 'Alleged efficiency in the pursuit of a good end replaced traditional morality in the conduct of war'.[68] A complementary and likely factor in the subordination of *jus in bello* principles was the construction of a profoundly destructive dichotomy of 'good guys' versus 'bad guys'. In the Pacific theatre, according to Sherry, the Americans'

> technological fetishism – whereby machines both unleashed and disguised the ferocity of their war making – stood in contrast to the human fanaticism they saw in their enemies, especially the Japanese. Dominant American attitudes toward the Japanese as a bestial, inferior race deserving of American revenge made the prospect of incinerating Japan's cities especially inviting, while Americans' isolation from aerial retaliation made bombing even more attractive to them.[69]

In the crucible of war, the emergence of such attitudes remains possible today, especially in a War on Terror in which the United States appears to pit its 'warriors' against 'criminals'. Nevertheless, atrocity based on 'good-versus-evil' is avoidable, as was demonstrated when Major General H. R. McMaster was commander of the US Army's 3rd Armored Cavalry Regiment during the Iraq War. There, McMaster

> forbade his soldiers from using dehumanizing and derogatory language when referring to Iraqis: both because such behavior is inconsistent with the shared values that define a soldier's moral identity, and because such behavior is potentially a verbal 'foot in the door' leading to more serious forms of abuse.[70]

The notion of 'shared values', consistent with the moral equality of combatants, is ethically important when it checks unjust conduct in war. As Coker has observed, 'How soldiers treat their enemies is the basis of the ethics of war.'[71] When it comes to the use of airpower specifically, however, the relationship between combatants on opposing sides of a conflict is arguably different from that which McMaster's soldiers experienced on the ground in Iraq. In particular, when airpower is used to wage post-heroic war in a radically asymmetric fashion, opposing combatants are starkly aware of power inequality. Whether such awareness is matched by a feeling of *moral* inequality is an issue explored in the next chapter: in the use of armed drones, is there a danger that the distance between combatants – physical, psychological and cultural – is conducive to mutual dehumanization?

Conclusion

In the perfectly symmetrical game that is chess, it is morally important for both players not to cheat while playing, but the outcome of the game itself (who wins and who loses) is of no moral consequence whatsoever. In war, which is never symmetrical, each side attaches great moral importance to victory, and there may be a strong temptation to cheat in order to win. Such is the potential tension between the morality surrounding the resort to armed force (*jus ad bellum*) and that which governs the conduct of violence (*jus in bello*), and it is compounded by the problem of radical asymmetry. When the technologically powerful United States uses armed drones against unsophisticated enemies who cannot contest airspace, it is applying force in a radically asymmetric fashion. Although there is no ethical requirement for war to be 'fair' in the sense of being roughly evenly balanced, it is the nature of war itself to be a contest. If there is no 'war' going on, there can be no just war, and many observers are likely to be morally troubled by the image of one side in a supposed contest inflicting harm with impunity. Depriving a state and people of the ability to exercise an inherent right of self-defence is to circumvent the *jus ad bellum* of principle of just cause, and any attack on those defenceless innocents would violate the *jus in bello* principle of discrimination. Nevertheless, even when the US Government uses armed drones exclusively in a theatre of operations like Pakistan, there is at least some reason to doubt that it is engaged in a non-war. A contest of sorts can and does occur, even if such contestation cannot immediately be directed against the US-based drone operators themselves. Rather it is directed against American non-combatants in the form of terrorism; an impermissible but nevertheless real reaction by the technologically weak to the provocation of radical asymmetry.

There is scope perhaps for the United States to be more proactive in lessening the grievance felt by its enemies in the War on Terror, but a critical first step would be to disentangle its warlike actions from the law enforcement paradigm. It must either be the case that terrorists are 'criminals' to be dealt with in accordance with ordinary peacetime justice measures (arrest, trial and sentencing), or they must be acknowledged as 'warriors' whose moral status is equal to that of US combatants. Drone strikes are highly unsuitable for law enforcement because their sole purpose is to kill. Even if the US Government were inclined to characterize a drone programme as such, it would be a highly implausible attempt to get around radical asymmetry; an exploding missile is 'war' to those in its vicinity. A better approach might be to characterize drone strikes as the stuff of war (and war alone) and perhaps, in a contest that is extremely and conspicuously unequal, the only way for the stronger party to fight justly is by being conspicuously observant of extremely strict *jus in bello* standards. The United States could choose, for example, to hold itself to a rigorous standard according to which harm (even if unintended) to just one non-combatant is unacceptable. This would go some way to addressing any 'fairness' objection to systemic risk-transfer, possibly to the point of lessening terrorists' motivation to perpetrate 'reciprocal' indiscriminate attacks on US civilians. Such punctiliousness in the conduct of drone strikes would be difficult to manage and maintain, however, and indeed it would likely be a huge impediment to US efforts to strike at legitimate (combatant) targets. Therefore, a third option – more attractive militarily and politically than the first two – might be to establish that the radically asymmetric use of armed drones is permissible because America's cause alone is just and Americans only are just combatants. If US drone operators were thus rendered morally immune from attack, but they remained morally bound to use force in pursuit of their cause, their ability to kill without experiencing physical risk would seem to be a perfect fit.

Placing an overriding emphasis on *jus ad bellum* (as McMahan does) nevertheless offers an imperfect escape from the problem of radical asymmetry. Historical and contemporary experience shows that the justice of resorting to force is virtually always subject to reasonable contestation, and weak and strong powers alike notoriously insist that only *their* cause is just. The principle that combatants in service to either side of a conflict are morally equal has traditionally applied precisely out of concern that *jus ad bellum* doubts should not affect *jus in bello* compliance. If the United States were to get carried away with the 'good guy' status of its drone operators, a warning from history is that drone strikes might come to be conducted with too little regard for the basic humanity of the 'bad guy' and those innocents around him. In circumstances where the necessity of advancing a just cause has ended up trumping rather than weighing against discrimination and proportionality considerations, the human consequences have been dire. By allowing and requiring the just use of force by *all* combatants, the notion of equal moral status plays an important role in preventing the abuse of military power inequalities. In some circumstances, however, the difficulty of characterizing drone strikes as war-as-contest could prove too great a burden for the ethics of *war* to bear. There can be no just war, and no justice in war, if the violence being perpetrated is not warlike. Are radically asymmetric drone strikes an exercise in 'law enforcement'? Do they more closely resemble 'murder'? No existing label, it seems, sufficiently captures the essence of such violence.

6 Drone operators and the warrior ethos

In circumstances of power inequality, and when there is doubt about the justice of going to war, opposing combatants are traditionally held to be moral equals. Each is as blameless as the other for the overall conflict (*jus ad bellum*), and all are equally required to fight justly (*jus in bello*). This moral equality is a point of commonality among combatants across countries and cultures, and even between armed enemies in war it is sometimes a source of mutual respect. The moral equality of combatants is, moreover, the basis for a warrior ethos; a sense of professional identity and purpose built around virtues and rules. The precise content and contours of this ethos vary across time and space, but it always has sociological significance too as a means of differentiating warriors and non-warriors (civilians) within a given society. Some authors prefer to draw a sharp distinction between the terms 'warrior' and 'military professional' because the former, they argue, evokes the caricature of someone who is old-fashioned, ethically non-constrained and even barbaric. Roger Wertheimer, for example, refers to 'pre-professional warriors [who] have often been enthusiastically ruthless, glorying in plunder, pillaging, raping, enslaving, massacring, torturing, untroubled by any doubt that the victor may despoil the vanquished at his pleasure'.[1] For present purposes, any such distinction is rejected in favour of the notion that ethical 'constraints and worries have *traditionally* been seen as part and parcel of the ideal military character'.[2] This then enables the warrior ethos to be seen as integral to military professionalism.

The previous chapter's discussion of radically asymmetric use of armed drones by the United States occasioned consideration of what counts as war. This chapter examines whether or how drone operators count as warriors, and the central themes for discussion are risk and courage. Mindful of the unique moral space that war potentially provides for killing someone justly, important questions include: is risk an essential characteristic of war, and is courage an indispensable characteristic of a warrior? Absent those characteristics, is killing rendered 'unwarlike' and thus divested of its moral potential? Arguably, by enabling risk-free killing, drone technology poses a fundamental challenge to war's precarious moral status. In the conduct of war (as a form of violence distinct from law enforcement or murder), the just war tradition demands that warriors use force in a manner that is militarily necessary, that discriminates between combatants and non-combatants, and that anticipates generating harm that is proportional to the expected military benefit. To require a drone operator to adhere to these principles is to assume, however, that he or she is waging war in the first place; that the killing being done has moral potential because it is warlike. The purpose of this chapter is to test that assumption by suggesting that it is not enough for a drone operator to use force in accordance with *jus in bello* principles. Rather, before being entitled to use force at all, there is a condition of reciprocity: a warrior is justly entitled to use force because and only when he or she is in a relationship of mutual risk with an enemy. This is consistent with the traditional notion that war must in some way be a contest. On the basis of that proposition, an argument can also be made that remote-control killing by drone operators challenges traditional notions (sociological as well as ethical) of what it means to be a combatant or 'warrior' within the military profession.

Unlike the pilots of in-theatre aircraft, ground-based US drone operators on the other side of the world experience no danger and are thus not required to exercise physical courage when using lethal force. But if the military profession's supposedly defining and much-admired characteristic is risk-taking, can drone operators be plausibly regarded as warriors with a moral (warlike) motivation? The chapter consists of four sections. The first explores the phenomenon of physical courage as a cardinal military virtue. Related to this, the second section advances the arguments that opposing combatants' equal right to kill in war is founded on the assumption of mutual risk, and that war necessarily involves some kind of contest in order to have any potential as a moral killing enterprise. The final two sections of the chapter examine the moral status of the drone operator whose mind is away at war but whose body is safe at home. Part of this discussion of 'disembodied warriors' focuses on the activity of killing in the absence of physical risk, and for the sake of completeness it is important also to consider drone operators as potential victims who experience psychological risks.

Military virtue and physical courage

In many societies, killing in war is regarded as not only morally permissible but also morally admirable. As Helen Frowe has observed: 'Children aspire to be soldiers. Parades are held for those returning from conflicts. We honour those who die in combat and decorate those who show particular courage or skill on the battlefield.'[3] Such are the rewards of and incentives for military virtue, which attaches to the warrior not only as a killer but also as a member of the profession of arms. In his 1957 book *The Soldier and the State*, Samuel Huntington wrote of professionalism: 'In our society, the businessman may command more income; the politician may command more power; but the professional man commands more respect.'[4] A person is a 'professional' not in the sense of doing something for monetary gain (i.e. not an amateur), but rather in the sense of being 'one who pursues a "higher calling" in the service of society'.[5] Among the members of any profession there is a sense of corporate unity and a consciousness of themselves as a group set apart from others in society. This collective sense has its origins, according to Huntington, 'in the lengthy discipline and training necessary for professional competence, the common bond of work, and the sharing of a unique social responsibility'.[6] Membership of a profession is also characterized by a commitment to a set of values that defines that profession and distinguishes it from others. Members of the military profession have a unique and demanding purpose – to deliver and receive death and destruction – and the profession's values are essential to that purpose.[7] In a lecture at the US Naval War College in 2010, H. R. McMaster described the warrior ethos – 'comprised of values such as honour, duty, courage, loyalty, and self-sacrifice' – as the basis of 'a covenant that binds [soldiers] to one another and to the society they serve'.[8] It is because they serve, and because they purportedly strive to embody the aforementioned virtues, that warriors are admired and respected; cheered when they march in parades, and mourned when they perish in battle.

Warriors are a breed apart from civilians, and they often find themselves a world apart too. It was Clausewitz's view that 'War is a special business... [which] always continues to be different and separate from the other pursuits which occupy the life of man'.[9] And Macchiavelli observed that once a man becomes a soldier 'he changes not only his clothing but he adopts attitudes, manners, ways of speaking and [becomes] himself quite at odds with the civilian life'.[10] In no other walk of life, according to Coker, do warriors find a comparable existential experience: 'For war generates those supreme moments of danger and intensity of emotion that enliven the spirit'.[11] In a post-heroic age especially, values like honour, courage, sacrifice and love of country must seem exotic to someone outside the military profession because these are values seldom rewarded in the civilian economy.[12] As Singer has observed

> Joining the military and heading off to war has long been viewed as a transformative act. It wraps together a deliberate choice of self-sacrifice, taking on a new identity, and adhering to a new code of behaviour, conduct, and honor. This experience changes how a person looks at the world and how the world looks at that person.[13]

Likewise, John Keegan has argued

> Soldiers are not as other men... War is fought... by men whose values and skills are not those of politicians and diplomats. They are those of a world apart, a very ancient world, which exists in parallel with the everyday world but does not belong to it.[14]

By contrast, the 'everyday world' of a US drone operator – firing a missile, watching it immediately hit someone who is thousands of miles away, then driving home to be with family – seemingly intersects closely with the 'world apart'. It does not follow from this, however, that US civilians living everyday lives would identify more closely with drone operators than with military personnel deployed overseas. To the contrary, the very fact that drone operators have not gone 'off to war' might cause civilians to spare them little or no thought: if someone is not at physical risk, why worry?

The notion of honour within the warrior ethos further distinguishes the military profession from civilian ones, and it is important from an ethical perspective as a potential source of restraint in the conduct of war. Historically, a code of honour – be it the Christian code of chivalry or the Japanese *Bushido* – is what has given warriors a sense of belonging to their profession, and this sense has been bound up in an ethic of responsibility to those within and beyond it. Critically, 'honour' has been the main point of reference by which warriors have sought to distinguished themselves from mere butchers. In his 1998 book *The Warrior's Honour*, Ignatieff observed

> Wherever the art of war was practised, warriors distinguished between combatants and noncombatants, legitimate and illegitimate targets, moral and immoral weaponry, civilized and barbarous usage in the treatment of prisoners and of the wounded. Such codes may have been honoured as often in the breach as in the observance, but without them war is not war – it is no more than slaughter.[15]

For Ignatieff, the 'decisive restraint' on unethical practice in battle 'lies within the warrior himself, in his conception of what is honorable and dishonorable for a man to do with weapons.'[16] There is a sense here that *jus in bello* principles get traction in war through the virtue of an individual warrior as well as through the application of learned rules. To kill a civilian, for example, offends a warrior's moral sensibilities not just because it breaches the Geneva Conventions but also because no courage is involved. On the latter point, Coker has observed that 'Cruelty against non-combatants is nearly always contemptible because it is so cowardly. And cruelty without extenuation… robs war of any moral charge.'[17] Courage, then, is a virtue central to 'the system of moral etiquette by which warriors judged themselves to be worthy of mutual respect',[18] and it is also one which ought to support the protection of non-warriors.

In Western civilization and dating from the time of Homer, the oldest source of a warrior's self-esteem is 'the belief that society is divided into two, between those willing to risk their lives and those who are not'.[19] In other times, places and cultures too, physical courage is the most important military virtue, commonly understood and appreciated in virtually every military organization. In his *Nicomachean Ethics*, Aristotle (who remains the foremost theorist of courage) stated that 'the courageous man will be one who is fearless in the face of an honourable death, or of some sudden threat of death; and it is in war that such situations chiefly occur'.[20] Courage, implying 'the presence of pain', is 'rightly praised', and

> it is the mark of a courageous man to face things that are terrible to a human being, and that he can see are such, because it is a fine act to face them and a disgrace not to do so.[21]

In *Art of War*, Sun Tzu advised that 'The principle on which to manage an army is to set up one standard of courage which all must reach',[22] and in *On War*, Clausewitz wrote of 'boldness' that 'this noble impulse, with which the human soul raises itself above the most formidable dangers, is to be regarded as an active principle peculiarly belonging to War'.[23] During World War I, former US President Theodore Roosevelt reportedly wished for his own sons to be tested in battle, so much so that he 'confided to a friend his hope that they might even be wounded or lose a limb as a mark of valor'.[24]

Aristotle conceived courage as manifesting in 'courageous acts, motivated by the love of virtue itself, and serving an honourable, that is morally just, cause'.[25] This resonates with Coker's view that 'War... like religion defines our humanity because it demands of some that they surrender the instinct of self-preservation in the present to make life better in the future'.[26] In like fashion, Artur Schopenhauer has written that 'Courage... implies that one is willing to face a present evil so as to prevent a greater evil in the future, while cowardice does the reverse'.[27] Today, however, it is probably setting the bar too high to require 'courage' to serve worthy causes, not least because military personnel generally 'do not have a say in what these causes are'.[28] Accordingly, the better approach is to adopt what Peter Olsthoorn describes as a 'scientific' view of courage, founded on the psychological phenomenon of fear: courage is 'acting despite fear'.[29] Fear of incurring injury or death relates to physical courage, and this is distinguishable from moral courage. The latter virtue – having the courage to speak out against perceived injustice, at the risk of losing (mere) esteem or dignity – is beyond the scope of this chapter. As for physical courage, which is capable of being exercised only in circumstances of physical risk, the central issue is: how should drone operators be regarded in the context of the ethics and sociology of war? Are these grounded aviators merely technicians of death, at best deserving only admiration for their competent application of technical skills? If not, by what measure can they be reasonably compared to warriors? The essential problem with reducing killing to a purely technical matter is that there exists no relationship of mutual risk as between killer and killed. Unless combatants on both sides experience at least a scintilla of risk, no contest can be said to exist between them as could plausibly count as war.

Mutual risk and war-as-contest

On the Western Front during World War I, commanders on both sides appeared to ascribe little or no value to their soldiers' lives when they routinely ordered them to advance in their thousands against withering machine-gun fire. By contrast, in the post-heroic warfare waged by the United States, the idea of 'cannon fodder' has given way to an enhanced concern to protect US combatants' lives.[30] Every military organization, and every individual military professional, understandably prefers to fight in a way that involves a maximum of risk to the enemy and a minimum of risk to one's own side. Indeed, just as it is important for commanders to try to reduce the risk of injury to their own forces, so it would be utterly immoral to require military personnel to assume unnecessary risks for a futile purpose. Ethically, however, there is a vital difference between risk reduction and risk elimination given that, as stated in the US Army's COIN field manual, 'risk taking is an essential part of the Warrior Ethos'.[31] Writing in 2002 about what he perceived as 'the paradox of riskless war', Kahn observed: 'Without the imposition of mutual risk, warfare is not war at all.'[32] It follows that any pre-meditated, organized killing that is risk-free must be called something else. Such killing might, for example, be the sentence component of a law enforcement process (capital punishment). Alternatively, to kill without experiencing risk might be murder (for example, a husband stabbing to death his sleeping wife).

According to the traditional conception and expectation of war as combat between combatants, those on one side may deliberately target those on the other side, and non-combatants in general are off-limits. Combatants are potential and (unlike non-combatants) legitimate victims of their enemy's uses of force, and it is this victimhood that requires and excuses violent action that is essentially defensive.[33] If a putative combatant is not a potential victim of some physical harm that is specifically attributable to his or her combatant status, the imperative and justification of killing is lost. A warlike killing is one for which the killer has a licence, but the indispensable condition for this licence is exposure to physical risk. At its most basic level, this is the stuff of give and take: a licence to kill in return for a preparedness to die. The notion of a 'bargain', founded on reciprocal risk between opposing combatants, has been well canvassed. As Cook has observed, volunteer military personnel 'live in a unique moral world' and enter into a special kind of 'contract' of service to the state.[34] This contract

> has an 'unlimited liability' clause – they accept ... the obligation to put their lives and bodies at grave risk when ordered to do so. Their contract also requires them to kill other human beings and to destroy their property when given legal orders to do so.[35]

This characterization resonates strongly with the views of other authors who regard war as a necessarily two-sided affair when it comes to physical risk. For example, John Keegan and Richard Holmes have observed that the 'heart of the military experience' is that the soldier, as 'both victim and executioner', runs the risk of being killed and wounded himself, 'but he also kills and wounds others'.[36] And McMahan acknowledges the argument that 'what makes all combatants legitimate targets for their military adversaries ... is that in one way or another they consent to be targets *in exchange* for the privilege of making other combatants their own targets'.[37] For Walzer, war is 'a moral condition that comes into existence only when armies of victims meet'.[38] As between opposing combatants, he records a prevailing attitude that those on the other side are 'poor sods, just like me',[39] each to the other representing danger at an institutional rather than a personal level. Such an attitude is well illustrated in Erich Maria Remarque's World War I novel *All Quiet on the Western Front*, in which the narrator (a German soldier) watches some starving Russian prisoners-of-war and thinks:

> An order has turned these silent figures into our enemies; an order could turn them into friends again. On some table, a document is signed by some people that none of us knows, and for years our main aim in life is the one thing that usually draws the condemnation of the whole world and incurs its severest punishment in law. How can anyone make distinctions like that looking at these silent men, with their faces like children and their beards like apostles?[40]

Mindful that, when actual fighting is under way, 'They can try to kill me, and I can try to kill them', the licence for soldiers is that they are 'entitled to kill, *not anyone*, but men whom we know to be victims'.[41]

In a variety of contexts, and with this 'contract' in mind, observers and practitioners of war have expressed distaste for killing that entails little or no risk to the killer. In war memoirs and letters from the front, there are numerous tales along the lines of 'a soldier on patrol or on sniper duty catches an enemy soldier unaware, holds him in his gunsight, easy to kill, and then must decide whether to shoot him or let the opportunity pass'.[42] In the case of sniper Robert Graves's reluctance to shoot a German taking a bath, Walzer offers the explanation that 'A naked man… is not a soldier'.[43] He also cites the reasoning of a nineteenth-century English student of war: 'No other term than murder expresses the killing of a lone sentry by a pot shot at long range. It [is] like shooting a partridge sitting.'[44] In his 1937 memoir *The Men I Killed*, former sniper Frank Percy Crozier described how he enjoyed game hunting in Africa but baulked at the bloodthirstiness of targeting humans: 'The game was dirty. I had to give it up. The cool, calculated murder of defenceless men was diabolical.'[45] He admitted to 'that sense of guilt, that conscious-stricken feeling of killing a man who at the moment was not menacing you and who was brought almost within hand-shaking distance by the telescopic sights'.[46] During the two world wars, snipers tended to be 'executed on the spot' for violating the 'condition of mutual risk',[47] and yet this itself shows that they did in fact experience some risk. When the 'sniper's dilemma' arises in the course of applying airpower in a highly asymmetric manner, however, the mutual risk that underpins war-as-contest becomes harder to discern.

In 1920 when British military aircraft were being used against Iraqi insurgents, one pilot remarked at the time: 'We can wipe out a third of the inhabitants of a village in 45 minutes, killed by four or five machines which offer them no real target, *no real opportunity [to be] glorious warriors*.'[48] Likewise, for the British pilots themselves, 'There was little glory in bombing unarmed civilians'.[49] Ignatieff is similarly scathing in his judgment of NATO's 1999 air-only campaign against Serbian forces:

> The Kosovo campaign achieved its objectives without a single NATO combat fatality. From a military standpoint, this is an unprecedented

achievement. From an ethical standpoint, it transforms the expectations that govern the morality of war. The tacit contract of combat throughout the ages has always assumed a basic equality of moral risk: kill or be killed. Accordingly violence in war avails itself of the legitimacy of self-defense. But this contract is void when one side begins killing with impunity. Put another way, a war ceases to be just when it becomes a turkey shoot.[50]

US pilots had engaged in a comparable application of airpower in the final days of the 1991 Gulf War. From 25 to 27 February 1991, there were repeated airstrikes on Iraqi soldiers and civilians retreating north from Kuwait City towards Basra along a road that became known as the 'Highway of Death'. Flying sorties against fleeing Iraqis was described by one US pilot as like 'shooting fish in a barrel',[51] and others pilots reportedly expressed misgivings about 'shooting up Iraqi troops who were powerless to defend themselves'.[52]

Even in circumstances as asymmetric as these, a pilot sitting in an aircraft cockpit nevertheless experiences some risk. This could take the form of mechanical failure or loss of consciousness leading to loss of aircraft control, or unexpected ground fire causing the aircraft to plummet from the sky. By contrast, none of these things endanger the operator of an armed drone. On the issue of whether this puts drone technology in a different ethical category, Strawser insists rather that remotely controlled weapon systems are 'merely an extension of a long historical trajectory of removing a warrior ever farther from his foe for the warrior's better protection'.[53] In his view, the 'fair fight' threshold was crossed long ago:

> How fair is the present fight between an F-22 pilot flying at altitude delivering a precision missile and a tribal warrior wielding a rocket-propelled grenade? If there is a moral problem here due to asymmetry, it seems to have occurred long before UAV implementation and is not endemic to them.[54]

Far from denying a 'moral problem' with drones, Strawser's logic implies it: even if this new form of airpower *is* unfair, it is no worse than what has gone before. And yet the threshold most worth considering here is not some vague notion of a 'fair' (evenly balanced) fight. As discussed in the previous chapter, such symmetry is apparent on a chessboard but is foreign to real war. Rather, what is ethically relevant is the crossing of the line between risk reduction and risk elimination. An F-22 pilot 'flying at altitude' assumes at least a scintilla of risk, and so there exists between him and a 'tribal warrior' a relationship of mutual risk. Controlling a Predator from a ground station in Nevada is, by contrast, 'the ultimate in standoff'.[55]

In circumstances where there is no mutual risk, at least in physical terms, drone strikes are perhaps more readily comparable to teleoperated hunting. In 2004 a Texas-based entrepreneur, John Lockwood, launched a website (www.live-shot.com) which allowed fee-paying users to log-in, and then aim a camera and fire a real rifle at real targets. The website was intended ultimately as 'a tele-operated hunting business'; live animals could be shot online by 'physically impaired hunting enthusiasts who could not go out into the woods themselves'.[56] Soon afterwards, 11 US states legislated against online hunting, insisting that a hunter had to be physically present when hunting. On the day before the ban came into force in Texas, however, a customer of Lockwood's used the website to shoot a sheep. Interest groups who had lobbied for the ban included both animal lovers (such as the Humane Society) and animal shooters (such as the National Assembly of Sportsmen's Caucuses). Scott Gunderson, an experienced hunter, and a representative in the Wisconsin State Assembly who supported the ban on online hunting, said in 2005:

> I just don't believe it was the right thing to do. People shouldn't use their credit card to buy a hunt and shoot an animal over the computer. To me, hunting is being out in nature and becoming one with the nature.[57]

From the perspective of animal shooters who consider themselves sportsmen, remote-control hunting is to be condemned as unsporting. The online hunter cannot be injured by a misfiring rifle or charged by a wounded beast; unless the hunter too is 'out in nature', only the hunted experiences risk. Analogizing between hunting and war is difficult, not least because animals do not bear the human right to life and they are incapable of politically motivated violence. Nevertheless, there is in both instances a common concern that mutual risk renders killing 'sporting' or 'warlike' – that is, a contest. If the risk-free (online) killing of a non-human can be deemed objectionable, it is reasonable to suggest that remote-control killing of humans might be objectionable too. Accordingly, the next section of this chapter examines the status of the drone operator as a killer whose mind is away at war but whose body is safe at home.

The drone operator as killer

At a conference in Washington in April 2011, Colonel Dean Bushey, deputy director of the Air Force Joint Unmanned Aircraft Systems Center, pointed out that USAF drone operators go through almost exactly the same routines that aeroplane pilots do prior to a mission. They pass through a restricted area, put on flight suits, and receive a mission brief, before stepping into a ground control station (rather than climbing into a cockpit).[58] From there, if the drone is armed, the operators apply their minds to the task of killing someone on the other side of the world (in Libya or Afghanistan, for example), while their bodies remain safe on the soil of their home country. From both a physical and sociological perspective, this is something genuinely new in warfare because, traditionally, an individual who 'chooses to leave the comfort of the community to go off to war ... becomes someone "exceptional"'.[59] In Shakespeare's *Henry V*, on the eve of the 1415 battle of Agincourt and vastly outnumbered by the French, the English king gathers his men around him and says:

We few, we happy few, we band of brothers.
For he today that sheds his blood with me
Shall be my brother; be he ne'er so vile,
This day shall gentle his condition.
And gentlemen in England now abed
Shall think themselves accursed they were not here,
And hold their manhoods cheap whiles any speaks
That fought with us upon Saint Crispin's day.[60]

Six centuries later, going 'off to war' is no longer so romantically straightforward. From the perspective of those military professionals who are in the field, is a drone operator someone who 'sheds his blood' and fights 'with us' or someone who is 'not here'? When a drone operator's mind alone goes to war while his or her body remains at home, he or she manifests as a 'disembodied warrior'. This is paradoxical because the warrior's body is arguably the indispensable pillar of his or her unique moral status: this person's right to inflict bodily harm on others is subject to a condition of mutual physical risk.

The disembodied warrior

The ethical rules of war arguably derive largely 'from our physical *embodiment*' which in turn gives us 'our sense of agency and responsibility for our actions'.[61] The human body makes experience meaningful because, according to sociologist Anthony Giddens, it is 'an object in which we are all privileged, or doomed, to dwell, the source of feelings of well-being and pleasure, but also the site of illnesses and strains'.[62] For Giddens, disembodiment has connections with 'reality inversion' as 'an attempt to transcend dangers and be safe'.[63] He cites the example of prisoners in Nazi concentration camps, subjected to 'horrendous physical and psychological pressures', who 'experienced states of dissociation of body and self'.[64] For them, feeling 'unreal', like being in 'a dream', or like being 'a character in a play', seems to have been a way to keep functioning, 'allowing distance from the physical deprivations which the body suffered'.[65] Disembodiment can sometimes be effected pharmacologically such as when US Army doctors prescribed tranquillizers for combat troops during the Vietnam War, and when 'many soldiers self-prescribed marijuana, opium, and heroin to deal with the stress they were facing'.[66] Beyond this, reality inversion – separating mind and body in order to keep functioning – might also occur through interaction with audio-visual technology. In the 1977 science fiction novel *Ender's Game*, the main character (a boy) is able to function as a killer only because his mind has been deceived into thinking the physical consequences of his 'actions' are imaginary. When it is revealed to Ender that he has not been playing a computer game after all, he struggles to process this terrible truth:

> Real. Not a game. Ender's mind was too tired to cope with it all. They weren't just points of light in the air, they were real ships that he had fought

with and real ships he had destroyed. And a real world that he had blasted into oblivion.[67]

The risk that drone operators, as disembodied warriors, will regard the killing they do as merely a game was raised in Alston's 2010 report as the UN Special Rapporteur on Extrajudicial, Summary or Arbitrary Executions: 'because operators are based thousands of miles away from the battlefield, and undertake operations entirely through computer screens and remote audio-feed, there is a risk of developing a "playstation" mentality to killing.'[68] The suggestion is a reasonable one, not least because some 'UAV systems are purposely designed to conform with PlayStation and Gameboy consoles to take advantage of the familiarity some individuals have with these systems'.[69] The essential concern is whether young military personnel, 'raised on a diet of video games' and 'removed from the human consequences of their actions', will 'value the right to life',[70] the ethical implication being that, without a proper appreciation of the value of human life, drone operators might be less capable of acting justly (e.g. refraining from indiscriminate violence) when extinguishing it. On the other hand, caring too little might sometimes be less of a problem than caring too much. Sparrow points to anecdotal evidence that some drone operators do experience strong feelings of anger, such as when US troops are observed taking fire,[71] but anger and airpower can be a dangerous combination. During World War I, for example, a Canadian pilot described how 'with hate in my heart... I fired every bullet I could' into the 'frightened faces' of the 'Huns' 30 feet below.[72]

None of the aforementioned claims is based on psychological expertise, so they would need to be substantiated by more research into the emotions of drone operators. The final section of this chapter explores the issue of emotional risk as a form of victimhood, but for now it is enough to note that at least one emotion – fear – cannot reasonably be felt by drone operators in their capacity as killers. In the absence of risk there is no reason to be fearful, and in the absence of fear there is no opportunity to be courageous. As Singer has observed, 'By removing warriors completely from risk and fear, unmanned systems create the first complete break in the ancient connection that defines warriors and their soldierly values'.[73] The alternative to maintaining that connection is perhaps to radically recast the notion of courage as a military virtue. Colonel Eric Mathewson, the commander of a drone squadron at Creech Air Force base in Nevada, did this in 2010 when he told the *Washington Post*: 'Valor to me is not risking your life. Valor is doing what is right. Valor is about your motivations and ends you seek. It is doing what is right for the right reasons. That to me is valor.'[74] Although such concern for worthy causes harks back to an Aristotelian notion of courage, Aristotle himself could not have conceived of courage manifesting in the absence of danger and fear. Today, warriors and civilians alike are also likely to perceive that risk-free killing is non-courageous. And if, by distancing themselves from those they kill, US drone operators attract disrespect, this might prove to be a longer-term ethical liability that outweighs the immediate operational advantages that armed drones appear to afford. Two perspectives are relevant. The first, the perspective from a drone operator's own society, concerns the risk of internally inflicted damage to the fabric of that society's military profession. The second perspective, that of those living in countries targeted by drone operators, concerns the risk of generating higher levels of destructive hatred towards a faraway enemy.

Distance and disrespect

The flight of human beings through the air has long been a spectacle attracting awe, admiration and respect. Ever since Wilbur Wright achieved powered and sustained flight in 1903, the 'death-defying feat of being in the air' has enthralled the popular and military imaginations.[75] When combat took to the air, this must have seemed a doubly dangerous affair, and from the time of World War I there began a romanticization of military pilots. British and German fighter aces, for example, sometimes dropped messages on each other's air bases, 'challenging their enemies to take off and fight in the manner of medieval knights'.[76] 'Aviators were "proof"', suggests Sherry, 'that the mechanical age possessed gallantry.'[77] In subsequent decades, inhabited military aircraft would come to be used in a seemingly ungallant and highly asymmetric fashion (in Iraq in 1991 and in Kosovo in 1999), but even this involved some physical risk to the pilots themselves. More recently, a British Air Chief Marshal who served in the Iraq War has argued that aircraft without on-board pilots are creating 'a virtueless war' requiring neither courage nor heroism.[78] Echoing this sentiment at a 2009 conference in the United Kingdom, Seb Cox warned that the advent of drones had implications for the future Royal Air Force that 'challenge the very nature of the Service, its self-image and the way it is perceived'.[79] His concern appeared to be that drone operators would not be of the same quality as their glorious 'forebears in Camels, Lancasters, Vulcans or Tornado GR1s'.[80] There could be nothing 'extraordinary' about fighting 'from a padded seat many thousands of miles away',[81] Cox argued, and he posed the question: 'Will there be serious issues of self-respect and motivation for such "warriors" if they come to regard it as just a job, or, conversely, will it dilute the meaning or the concept of the warrior?'[82] Meanwhile, in the United States, the relative importance of courage in the face of physical risk has been a point of contestation inside parts of the US military. Drone warfare is intruding into military doctrine, and drone operators are increasingly encroaching on the space of those swaggering pilots who have long dominated military aviation; those magnificent men *in* their flying machines.

When Frank Barrett researched the construction of masculinity in the US Navy in the 1990s, he found that aviators had the highest status among naval officers. They came 'closest to embodying the ideal of hegemonic masculinity' by representing 'aggressiveness, technical mastery of complex machinery, courage, and autonomy'.[83] Each of the pilots interviewed by Barrett confirmed that his life was marked by a degree of recklessness; behaviour attributed to the danger associated with flying. One pilot remarked: 'Each time we go out, we never know if we'll be back.... So, we live for today. We do tend to be wild and take more risks. It's a mortality thing.'[84] By contrast, one USAF veteran of Iraq and Afghanistan has claimed that operating a drone is 'like being a pilot for nerds. Where is the sense of adventure, the sense of danger?... Let's put it this way: I don't think they're going to make any movies about guys who fly Predators.'[85] Similarly, a former US Defense Department analyst has joked that 'no fighter pilot is ever going to pick up a girl at a bar by saying he flies a UAV'.[86] Strawser dismisses as 'wrong-headed machismo' the notion that drone operators are weak, cowardly or somehow not tough enough, and he expresses the hope that such attitudes 'are not taken seriously by any military policy decisionmakers'.[87] However, it would be a mistake to ignore the strong emphasis on masculinity that pervades US military culture, bearing in mind that war has historically been 'the prime place to define oneself as a man'.[88]

In July 2010, General James Mattis was named head of US Central Command, overseeing the Middle East and Central Asia. Nine years previously, he had commanded the first forces in the US invasion of Afghanistan.[89] At a public forum in 2005, Mattis reportedly commented:

> It's fun to shoot some people when you like brawling. When you go into Afghanistan, you got guys who slapped women around for five years because they didn't wear a veil. You know, guys like that *ain't got no manhood* left anyway. So it's a hell of a lot of fun to shoot them.[90]

To belittle or deny the manhood of other men as Mattis did (and as Shakespeare's King Henry did on St Crispin's Day) is to portray them as lacking courage. In the case of drone operators, the accusation might be that they, as well as their aircraft, are 'unmanned'. At the very least, the drone operator arguably does not share with a traditional pilot the same sense of 'being different from other [civilian] people'.[91] New recruits can become certified drone operators in under two years and without first having to qualify as a pilot of manned aircraft.[92] And although a drone operator requires good concentration and coordination, physical fitness and keen eyesight are much less important.[93]

Whether it is to counter the disrespect that traditional pilots might feel towards drone operators, or simply to meet rising operational demand for drone strikes, there has been a great effort to make drone operators feel like full members of the military profession. In early 2009, when the USAF began a training programme for officers with no aviation background to 'fly' the Predator, Air Force chief Norton Schwartz controversially decreed that the graduates of this training programme should be called 'pilots'. At their graduation ceremony, he pinned on each trainee's uniform a specially designed set of wings featuring lightning bolts to signify the satellite signals that connect drones to their operators.[94] Alongside uniforms, and touching on the military virtue of courage, is the matter of decorations. USAF colonel Luther Turner, a former fighter pilot who had flown Predators since 2003, told the *Washington Post* in 2010: 'There is no valor in flying a remotely piloted aircraft. I get it. But there needs to be an award to recognize [drone] crews for combat missions.'[95] Already, as reported in the *Army Times* in 2007, US drone operators are eligible to be awarded the Air Medal and the Distinguished Flying Cross (DFC). The former, ranking behind the Bronze Star, is awarded 'for heroism, outstanding achievement or meritorious service', and the DFC ranks just below the Silver Star 'as a valor medal... awarded for heroism or extraordinary achievement'.[96] In early 2013 Leon Panetta, as the outgoing US Defense Secretary, introduced Distinguished Warfare Medals for 'drone pilots and cyberwarriors', although his successor Chuck Hagel suspended the production of these following complaints from veterans' organizations.[97] A country that awards medals for valour to its own drone operators cannot, however, thereby control outsiders' perceptions of whether remote-control killing is courageous. Even if the US military can protect the fabric of its professionalism by persuading Americans at home that drone operators are true warriors, many foreigners are likely to remain unconvinced. As Ignatieff wrote in 2000, 'the future depends not on us alone but on our enemies. They, like us, are drawing their own conclusions from the way we seek to avoid the mortal hazard of war.'[98] To the extent that the populations of US-targeted territories react to drone strikes with scorn and derision, rather than with awe and meekness, the use of this technology is arguably counterproductive.

High technology can dazzle an enemy into submission, as was demonstrated in August 1945 when the dropping of two atomic bombs caused the swift surrender of Japan. With regard to present-day drone technology, the view of one US drone operator is that it will discourage the enemy: 'I know that if I was out on a future battlefield risking my life, my emotions would be out of whack knowing that I could be killed and the only damage I could inflict was to a robot.'[99] It is no straightforward matter, however, to transpose one combatant's worldview and way of thinking onto a faraway combatant from a radically different culture. Sun Tzu's pithy injunction was to 'Know the enemy and know yourself; in a hundred battles you will never be in peril', but Mahnken has warned that the acquisition of such understanding is challenged by 'imperfect information, ethnocentrism and mirror-imaging'.[100] There is a preference in the United States and elsewhere in the West to perceive the violence meted out in war in utilitarian, means-and-ends terms. But if the War on Terror is in part a 'war' of ideas, the question of what Western violence 'signifies', 'says' or 'expresses' seems relevant too.[101] The will to martyrdom on the part of some members of the Islamic faith has the appearance of fanaticism to many Western eyes, and yet equally it could be said that 'many Muslims see the West's wish to avoid human suffering and pain as grossly materialistic'.[102] Coker has described how, in Somalia in the early 1990s, even a mode of dress sent the wrong signal:

> the Americans... always went around in flak jackets and wore helmets, and were described by the Somalis as 'human tanks'. Without the Americans realising it, this was a constant irritant and a definite factor in Somali aggressiveness towards them.... The Americans both inspired fear and were perceived as being fearful: a fatal combination.[103]

90 *Drone operators and the warrior ethos*

In the War on Terror too, at the level of one combatant's perception of another, the mutual respect that supposedly derives from the moral equality of combatants is severely tested. As Singer has observed

> conflicts in places like Iraq and Afghanistan are bringing together combatants with vastly different understandings of war, the role of the warrior, and the meaning of sacrifice. One side looks at war instrumentally, as a means to an end, while the other sees it metaphysically, placing great meaning on the very act of dying for a cause.[104]

The instrumentalist understanding of war was starkly encapsulated by Colonel Mathewson who, while commanding his drone squadron, reportedly had a three-word mission statement for his unit: 'Kill [Expletive] Heads', or 'KFH' for short.[105] For all that this statement might be intended to convey an attitude of casual omnipotence, the message sent might well differ from the message received. Although Americans themselves might describe US Predators and Reapers as efficient and cutting-edge, people in other parts of the world would describe the use of such technology as dishonourable. Even if the latter notion sounds old-fashioned, honour is part of the warrior ethos even for Western warriors, and a foreign perception of dishonour is a reality to be taken seriously by the US Government if it feeds into its enemies' propaganda and recruiting efforts. David Kilcullen, a COIN adviser to the US Government, argued in 2009 that 'While violent extremists may be unpopular, for a frightened population they seem less ominous than a faceless enemy that wages war from afar'.[106] In 2010 Edward Barrett testified before a US congressional committee that COIN efforts could be undermined by 'perceptions that these [unmanned] weapons... are indicative of flawed characters and/or tepid commitments'.[107] And a 2011 British Doctrine Note warned that:

> the ill-considered use of armed unmanned aircraft offers an adversary a potent propaganda weapon. This enables the insurgent to cast himself in the role of underdog and the West as a cowardly bully – that is unwilling to risk his own troops, but is happy to kill remotely.[108]

The risk of generating the impression that Americans, unable to 'stand the sight of their own blood',[109] are too afraid to fight – that theirs is a creed of dishonour before death – must of course be weighed against the chance that drone strikes will bring valuable military benefits. In the case of the undeclared US programme of drone strikes in Pakistan, for example, Panetta might still be correct in the view he expressed in 2009: that this is 'the only game in town' in terms of confronting the enemy.[110] But there are others, especially COIN enthusiasts, who prefer to play a long game that is more responsive to local sensitivities, and to whom drone strikes seem ill-suited to such a task. Singer recounts the tale of an elder, from Pakistan's tribal regions near Afghanistan, who met with US military officials and told them that the Americans must be working with forces of evil.

Given the way that America's enemies were being killed from afar, in an almost inexplicable fashion, the elder commented: 'They must have the power of the devil behind them.'[111] Along similar lines, the *New York Times* has reported that, according to the lyrics of a popular Pakistani song of protest, US drone strikes are 'America's heartless terrorism / Killing people like insects'.[112] The latter phrase sounds like hyperbole, and yet it is arguably not so very far removed from the perspective of those who operate the drones. At a conference in Washington in 2011, former CIA director Michael Hayden reportedly described how, with an armed Predator circling overhead, those ordering the launch of a Hellfire missile are able to call up computer maps showing the potential effects of the weapon. Before any launch, Hayden said, 'the backup team asks for "the bug splat" of the attack – a readout of the impact the missile would have on its ground target'.[113]

As between a drone operator who kills and the person being killed, there is no relationship of mutual risk. The 'war' that this disembodied warrior engages in is no more a contest, one could argue, than is pressing the sole of a shoe on an insect. In the absence of physical risk and an opportunity thus to exercise courage, the military virtue of the drone operator is diminished. This is a problem if, from the perspective of those living in targeted foreign countries, drone strikes precipitate more contempt and defiance than fear and submission. Moreover, from a 'home front' perspective, the diminished moral status of a drone operator is a problem if it damages the ethos and integrity of the military profession as a whole. An examination of the status of a drone operator as a killer occasions contestation of the notion that 'warriors' can wage 'war' without experiencing physical risk. For the sake of completeness, however, it is important to acknowledge that drone operators can and do experience non-physical risks. Accordingly, the final section of this chapter explores the status of the drone operator as a victim.

The drone operator as victim

If the operators of armed drones are combatants, and if opposing combatants are moral equals, it follows that their enemies may legitimately inflict harm upon them.[114] However, 'may' implies 'can', and realistically the physical safety of US-based drone operators is not in doubt. This makes for a difficult starting point when contemplating the status of drone operators as potential or actual victims in war. The mutual risk experienced in war-as-contest must be risk that is specifically attributable to a person's combatant status. Therefore, it is irrelevant that a US drone operator risks being harmed in a transport accident while travelling to and from work, because this is a risk assumed by every commuter. Likewise, the risk of being killed in a terrorist attack aimed at Americans in general is one that a drone operator experiences as a citizen rather than as a combatant. A drone operator experiences *relevant* physical risk only if he or she is attacked for *being* a drone operator. This seemed a highly unlikely prospect in August 2009 when two Nevada-based USAF drone operators (Lieutenant

Colonel Chris Gough and Colonel Chris Chambliss) openly displayed their faces and name-tags during a television documentary. Significantly, Chambliss also agreed to be filmed at home with his wife in suburban Las Vegas.[115] By 2012, when journalists conducted interviews at a USAF training facility in New Mexico, drone operators wore black tape over their name tags, ostensibly because of security concerns.[116] Even so, the risks that have appeared to concern the US Government and drone operators themselves the most have been not physical but psychological. In the latter sense only, perhaps, can drone operators be victims. In particular, the experience of killing someone and then driving home is one with which some drone operators appear to struggle emotionally.

Being simultaneously 'present' in and absent from the battlefield is, according to Sparrow, 'likely to generate significant psychological stress', not least because drone operators witness and sometimes participate in highly distressing situations.[117] Ordinarily, the fact of being physically present in a theatre of operations provides scope for a combatant to prepare for combat 'through a process of anticipation that makes reference to local circumstances', and 'conversation and interaction with others who may have shared similar experiences' is available as a post-combat coping mechanism.[118] By contrast, on either side of an eight-hour shift, a drone operator quickly moves out of and back into an essentially civilian existence. At a US congressional committee hearing in March 2010, the chairman noted in his opening statement:

> If unmanned systems are changing the way that we train our military personnel, so too should they change the way that we respond to the stress of combat. We already know that unmanned pilots are showing signs of equal or greater stress from combat compared to traditional pilots. The stress of fighting a war thousands of miles away, then minutes later joining your family at the dinner table presents mental health challenges that we must address.[119]

Among these challenges are reported cases of 'impaired domestic relationships' as well as 'chronic fatigue'.[120]

Beyond the seeming unreality of being at once here and there, it is also a 'psychological burden' to have 'lives on the ground depending on [a drone operator's] flawless performance'.[121] A drone operator might feel guilty in circumstances where he or she was unable to achieve a desired outcome, such as were described by USAF Major Bryan Callahan:

> you're trying to protect those guys on the ground. You try to help those guys with whatever situation they're in. There are cases where you can't do anything immediate, and you may feel helpless.... It sounds strange but being far away and safe is kind of a bummer. The other guys are exposing themselves, and that to me is still quite an honorable thing to do. So I feel like I'm cheating them. I'm relatively safe. If I screw up or miss something, if I screw up a shot, I wish it was me down there, not them. Sometimes I feel like I left them behind.[122]

In April 2011 a US drone operator did indeed 'screw up a shot' in the first reported instance of friendly fire. Pentagon officials confirmed that two Americans, a marine and a navy medic, were killed by a Predator-launched missile in southern Afghanistan after 'apparently being mistaken for insurgents moving to attack another group of marines'.[123] It is reasonable to suppose that the drone operator who released the missile felt a sense of guilt at having made a fatal mistake. Beyond the realm of accidents, however, it might also be the case that drone operators can be victims of emotional damage derived from the killing they do deliberately. According to Nick Floyd, an Australian army officer, 'the justification of self-preservation... diminishes as physical separation between killer and killed grows, leaving increasing room for self-doubt and, potentially, loss of psychological integrity'.[124]

In his 1995 book *On Killing*, US Army psychologist Dave Grossman argues that 'the act of killing an armed enemy who is trying to kill you... is not atrocity at all, but serves as a standard against which other kinds of killing can be measured'.[125] This resonates with the argument that killing only has moral potential in being 'warlike' if it occurs in circumstances of mutual physical risk. At the extreme end of Grossman's 'spectrum of atrocity' is the cold-blooded, close-range, execution-style killing of someone 'who represents no significant or immediate military or personal threat to the killer'.[126] Such a kill is intensely traumatic for the killer, who

> has limited internal motivation to kill the victim and kills almost entirely out of external motivations. The close range of the kill severely hampers the killer in his attempts to deny the humanity of the victim and severely hampers denial of personal responsibility for the kill.[127]

At the other end of the spectrum, Grossman refers to bomber crews who, during World War II, were able to bring themselves to kill non-combatants 'primarily through application of the mental leverage provided to them by the distance factor'.[128] Although the crews understood at an intellectual level the horror of what they were doing, the distance factor 'permitted them to deny it' emotionally.[129] Physical remoteness and reduced sensory perception can, according to Grossman's findings, facilitate killing that would not otherwise be stomached. Using the example of the British bomber attack on the German city of Hamburg in 1943, he suggests:

> If bomber crew members had had to turn a flamethrower on each one of these seventy thousand women and children or, worse yet, slit each of their throats, the awfulness and trauma inherent in the act would have been of such a magnitude that it simply would not have happened. But when it is done from thousands of feet in the air, where the screams cannot be heard and the burning bodies cannot be seen, it is easy.[130]

Drone operators are even more physically remote than bomber crews, and they too cannot hear screams or smell burning bodies, but they can certainly see. As one US drone operator told the *Los Angeles Times* in 2010, 'You see a lot of detail. We feel it, maybe not to the same degree as if we were actually there, but it affects us. Part of the job is to try and identify body parts.'[131] It is not clear, therefore, whether or how Grossman's 'spectrum of atrocity' model would apply to killing that is done by the operator of an armed drone. He or she is distant (thousands of miles away) from the person being killed, yet the vision (transmitted via camera, satellite and screen) of a body blown apart in a missile strike arguably renders such killing a 'close-up' experience of sorts. In addition, for hours or days prior to such killing, a drone operator might have been witnessing the ordinariness of the life being lived by the targeted individual. Further to his notion of 'naked soldiers', Walzer has argued that an enemy 'alienates himself from me when he tries to kill me, and from our common humanity', but 'the alienation is temporary, the humanity imminent', and it is 'restored... by... prosaic acts'.[132] The operator of a Reaper flying over Afghanistan (and controlled from a base in New York) has described how, while capturing hundreds of hours of video footage of a particular compound, 'I see mothers with children, I see fathers with children, I see fathers with mothers, I see kids playing soccer.'[133] The 'common humanity' exhibited through 'prosaic acts' is further evidenced by the observations of a drone operator based in Las Vegas:

> you wind up watching a house for hours, and all you see is a guy walk into the courtyard at night to take a crap, registered by the heat signature picked up on the ground after he gets up from his squat.[134]

According to a medical officer at the US Air Education Training Command, witnessing these 'regular old life things' can cause stress on drone operators because, 'At some point, some of the stuff [you watch] might remind you of stuff you did yourself. You might gain a level of familiarity that makes it a little difficult to pull the trigger.'[135] A 2011 study by the USAF School of Aerospace Medicine found that drone operators experienced stress from watching hours of close-up video footage of people killed in missile strikes. In the words of one of the study's authors, neuropsychiatrist Colonel Kent McDonald: 'Collateral damage is unnerving or unsettling to these guys.'[136]

Regarding the psychological risks that attach to the use of force more generally, evidence has recently emerged that US soldiers who report killing in battle suffer more symptoms of post-traumatic stress disorder (PTSD) than those who do not. However, it has also been suggested that soldiers who kill in self-defence seem to cope better than those who kill without experiencing any personal threat.[137] As the operators of armed drones fall into the latter category, it is reasonable to suppose that they too might face a higher PTSD risk. Nevertheless, drawing a comparison between them and soldiers is difficult, and where emotions are concerned it is possibly also unhelpful. Because the killing in which drone operators engage is *always* divorced from physical risk, the protection of their psychological integrity is perhaps more suitably approached by comparing them to executioners. To do so, however, would be to cast drone operators into a profession with an ethos quite different from that of the warrior. According to Wertheimer,

> An executioner's proficiency may win admiration from her peers but not public adulation and glory.... Society pays executioners a fair wage, convinced that this work is worth it, that it must be done. Society cannot well call it dishonorable work. But it doesn't honor it either. Even when deemed needed, it seems ignoble.[138]

An argument could nevertheless be made that executing someone is something extraordinary, and that an executioner's sensibilities must in some way be recognized respectfully if such grisly work is to go on. Such was the case in June 2010 when prison authorities in the US state of Utah organised the execution by firing squad of convicted murderer Ronnie Lee Gardner. Five anonymous, volunteer marksmen (all local law enforcement officers) were each handed a rifle, and none could ever know for sure if he fired a lethal shot because one of the rifles was loaded with a dummy round. An additional marksman was on standby in case one of the others lost his nerve, and afterwards, for 'service beyond their ordinary daily duties', the marksmen were given a commemorative Ronnie Lee Gardner coin.[139] Perhaps the coin was rather like a medal awarded to men who had 'courageously' dared to hazard the emotional toll of executing a fellow human being.

The psychological risks experienced by drone operators is an area deserving of further research, and from this it might emerge that the comparison to executioners is odious or unhelpful. For present purposes, it is enough to acknowledge that, while the experience of physical risk in drone strikes is inherently one-sided, this is tempered by non-physical risks that make drone operators victims as well as killers. Ultimately, however, the victimhood of drone operators caused by non-physical risks might not be enough to satisfy the moral requirement that war is a contest between warriors experiencing mutual risk. It is difficult enough to weigh the loss of psychological integrity against the loss of a limb, much less the loss of a life.

Conclusion

In the 1955 novel *Catch-22*, Orr and Yossarian are airmen in a fictitious American bomber squadron based in Italy in 1944. Yossarian, unlike Orr, is anxious not to fly missions over Italy on account of his 'morbid aversion to dying', but there is a catch:

> Catch-22... specified that a concern for one's own safety in the face of dangers that were real and immediate was the process of a rational mind. Orr was crazy and could be grounded. All he had to do was ask; and as soon as he did, he would no longer be crazy and would have to fly more missions. Orr would be crazy to fly more missions and sane if he didn't, but if he was sane, he had to fly them.[140]

By removing the 'pilot' from any danger, drones render Catch-22 obsolete; operating a drone requires neither craziness nor courage. If the drone is armed and its ground-based operator is a killer, however, this arguably creates a new catch: removing oneself from risk completely is the most rational thing a person could want, and yet only by experiencing at least a scintilla of risk can a killer claim to be engaged in a warlike activity invested with moral potential.

The peculiar characteristic of war is that it is a potentially lethal contest. Combatants on one side use force in a relationship of mutual risk with those on the other side. The 'bargain' among warriors is that the moral licence to kill may be exercised only by someone who in return is prepared to die. In no profession save the military is killing and being killed integral to the purpose of that profession. Risk is an indispensable characteristic of war, and courage is an indispensable characteristic of a warrior. When there is no contest between killer and killed, no relationship of mutual risk, it is difficult to see how any killing that takes place can attract the moral imprimatur that *war* potentially bestows. The use of armed drones is therefore something that is genuinely new and arguably anathema to the reputed virtues of the military profession. The drone operator kills without experiencing any physical risk, thus requiring none of the courage that for millennia has distinguished the warrior from all other kinds of killer. As such, the moral status of the drone operator is diminished. With their minds away at war and their bodies safe at home, these killers are disembodied warriors. This paradox is confusing and potentially damaging to the military profession of which drone operators are supposedly a part, and it can generate dangerous derision from those living in targeted foreign countries. Although drone operators may legitimately be subjected to harm by their enemies, in practice the victimhood of drone operators is attributable to psychological rather than physical risks. The emotional toll endured by drone operators who kill is a subject worthy of concern and redress. It should not, however, distract attention from the human suffering that overwhelmingly occurs at the missile end of a drone strike, lest more effort be directed to protecting the feelings of killers than to mitigating the plight of those facing death. In a physically one-sided contest, drone operators can be victims of psychological harm, but this is probably not enough to make them warriors.

7 Autonomous drones and post-human war

In the discussion of ethics, armed drones and post-heroic war thus far, the focus has been on human decisions and actions. The availability of technology for remote-control killing presents opportunities for political leaders to convince themselves and their citizens that resorting to armed force carries no risk, and in the physical separation of weapon and warrior there is scope both to enhance and to degrade adherence to principles governing the conduct of war. In this chapter, the discussion turns to an as-yet theoretical circumstance in which the weapon *is* the warrior. In the United States, there is strong technological and institutional momentum towards the development and use of autonomous drones, but there is also deep concern there and elsewhere over the prospect of machines that can decide to kill humans. From an ethical perspective, an argument in favour of autonomy might be that, given the poor record of human adherence to just war principles, an armed drone could be programmed to do a better job. An alternative would be to hold fast to the notion that both war and ethics are necessarily and inescapably a human affair. Thus, when contemplating autonomous drones as a seemingly 'post-human' approach to war, the critical issue is whether or how technology can overcome ethical shortcomings in the use of force while preserving the moral influence of human responsibility. In government documents and academic literature on military robotics, little differentiation is made between machines that operate on land, in water or in the air. The latter element, however, is arguably worthy of special attention when considering the post-heroic appeal of low-risk uses of force. Not only does an airborne robot relieve a human pilot of a potentially dangerous job, it is itself less vulnerable to the attacks of earth-bound adversaries. Autonomous drones – having greater capabilities for speed, penetration, perception and manoeuvre – are likely therefore to be preferred over land-based robots in much the same way that traditional aircraft are currently often preferred over ground troops. The making of this distinction on a strategic or operational basis does not, however, preclude ethical consideration of autonomy in robots more generally. What matters most for present purposes is the capacity of any machine, airborne or not, to decide to kill.

At the outset, given that the subject for analysis lies on the cusp of state-of-the-art science and science fiction, it is worthwhile recalling Isaac Asimov's view on the moral relationship between humans, robots and violence. In his 1950 novel *I, Robot* the Three Laws of Robotics are intended to preclude the very idea of a 'killer robot'. The First Law is that a robot may not injure a human being or, through inaction, allow a human being to come to harm; second, a robot must obey any orders given to it by human beings, except where such orders would conflict with the First Law; and third, a robot must protect its own existence as long as such protection does not conflict with the First or Second Law.[1] In Asimov's futuristic vision, society is divided into two categories – humans and robots – and the applicability of his Three Laws is universal. There is no category of humans to which a robot owes a greater duty than it does to another, and nor is there a category of robots to which the Three Laws apply differently or not at all. As between all humans and all robots, therefore, there is necessarily and immutably a master–slave relationship. Such a relationship is consistent with the derivation of the word 'robot' from the Czech words *robotnik* (slave) and *robota* (forced labor),[2] and it renders impermissible any circumstance in which a human and a robot are enemies using violence against one another. Whether inspired by Asimov or not, many roboticists today take the view, as Peter Asaro does, that the overall purpose of robot ethics 'ought to be the practical one of preventing robots from doing harm' to humans.[3] For this reason, the idea of robot warriors fighting wars in which humans are potential victims is one that generates controversy. Even if a machine were to use force against a human being only for the purpose of defending itself (Asimov's Third Law notwithstanding), in that instant would be a realization of the radical notion that a life must be extinguished so that a non-living machine might 'live' on. In exploring the ethical implications of robot autonomy in war, there is occasion to consider anew what it means to be 'alive' and to be 'human'.

This chapter consists of three sections. The first describes the technological momentum and operational imperatives driving US military enthusiasm for armed drones that can operate with reduced human control. The second section examines whether or how justice in war can be programmed into and processed by autonomous drones, and the third addresses the critical issues of moral responsibility and punishment for wrongdoing. The chapter then concludes by exploring the proposition that a human element is necessary (perhaps tragically so) if war is to have any moral potential.

From remote-control to autonomy

When an aircraft has a pilot on board, there is a need to accommodate and protect frail human flesh in the engineering, construction and use of that aircraft. By contrast, a drone requires no cockpit pressurisation and temperature control, and it has more space and payload capacity for fuel so that it can stay in the air (and at high altitudes) for longer. This long-dwell capability has been advantageous for US military purposes (air surveillance and strike) in Afghanistan, Iraq and Libya, as well as for the CIA's purpose of hunting and killing enemies in Pakistan, Yemen and Somalia. In the uncontested or largely uncontested airspace of these territories, the use of armed drones not only avoids physical risk to pilots, it also provides a more persistent aerial presence than inhabited aircraft do. In contested airspaces, however, and as other countries acquire more drones of greater technical sophistication, the United States is less likely to enjoy an advantage. As one USAF drone operator, Major Bryan Callahan, told *Der Spiegel* in 2010: 'we operate in a war that highlights the strengths of RPAs [remotely piloted aircraft]. Their weaknesses are not much of a problem right now. They may be in future conflicts.'[4] Propeller-powered Predators and Reapers are slower than jet-powered aircraft, their long-range (satellite-based) communication systems are vulnerable to overload or interference, and drone operators are unlikely to prevail in air-to-air 'combat' against fighter pilots. At the time of writing, a jet-powered drone (the Avenger) was under development by General Atomics,[5] but it is not enough for a drone to have the same or better speed and manoeuvring capabilities as an inhabited aircraft. Even if the operator of such a drone possessed airmanship skills equal to any pilot, the fact that drones are controlled remotely means a reliable and secure communication system is required.

In late 2011 the Iranian government displayed images on national television of a captured US drone. Iran's military claimed that it had brought down an unarmed RQ-170 Sentinel (a stealth aircraft manufactured by Lockheed Martin) in an electronic attack, but US officials insisted at the time that the drone was lost due to a technical malfunction.[6] Either way, the prospect of control being lost or stolen due to communication problems is a primary driver of US efforts to develop a drone that can keep operating with little or no human input. An 'autonomous' drone would thus in a sense be less like an aircraft and more like a pilot who, knowing a mission's objective, can keep flying and fighting without instructions from ground crew. Finite bandwidth (the amount of data transmittable over a communications link in a given amount of time) would be less of a constraint if a drone needed to receive smaller amounts of information and less often,[7] and the continued operation of such a drone would also be less vulnerable to attacks on communications infrastructure (e.g. satellites and transmitters). Moreover, minimizing or eliminating human input would reduce the likelihood of control of a drone being wrested away by an adversary. In 2011 the spectre of this problem was raised by *Wired* magazine when it reported on a computer virus at Creech Air Force Base in Nevada that had been logging US drone operators' every keystroke.[8] Even if reliable and secure communication were assured, however, the information being acquired and transmitted by a drone could become so voluminous and so complex as to be beyond human capacity to comprehend and use in a timely fashion. Arguably, human brains – unable to think and decide quickly enough – are 'bottlenecks' in a modern military's otherwise fast-flowing system of information-processing. In 2010 the USAF Chief Scientist predicted that 'by 2030 machine capabilities will have increased to the point that humans will have become the weakest component in a wide array of systems and processes'.[9] And as the deputy director of the US Defense Department's Unmanned Aerial Systems Taskforce reportedly said the previous year, 'There's really no way a system that is remotely controlled can effectively operate in an offensive or defensive air combat environment'.[10] For these and other reasons, the Pentagon's position as set out in its 2011 *Unmanned Systems Integrated Roadmap* (*USIR*) is that it must 'continue to pursue technologies and policies that introduce a higher degree of autonomy to reduce the manpower burden and reliance on full-time high-speed communications links while also reducing decision loop cycle time'.[11]

The US military's use of the term 'autonomous' tends to connote a negative; that is, the reduction or elimination of human control over a drone. It is also the case, however, that the term has a positive connotation: the increase or achievement of a drone's control over itself. Recognition of this duality is important when contemplating moral responsibility for actions taken in war, even though it might not be the case that the transition of control (and responsibility) from human to drone is seamless. A later section of this chapter examines whether a human, an autonomous drone or neither can be fairly held responsible for ethical transgressions in the conduct of drone warfare, but it is necessary first to consider briefly the meaning of 'autonomy' itself. The word is derived from the Greek words *auto* (self) and *nomos* (rule), and the city states of ancient Greece were politically autonomous in the sense that they were governed by their own laws rather than the laws of others. According to Jean-Jacques Rousseau, there is individual autonomy when a person 'is obedient to a law that he prescribes to himself',[12] and Andrew Reath has argued more recently that the concept of autonomy has evolved to refer to 'the capacity to govern one's actions, preferences, and values through rational, critical reflection'.[13] Philosophical disagreements persist, and 'autonomy' will mean different things depending on whether the term is being used by an ethicist, a biologist, an engineer or a military commander, but some underlying notion (true to its etymology) of 'self-governance' is common to all such uses. Strictly speaking, 'full' autonomy is nonsensical. To be governed entirely and only by one's own rules is an impossible state of being for anyone, except perhaps for a hermit in the wilderness. Therefore, whether referring to humans or machines, it is more useful to conceive of autonomy in degrees.

If an autonomous machine is one that is capable of unsupervised operation, a machine with a lesser need for human supervision and intervention is one that can be said to have greater autonomy.[14] The US Defense Department recognizes four levels of autonomy (see Table 7.1).

The first level, which essentially describes a state of non-autonomy, is commonly referred to as 'human-in-the-loop', and levels two and three are variations of 'human-on-the-loop'. The fourth level might be called 'human-out-of-the-loop' except that, even in a 'fully' autonomous system, 'a human could still enter the loop' in time to make a difference.[15] The Pentagon's scheme implies, nevertheless, that a fast-paced and complex combat scenario would afford no opportunity for human intervention in a weapon system that independently identifies and attacks targets. In this vision of autonomy advancements into the future, it is unclear when (or even if) a level four system would enter into service, although something called 'Intelligent Control' is planned to be achieved sometime between 2020 and 2025.[16]

Table 7.1 Levels of autonomy

Human operated	A human operator makes all decisions. The system has no autonomous control of its environment although it may have information-only responses to sensed data.
Human delegated	The vehicle can perform many functions independently of human control when delegated to do so. This level encompasses automatic controls, engine controls, and other low-level automation that must be activated or deactivated by human input and must act in mutual exclusion of human operation.
Human supervised	The system can perform a wide variety of activities when given top-level permissions or direction by a human. Both the human and the system can initiate behaviours based on sensed data, but the system can do so only if within the scope of its currently directed tasks.
Fully autonomous	The system receives goals from humans and translates them into tasks to be performed without human interaction. A human could still enter the loop in an emergency or change the goals, although in practice there may be significant time delays before human intervention occurs.

Adapted from US Department of Defense, *Unmanned Systems Integrated Roadmap FY2011–2036*, Reference no. 11-S-3613, 2011. Available online at www.defenseinnovationmarketplace.mil/resources/UnmannedSystemsIntegratedRoadmapFY2011.pdf (accessed 10 January 2013), p. 46.

Regarding drone systems specifically, US technology appears to have a long way to go. Some drones, including the Global Hawk and Scan Eagle, are capable of automatic take-off and landing, and they can follow a pre-programmed flight path for extended periods of time provided that poor weather conditions do not require continuous operator intervention.[17] For a drone to identify a target on the ground, however, is more complicated, such that fighting by itself seems a prospect more distant (or a possibility more remote) than flying by itself. In 2011 an experiment was conducted at the US Army's Fort Benning in Georgia, in which two model-sized aircraft flying at 800 and 1,000 feet, without any human control, flew back and forth across the military base in search of a multi-coloured sheet of tarpaulin. Twenty minutes after take-off, one of the aircraft used its on-board camera and image-processing computer to locate and fly towards the tarpaulin. It also contacted the second aircraft, which flew closer and used its own sensors to focus on the coloured object below. Finally, one of the aircraft transmitted a signal to an uninhabited ground vehicle instructing it to move close to the tarpaulin and confirm the location thereof with its own camera. All told, target confirmation was achieved without any human involvement.[18]

Similar and more challenging experiments are presumably planned to take place over the long term, although the US Defense Department has acknowledged that 'public opinion' (in addition to technological factors) is a possible constraint on the introduction of 'increased unmanned system autonomy'.[19] Thus, it was probably not just a comment on likely scientific progress but also a political gesture of reassurance when the 2011 *USIR* predicted 'For the foreseeable future, decisions over the use of force and the choice of which individual targets to engage with lethal force will be retained under human control in unmanned systems'.[20] The previous *USIR* had contained the same prediction, adding that 'the decision to fire will not likely be fully automated *until* legal, rules of engagement, and safety concerns have all been thoroughly examined and resolved'.[21] The use of the word 'until' (rather than 'unless') suggests that a final resolution of these concerns is possible, yet debate persists over the feasibility and desirability of a machine's autonomy reaching a point at which humans are divested of moral responsibility for its actions. Among those who favour the advent of 'fully' autonomous weapon systems, and also among those who abhor the idea, there are some who appear resigned to its inevitability.[22] If indeed the technological momentum towards autonomous drones is irresistible, ethical consideration of its implications for war could provide a critical opportunity to prepare rules in advance of actual use. An alternative view, however, is that the outcome of ethical consideration could be a political determination to halt 'progress' towards autonomy.[23] As the remainder of this chapter will show, the moral case for introducing mechanical warriors into war depends, first, on their improving the conduct of war from a *jus in bello* perspective. Second, justice in war requires that responsibility for any misconduct that does occur can be fairly attributed and punishment meted out accordingly.

Programming and processing *jus in bello*

In November 2005, in the Iraqi village of Haditha, a roadside bomb killed a US marine – Lance Corporal Miguel ('TJ') Terrazas – and injured two others in his patrol.[24] Afterwards, according to witnesses, the marines 'went on a rampage in the village', killing 15 Iraqi civilians including seven women and three children.[25] Sergeant Sanick Dela Cruz, who 'pissed on one Iraqi's head', knowing it was wrong, later said: 'I done it because I was angry TJ was dead.'[26] Every student of military history knows that, the warrior ethos notwithstanding, warriors sometimes behave unethically. Whether due to lack of ethical awareness, inadequate training, and/or the emotional stress of combat, humans have on numerous occasions used force in a manner that is militarily unnecessary, indiscriminate and/or disproportionate. But if, for example, a human pilot's standard of ethical performance could be surpassed by an autonomous drone, might not this make for a kinder and gentler war? The best and most conspicuous proponent of such improvement is the roboticist Ronald Arkin. He argues that 'lethal autonomous unmanned systems... will potentially be capable of performing more ethically on the battlefield than are human soldiers'.[27] And by pointing to the historical and contemporary record of human ethical failings in the conduct of war, Arkin implies that the standard to be exceeded is not high.[28] His vision is to design 'Robots... without emotions that cloud their judgment or result in anger and frustration with ongoing battlefield events',[29] and the US Department of Defense has funded a project to provide design recommendations for the implementation of an ethical control and reasoning system potentially suitable for constraining lethal actions in an autonomous robotic system so that they fall within the bounds prescribed by the Laws of War and the Rules of Engagement.[30]

The system envisaged by Arkin is an embedded 'ethical governor component' by reference to which a robot warrior would be able to 'conduct an evaluation of the ethical appropriateness of any lethal response that has been produced by the robot architecture prior to its being enacted'.[31] Considered in the abstract, bringing about a higher degree of overall adherence to *jus in bello* principles seems a worthy and important goal, but there are at least two flaws in Arkin's project that go to feasibility and desirability respectively. First, the problem of poor ethical performance in war is not amenable to a technical solution because the rules in question are inherently unprogrammable. Second, the moral justification for deploying autonomous machines (in place of human warriors) is of a kind that effectively *lowers* the expected standard of ethical conduct in war.

On the issue of programming, Arkin's goal is 'to provide robots with an ethical code that has been already established by humanity as encoded in the Laws of War and Rules of Engagement'.[32] It is not the case, however, that 'humanity' in general has rules of engagement; rather, the militaries of individual states do, and these vary markedly from state to state and from one conflict to another. As for 'the Laws of War', Arkin appears to assume that *jus in bello* principles have been settled and are now manifested in the letter of international humanitarian law treaties, such that it remains only for engineers to translate those texts into the language (computer code) of machines. For better or for worse, it is rather the very nature of law (and international law especially) that the meaning of written rules is open to challenge and subject to differing interpretations. Even a rule which at first seems easy to apply – the rule against torture – leaves room for arguments about whether specific interrogation techniques are torturous as distinct from merely discomforting.[33] Moreover, international treaties are routinely and deliberately drafted using vague language so as to attract the greatest number of signatures, and sometimes a signatory state will lodge a reservation indicating how it intends to interpret its legal obligations. As much as such vagueness and inconsistency are a reality of international politics, it is nevertheless consistent with the way ethical principles 'require people to think about the ethical implications of their actions in certain ways, rather than dictating to them a specific action in a specific situation'.[34] The discussion of armed drones in Chapter 4, for example, suggested that applying the principles of necessity, discrimination and proportionality at a given time and place is more a matter of making subjective and plausible judgements than of making objective and precise calculations.

Good intentions notwithstanding, robotics engineers eager to achieve a programmed 'solution' to human atrocity at the earliest opportunity could be tempted to see the ethics of war as less complicated and less contestable than they are in practice. At the nexus of ethics and technology, the danger is that ethical principles will be distorted or truncated by a perceived need to 'implement them in an algorithmic form suitable to machine architecture'.[35] However, an electronically embedded code of ethics might never be a substitute for innate humanity if, as Sharkey has insisted, 'Humans understand one another in a way that machines cannot'.[36] In seeking to fight a war justly, so much depends upon a warrior being able to discern the true intentions behind apparently dangerous acts, and yet ambiguity is so often a foil to discrimination between combatants and non-combatants. What is the ethically appropriate response, for example, to the sight of a child carrying a grenade-launcher or a tank towing an ambulance? An understanding of the social, cultural, religious, economic and political contexts of a conflict could usefully inform an answer, as could familiarity with an odd expression on the child's face, but these factors are arguably just as unprogrammable as is the law. For a programmer seeking to encode an algorithm for discriminate use of force against non-uniformed combatants, it is little help that the ICRC's non-binding guidance on 'direct participation in hostilities'[37] does not even qualify as law. Neither would it be a solution to programme an autonomous machine to attack identified weaponry rather than dangerous individuals, because mere possession of a particular weapon (for example, an AK-47 rifle) is not proof positive of the possessor's hostile purpose.

Overall, there is little scope for optimism that autonomous drones could be programmed to exercise and act upon better ethical judgement than on-board pilots or ground-based operators, and a more serious concern is that they might be deployed before achieving even a roughly equal standard. The latter prospect, involving *increased* risk of death or injury to non-combatants during armed conflict, led Human Rights Watch to recommend in 2012 that governments urgently pursue a 'preemptive prohibition on [the] development and use' of autonomous weapons.[38] In the unlikely event, however, that an autonomous drone is somehow designed and deployed to use force 'more ethically' – that is, at a standard demonstrably superior to what would in practice be expected of human warriors – this would still present a moral problem. When Arkin argues that 'autonomous armed robotic platforms may ultimately reduce casualties... by their ability to better adhere to the Laws of War than most soldiers possibly can',[39] he uses as his moral benchmark the record of human frailty rather than the ideal of human perfection. In other words, he is lowering the bar, ethically speaking. Doing something better (than humans) is not the same as doing it 'well' *per se*, and it is important to recall that humans themselves are required to aim for complete adherence to every rule. As George Lucas has observed, 'we expect and demand that every human combatant will comply *fully* with the law, even though we realize statistically that not all will as a matter of experience'.[40] There is neither accommodation nor congratulations for a person who is only 99 per cent compliant with the law; rather their 1 per cent non-compliance attracts punishment (in theory if not in practice), and it would be no defence to argue, say, that people in general are understood to be only 98 per cent compliant.

A random selection of fighter and bomber pilots from any country or around the world is unlikely to yield a perfect record of ethical conduct across the board, yet such perfection by any and all pilots remains a theoretical possibility, and indeed it is a military virtue to strive for it. In the case of autonomous drones, by contrast, perfection is neither possible nor required. Arkin's benchmark seems rather to be that they need only behave better than the average pilot, even if that standard of behaviour declines in the future. Moreover, in a conflict in which one side deployed autonomous drones against the other side's human pilots, only the latter (if captured) could be punished for conduct that was less than perfectly compliant with *jus in bello* rules. Such a prospect conflicts with the notion discussed in Chapter 5 that, in circumstances of radical asymmetry, it is the technologically *superior* users of force who should be held to a higher standard. In addition, for present purposes, this prospect occasions hypothetical consideration of whether autonomous drones are moral agents capable of bearing responsibility for ethical transgressions in war. Closely related to this is the issue of whether they could be subjected to meaningful punishment.

Moral responsibility and meaningful punishment

If US military robotics technology progresses through the Pentagon's four levels of autonomy and beyond, a point can be imagined at which a drone makes and acts upon a decision to kill a human being. At that point, and if such killing is morally wrong because the drone knew the human in question to be a noncombatant (e.g. an infant), it will be vital to establish who is responsible. For *jus in bello* principles to have any practical effect in guiding violent actions, responsibility for breaches must be fairly assumed by or assigned to a moral agent. The alternative, if a responsible agent cannot be identified and punishment meted out accordingly, is that unethical forms of violence can occur with impunity. If, in the deployment of an armed autonomous drone, any such responsibility gap remained unfilled, this would constitute a complete denial of respect for an enemy. Failing to take responsibility for the taking of life would be, according to Sparrow, to 'treat our enemy like vermin, as though they may be exterminated without moral regard at all'.[41] In the hypothetical case of an autonomous drone perpetrating an atrocity, the language of the US Defense Department's definition of 'autonomous systems' suggests that there are three possible loci for blame:

> autonomous systems are self-directed toward a goal in that they do not require outside control, but rather are governed by laws and strategies that direct their behavior. Initially, these control algorithms are created and tested by teams of human operators and software developers. However, if machine learning is utilized, autonomous systems can develop modified strategies for themselves by which they select their behavior. An autonomous system is self-directed by choosing the behavior it follows to reach a human-directed goal.[42]

One possible bearer of moral responsibility is the drone's programmer ('control algorithms are created and tested'), and another is its commander ('a human-directed goal'). A third possibility, and one that seems exotic in today's world, is that blame could be assigned to the drone itself ('autonomous systems ... select their behavior'). If it were the case, however, that no one could fairly be held responsible and punished for an autonomous drone's misdeeds, this would render their use/participation in war impermissible from the outset.

Holding a human programmer responsible and punishable for the unjust behaviour of an autonomous drone seems at first both plausible and desirable. From the design stage onwards, it would concentrate a programmer's mind to know that his or her role was to prevent the deaths of innocents in war.[43] Any failure in this regard could be held to constitute criminal negligence or, as Lucas has suggested, an accountability mechanism could be modelled on existing product liability laws.[44] In circumstances where, for example, the law insisted on a drone programmer's strict or 'no fault' liability for injury or death resulting from any use of that drone, this 'daunting prospect ... might serve as a powerful disincentive to proceed with the requisite research, development, and manufacture of autonomous lethal systems'.[45] One problem with such an arrangement, however, is that if autonomous drones were used anyway, it would be difficult for the families of anyone unjustly killed to regard a product liability lawsuit as justice being served. Prosecution and punishment of an individual programmer for criminal negligence would perhaps more closely resemble just retribution, but if responsibility was assigned to the programmer's corporation (as a legal 'person'), no human would end up suffering much more than embarrassment and disgrace. A second problem is that the very countries whose militaries are most keen to deploy autonomous drones are probably those least likely to implement liability laws that effectively prohibit the participation of programmers in research, development and manufacture. In any event, assigning responsibility to a drone's programmer is probably unfair given that the whole thrust of autonomy technology is to enable a machine to operate with little or no human intervention. Precisely because programmers cannot know or predict everything a robot might encounter in performing its task, the purpose of programming an autonomous drone would not be to anticipate every circumstance and prescribe an ethical response to each. Rather, there is greater operational value in a drone that can 'learn' from its experiences and adapt its behaviour accordingly without first needing to be reprogrammed by a human. In a sense, such a machine would be *designed* to render itself capable of making 'choices other than those predicted or encouraged by its programmers'.[46] In a complex and fast-paced combat scenario especially, the in-built learning capacity of a drone could give a military commander some confidence that this machine (like a human warrior) will keep fighting in circumstances where it is unable to receive an order.

One imaginable circumstance is that, despite general programming and standing orders to direct fire away from individuals registered as non-combatants, a drone that finds itself beyond contact with its commander might learn to characterize those individuals differently and decide to fire upon them. If such learning precipitated a moral wrong, arguably it is the commander who would be responsible because he or she knew that attacks on the wrong targets are an inherent possibility when using an autonomous drone. According to John Sullins, it is apt to compare responsibility for the actions of 'complex robot agents' with that applicable to 'trained animals such as guard dogs' because 'The decision to own and operate them is the most significant moral question'.[47] Nevertheless, it seems an unfair prospect, especially from the perspective of military personnel, that human actors in war would be held responsible for a process of machine decision-making that the machine's programmer had deliberately sought to place beyond human control. This is perhaps why the Pentagon has insisted that 'Robust safeties and control measures will be required for commanders to trust that autonomous systems will not behave in a manner other than what is intended [by commanders] on the battlefield'.[48] Such measures are potentially important for ethical reasons too if they reduce the likelihood of harm to non-combatants, and for this reason Armin Krishnan has argued that 'any military computer system that controls weapons and could change its original programming by itself should be prohibited'.[49] There is an irony here, however. On the one hand, limiting drones' autonomy can be seen as a way of heading off a refusal by US military commanders to use them (for fear of being punished for any injustices perpetrated). On the other hand, the logic behind the US pursuit of technical advancement in this area is that maximizing military utility means maximizing autonomy. A radical option for escaping this apparent contradiction might be to accept that 'autonomy' for a drone means exactly what it means for a human, and in so doing to shift moral responsibility away from commanders and towards the drones themselves.

If one takes the view that moral agency can reside only in human life, the idea of assigning responsibility to a drone is nonsense. A comparison might be drawn to the transition from childhood to adulthood whereupon a person's moral responsibility crystallizes, but the analogy to machine autonomy is arguably a poor one; not only does a child progress *naturally* to adulthood, he or she is flesh and blood. An alternative view is that it is consistent with the vision of progress towards 'full' autonomy that a machine would one day acquire the moral responsibility that attaches to an autonomous human being. If autonomy *per se* is the morally significant characteristic of an entity when attributing responsibility for deliberate actions, why should it matter that the entity in question is non-human and non-living? The answer lies in the difficulty that arises when taking responsibility for wrongdoing means being subjected to punishment. The moral argument in favour of using robots in war is based on the proposition that they exhibit none of the physical and emotional frailties of humankind, and yet it is precisely these frailties that make punishment meaningful for humans. The prospect and actuality of punishment are what in large measure imbues a *sense* of responsibility, but if a machine can feel nothing (physically or emotionally), punishment is impossible. Sparrow has entertained the possibility that 'any robot that is capable of "intelligent" behaviour will have internal states which function like desires as well as an internal structure which motivates them to pursue these'.[50] If so, the frustration of these desires might serve as a mechanism for punishment. If, for example, an autonomous drone maintained a bank account, the imposition of a financial penalty would frustrate any desire it might have to purchase maintenance, cleaning, repairs, refuelling or decoration to its fuselage. However, if the cause of the fine was attribution of responsibility for a deadly wartime atrocity, it is highly doubtful that any human witness to this would be satisfied that justice had been done. From a human perspective, informed by human history and personal experience, the appropriate punishment for serious wrongdoing is serious suffering by the wrongdoer. The loss of liberty, bodily integrity or life is usually seen as serious enough, but the imprisonment, flogging or execution of an autonomous drone would likely seem futile unless humans felt empathy for the 'suffering' of a machine. There is precedent for such feeling in science fiction, such as the scene in the 1977 film *Star Wars* when Luke Skywalker removes restraining bolts from the droids C-3PO and R2-D2, but even state-of-the-art robots in the real world are insufficiently lifelike to elicit much fellow-feeling on the part of humans.

If a machine is inherently unpunishable and therefore incapable of moral responsibility, and if the programmer and commander of an armed autonomous drone cannot fairly be held responsible for its wrongdoings, the result is a responsibility gap. In war, a similar predicament arises in the case of child soldiers. Although they cannot fully comprehend the moral significance of their violent actions, they exhibit a degree of autonomy high enough to problematize the attribution of responsibility to their commanders, such that neither can fairly be held responsible.[51] However, whereas children can grow into responsible adults, a robot might never advance from its 'child-like' state. Unless or until the responsibility question can be resolved, there must be a presumptive prohibition against the deployment of armed autonomous drones. The alternative is to court injustice by failing to provide a means to punish it. From a technological perspective, the rise of autonomous robot warriors is often described as inevitable, but there is no reason why ethical arguments could not make this a self-denying prophecy. Scientific progress towards the militarization of machine autonomy can continue only for so long as individual scientists have the will to participate in research and development, and scientists have in the past shown themselves capable of abstaining on ethical grounds. In February 2009, at a conference convened by the Association for the Advancement of Artificial Intelligence, a group of computer scientists met at Asilomar, California, to debate whether there should be limits on research that might lead to loss of human control over computer-based systems. Asilomar was a deliberately chosen venue because there, in 1975, the world's leading biologists met to discuss a moratorium on possible biohazards and ethical concerns related to recombinant DNA research.[52] In early 2012, a similar moratorium was voluntarily instituted by the world's leading influenza researchers after scientists in two laboratories caused public alarm by creating a human-to-human transmissible (pandemic) form of avian influenza virus.[53] It appears that 'progress' sometimes can be stopped, and the dangers and uncertainties surrounding the use of autonomous drones in war are sufficiently profound to warrant caution on the part of roboticists and military planners.

Conclusion: the paradox of post-human war

In 1995 Robert Pepperell used the term 'post-human' in the context of a 'general convergence of organisms and technology' which he saw as leading to a profound transformation of 'our own view of what constitutes a human being'.[54] The idea of an autonomous machine challenges that view because it suggests that intelligence and morality are characteristics not exclusive to humanity. The challenge is compounded by the possibility of such a machine using force as a participant in war, because humans think of themselves alone as being capable of *politically* motivated violence. On one view, the anticipated rise of autonomous drones and other robot warriors heralds the rendering of both war and the ethics of war as post-human in the sense that the human element therein is removed. Given the demonstrated capacity of humans to wreak widespread destruction and suffering, it would perhaps be a positive development for non-human, morally superior entities to take over the business of war. An alternative view is that post-human war is a paradox; only humans can wage war and give it moral meaning. If ethics can inhere in humans only, post-human war is necessarily devoid of ethics and, arguably, it does not count as war at all. Gray has insisted upon 'the centrality of the human factor', arguing that 'Only people can be passionate, not their machines or organisations. The only source of creativity in war has to be human, just as most of the causes of chance events are traceable to human choices.'[55] A similar view was expressed by the former Chairman of the US Joint Chiefs of Staff, Admiral Mike Mullen: 'Because war is a clash of opposing wills, the human dimension is central. War may involve the use of technology, but it is waged by people.'[56]

In the planned shift from remote-control to autonomy for armed drones, the US military sees value in overcoming the physical and mental limitations of human participants in high-technology war. However, it is less certain that autonomous drones, programmed to be emotionless, would generate better ethical outcomes. From a *jus in bello* perspective, although an emotion like anger can be shown to undermine a warrior's adherence to ethical principles, the emotion of compassion can enhance it. Because a machine is not and cannot be a parent, for example, it arguably lacks a powerful check on human's willingness to kill:

> a robot in a combat zone might shoot a child pointing a gun at it, which might be a lawful response but not necessarily the most ethical one. By contrast, even if not required under the law to do so, a human soldier might remember his or her children, hold fire, and seek a more merciful solution to the situation, such as trying to capture the child or advance in a different direction.[57]

It is possible, more generally, that 'emotions may be *necessary* to ethical judgement', as Kaag and Kaufman have argued, because 'one who could not feel compassion for the sufferings of others might not be capable of making good moral decisions'.[58] If that is the case, it has even been suggested that present-day drone operators *ought* to experience 'high levels of psychological stress... in order to improve their ethical performance',[59] yet the US Government is clearly concerned rather to reduce that stress.

A project to engineer a robot warrior without human frailties and possessing ethically superior warfighting abilities must be a fascinating one for a roboticist like Ronald Arkin, but the reduction or removal of human participation in war threatens to preclude improvement in human adherence to war's rules. Such improvement is vital, not only because human standards of conduct are the benchmark to be exceeded by Arkin's robot warriors, but also for its own sake. As Ryan Tonkens has argued, machine autonomy in war could be challenged on the grounds that it 'unduly threatens the ability of human soldiers to exhibit morally exceptional behaviour, and undermines important aspects of the military profession'.[60] With fewer opportunities for soldiers, sailors and airmen to demonstrate courage and 'selfless sacrifice' for the society they serve, 'morally praiseworthy aspects of *human* warfare might be lost'.[61] It is certainly not the case that the alternative to deploying autonomous robots is to do nothing. Any deficit of human adherence to *jus in bello* principles could also be addressed by, for example, 'having shorter tours of duty... tightening up psychological screening of soldiers... [and] holding more rigorous training on the ethics of warfare'.[62] To do any or all of these things would be to build upon or improve existing practices, and as a way of reducing injustice in the conduct of war it might be cheaper, simpler and better than deploying robots.

Adherence to the principles of necessity, discrimination and proportionality is intended to prevent unjust victimhood in war, but the problem of non-adherence is not amenable to a technical solution. Rather, it is in the nature of ethics and laws that they are inherently unprogrammable. They tend to be vague rather than precise, and they can only serve as a general guide for behaviour rather than as an exhaustive list of specific actions required in specific circumstances. Moreover, even if *jus in bello* principles could somehow be programmed and processed, the *jus ad bellum* dimension would remain. As the discussion in Chapters 3 and 6 showed, the principle of just cause alone is so notoriously contested as to defy its reduction to an algorithm. Arkin correctly observes that norms of just conduct 'are often cast aside in the heat of combat, for reasons such as vengeance, anger, frustration, and the desire for victory at any cost',[63] but it remains the subject of debate whether victory itself can sometimes be a goal of overriding moral importance.[64] It is therefore significant that, although Arkin's prototype 'ethical governor' provides a robot with the ability to refuse an order it deems unethical, there is an option for a human to override the robot's refusal.[65] Broader military and political considerations might necessitate such intervention if, for example, the morally important goal of victory could only be achieved by a drone perpetrating a 'minor atrocity' like the intentional killing of a single infant. If a machine's refusal to fire upon this non-combatant, in accordance with the discrimination principle, were allowed to stand, a *jus ad bellum* imperative would be thwarted. Thus, the deliberate attenuation of a drone's autonomy by means of an override mechanism leaves the human element of war intact, albeit tragically so for the infant human concerned. The importance of victory notwithstanding, a human who in this way forced a drone to violate a *jus in bello* principle would clearly be morally responsible for that wrong. However, assigning responsibility for a drone's *own* decision to do so is difficult at best and probably impossible given its inability to understand punishment through the experience of suffering. Such a responsibility gap renders impermissible the use and perhaps the very existence of a machine that can decide for itself who to kill. War, to be just, would have to remain a human affair.

It seems unlikely that, through a combination of technological advancement and general human acceptance, an autonomous drone would attain full status as a moral agent capable of bearing responsibility for wrongdoing. Nevertheless, if that were to occur, the paradox of post-human war might still be evident. The scenario that comes to mind is one in which the very post-heroic impulses that caused a society to remove its human warriors from war would cause it also to abhor the notion of robot casualties. In other words, the military pursuit of robot autonomy would become self-defeating. Human Rights Watch has argued that the availability of autonomous robot warriors would 'make it easier for political leaders to resort to force since their own troops would not face death or injury',[66] yet this would only be the case if a robot's suffering were unimaginable. If a human could appreciate and be satisfied by the suffering of a drone who is punished for moral transgressions in war, it is a short step then to accept that a drone could suffer during war itself – experiencing injury (damage) or death (destruction) – just like a human could. And if physical risk both to humans *and* their mechanical moral counterparts became unacceptable, there would no one left to do the fighting. Already, humankind's 'remarkable tendency to anthropomorphise' has manifested in mourning for the loss in battle of 'today's relatively dumb robots'.[67]

Both within and beyond the realm of war, a 'robot' is 'an engineered machine that senses, thinks, and acts'.[68] Humans sense and act in largely the same way, but contemporary robots' 'thinking' does not extend to daydreaming or taking delight in wonder. Not only do their thoughts not wander, they are strictly in the binary form 'if X, then Y'. However, if ever the imaginings and moral ruminations of a machine became as rich and mysterious as a human's, such a machine could find itself relating to humans as closely as they relate to each other. It would be the encounter, perhaps, of *Homo sapiens* and *Robo sapiens*,[69] and a robot who felt a sense of responsibility to a human (along the lines of Asimov's Three Laws) could find that feeling reciprocated. If each in the other recognized life and therefore a right to life, both could claim to be deserving of protection from the dangers of war.

8 Conclusion

The United States has a self-interested desire to wage post-heroic war, and it has a moral duty to do so justly. To the extent that the world is an orderly society governed by rules, a concern for justice can and should act as a restraint on states' pursuit of self-interest, especially when the means of pursuit is violence. The history of war has frequently demonstrated, however, that the relationship between self-interest and justice is one mediated by technology and technological advantage. Where technology lowers one side's expectations of loss resulting from the use of force, the pursuit of self-interest is made easier and the temptation to use force unjustly can increase. In particular, the combination of technologies underpinning airpower and long-range communication, by moving the practice of war far beyond its hand-to-hand combat origins, has made it easier for some states to apply force from a great distance. In the case of America's use of armed drones, remote-controlled killing is carried out in a way that is also largely unseen by would-be targets, unintended victims, US citizens and outside observers alike. Such invisibility can enable the surmounting of erstwhile obstacles to the achievement of self-interest, and justice too could thereby well be served. Alternatively, the increased power afforded by invisibility could generate a powerful temptation to act without regard to what other actors might think is unjust. In Plato's *The Republic*, Glaucon observes that a system of morality is a compromise between people's 'natural' pursuit of their own interests 'regardless of others' and the need to 'run an orderly society'. He then argues that, if the sanctions of that system are removed, it would profit a person more to act unjustly.[1] Glaucon illustrates the power of unrestrained liberty to pursue self-interest by recounting the tale of a shepherd, named Gyges, employed by the king of Lydia. One day, after an earthquake, Gyges discovered a gold ring in a chasm in the earth. He wore the ring at a meeting of shepherds who reported monthly to the king on the state of his flocks. When Gyges happened to twist the ring on his finger, 'he became invisible to his companions', and he became visible again when he twisted the ring in the other direction. Soon afterwards, empowered by the ring to act unseen, he was able to enter the king's palace, seduce the queen, murder the king and seize the throne of Lydia for himself.[2] With such a magic ring, Glaucon suggested, a man could 'generally behave as if he had supernatural powers', and acting unjustly (seducing, murdering and stealing) would pay better than acting justly.³

This technology of invisibility, although itself morally neutral, became morally relevant once it was in the hands of a potential user who felt he could then recast the relationship between self-interest and justice. Gyges could have chosen not to wear the ring, or he could have used it for good, but unjust action was made more likely by the temptation to seize what would otherwise be unattainable. Absent the prospect of being thwarted in the pursuit of self-interest in a manner that others would regard as unjust, the distinction between pursuing good purposes and pursuing bad purposes had become less meaningful. Technology, it could be argued, had opened the door for Gyges to forsake his virtue for the sake of profit. The magic ring made the achievement of Gyges' goals more feasible, but it did not magically make legitimate the goals themselves or the violent means he chose to achieve them. Rather, Gyges' decisions and actions alone attract moral judgement. Likewise, the mere fact that drone technology makes violence easier for and less risky to its unseen user is not to be confused with moral permission to engage in drone warfare. The US Government ought to be capable of using any military technology for just purposes and in a just manner, but its challenge is to avoid the technology-driven temptation to do otherwise. Where Gyges failed (morally), the United States might yet succeed, and so it is important now for war's analysts and practitioners to explore or anticipate the ethical challenges associated with armed drones. Hitherto, technical and operational discussions of drones have tended to emphasize the immediate advantages that this technology appears to afford. In bringing an ethical perspective to bear, there is more scope to consider longer-term disadvantages. The evidence and arguments presented in this book indicate that, in some respects, the use of armed drones is to be welcomed as an ethically superior mode of warfare. Over time, however, their continued and increased use is likely to generate more challenges than solutions and perhaps more harm than good.

In the United States, financial and operational commitments are nevertheless increasing, and drone technology continues to advance. This reinforces a trend in the American way of war away from the heroic and towards the post-heroic. In large measure, this trend is being driven by a political desire both to manage strategic risks as much as possible from the air and to avoid exposing America's tactical users of force to physical risk. In a post-heroic age, every American life is more precious and less able to be sacrificed for a grand purpose. Even the War on Terror, which might have begun as a heroic one, could not long withstand the conscientious impulse to reduce risks to US personnel. As ground troops have departed the scene of conflict in the Middle East and Central Asia, it is ground-based drone operators who have maintained an American presence there. The advantage conferred by remote control of the skies could nonetheless turn out to be fleeting. In all the places where the United States has to date deployed armed drones, these aircraft have flown unmolested, but air superiority is less likely in other places and in the future. The US Government clearly anticipates a need to increase the scale and intensity of its drone use, not least because hundreds of non-US drone programmes have emerged worldwide in the last decade. A global race appears to be under way to build more drones to higher levels of technical sophistication, and this increases the urgency of ethical consideration. States and individuals everywhere have a long-term interest in maintaining international norms of war, not only because they promise to make conflict less frequent and more humane, but also because they promote stability in the global order. The appearance or actuality of unrestrained US use of armed drones would set a dangerous and destabilizing precedent because other states might feel they are morally entitled to act in like fashion. As American superiority comes to be challenged by other actors, however, the US Government is likely to acquire a greater grasp of the wisdom as well as the virtue of championing limitations on the use of armed drones. The overall objective of such limitations, in accordance with just war principles, is to prevent any unjust increase in the incidence and lethality of armed conflict.

For better or for worse, the availability of drone technology can affect political decision-making on whether and when to cross the war threshold and resort to force. As more armed drones become available to more actors, there is likely to be a widespread increase in the degree of willingness and the number of perceived opportunities to use them. This in turn would carry the risk of an overall rise in the number of unjust decisions to wage war in the first place, notwithstanding any description of drone warfare as small in scale and precise in its effects. From a *jus ad bellum* perspective, such an increase would be unjust if force was resorted to without a just cause. The recent record of drone use by the United States has included its interventions in Libya for humanitarian purposes and in Afghanistan for self-defence purposes, but elsewhere America's pre-emptive use of armed drones is less easy to justify because it appears to exceed what is required for self-defence. On the matter of right authority, UNSC authorization is required when drones (like any other military technology) are used for humanitarian purposes. When it comes to the exercise of a state's inherent right of self-defence, however, recent US experience suggests that the standard of domestic authorization is changing with the post-heroic times. Where civilian Americans are mostly disengaged from the risk-free, drone-based killings that are carried out on their behalf by their government, there is reason to doubt whether such use of force has really been adequately authorized and whether it is truly a last resort. At the same time, if drone technology enables minor uses of force in response to minor threats, and if this is done with the intention of forestalling the emergence of major threats, this would appear to satisfy *jus ad bellum* requirements that force be resorted to in a proportionate fashion and with a genuine desire to achieve a better post-war peace. As for whether the use of armed drones in the War on Terror has a reasonable prospect of success, recent empirical studies leave room for doubt about the long-term effectiveness of using drones to decapitate enemy organizations. Moreover, when US drone strikes generate non-combatant casualties, this arguably decreases the likelihood that drone strikes will bring strategic success; local and external dismay at seemingly excessive victimhood in war can be a potent political liability for the user of force. Adherence to ethical principles governing the conduct of hostilities is therefore of instrumental value to the United States, as well as being morally important in itself.

From a *jus in bello* perspective, any drone-driven increase in the lethality of armed conflict is unjust if more non-combatants are deliberately killed or if the numbers unintentionally killed are excessive in relation to what is militarily necessary. It is no straightforward matter to claim that drone strikes in general kill fewer non-combatants than other forms of warfare, because so much depends upon the context. If a drone war is of long duration, for example, the total number of non-combatant deaths might be greater than a shorter war that features other military technologies. Moreover, if the availability of drones strengthens the political preference for force over non-violent alternatives, the outcome might be larger numbers of non-combatant deaths than would result if, because of technological hurdles, force were resorted to less often. Drone technology, incorporating powerful cameras and other advanced means of target identification, is theoretically more capable than other weapons platforms of enabling adherence to *jus in bello* principles. In practice, however, unofficial statistics differ markedly on the ratio of combatant to non-combatant deaths resulting from drone strikes, and ethical judgement is made more difficult when there is uncertainty over what kinds of people get counted as non-combatants in the first place. An examination of Pakistan, where the US Government has used armed drones most extensively, reveals uncertainties regarding the ethical soundness of drone strikes. The military benefit derived from disrupting enemy activities in that country is real, but weighing against this is an immediate and growing human cost measured in innocent lives lost. This in turn brings a strategic cost in COIN terms because of a persistent and widespread perception among Pakistanis that drone strikes kill too many non-combatants. The problem this presents is a moral as well as a practical one, and so the Pakistan case highlights the need for greater official transparency. Although the US Government professes its intentions to use force justly, this does not obviate the need to demonstrate its sincerity. It could do this, first, by conspicuously inquiring into and reporting on the human effects of drone strikes. Second, it could publicize its implementation of measures to prevent and punish any unjust behaviour by US drone operators. For so long as the US Government eschews transparency, it is in a weak position to argue for restraint in the use of armed drones by other actors, and such restraint will likely become more important to the United States as its technological dominance erodes.

For the time being, such dominance remains a reality, and this is what has enabled the United States to use armed drones hitherto in a radically asymmetric manner. From the perspective of a state bringing to bear vastly superior strength, the circumstance of radical asymmetry is such that the risks that usually accompany the conduct of war are not as great an impediment to resorting to war. In an uncontested airspace, with remotely located drone operators experiencing no physical risk, force can be applied with apparent impunity. Nevertheless, ethical difficulties might arise if this affects an enemy's ability to exercise the right of self-defence (*jus ad bellum*) and if it constitutes systemic risk-transfer from combatants to non-combatants (*jus in bello*). The radical asymmetry manifested in drone strikes does not avail targeted enemies of moral permission to suspend or curtail their own adherence to *jus in bello* principles, but it would be prudent nonetheless for the United States to be ethically proactive rather than stand idle in the hope that reality will match morality. Terroristic violation of *jus in bello* principles is likely to remain a threat to American non-combatants, but the impetus for such violence might be lessened if the US Government were to hold itself to a stricter ethical standard of conduct. That standard could involve a requirement for greater care in the drawing of distinctions between combatants and non-combatants, and it could see the lives of non-combatants accorded greater weight in proportionality calculations. US military objectives would thereby be made harder to achieve, but the likelihood of enemies being able to use non-combatant deaths as a pretext for terrorism would arguably be lessened.

An extreme alternative when it comes to surmounting the ethical difficulties posed by radical asymmetry is to abandon the traditional notion that combatants on each side of a conflict are morally equal in terms of their licence to kill and their liability to be killed. On this view, if it is morally important for US drone operators, as just combatants, to succeed in their just cause, it is only right that they be spared any physical risk in order to continue using force unhindered. The flaw in this argument is that it is seldom if ever easy to determine whose is a just cause and who is a just combatant in war. If America's cause is unjust, it follows that neither armed drones nor any other kind of force may be used. It might therefore be better, just in case, for US-based drone operators and their distant enemies to be regarded as moral equals. The former would thus in theory be legitimate targets for violence, even though they are virtually untouchable in practice. It remains difficult to account for this last detail, however, if one cleaves to the traditional concept of war as a contest; not a fair fight, but a fight *per se*. The bleakest ethical assessment is that a drone campaign, if it does not count as war, cannot be a just war. A more plausible assessment is that a contest of sorts can and does occur when the US Government uses armed drones exclusively in a theatre of operations like Pakistan. In practice, albeit impermissibly, the enemy's retaliatory violence is able to be directed against American non-combatants rather than against the drone operators themselves.

The absence of a relationship of mutual risk between putative combatants nevertheless militates against classifying drone strikes as war and drone operators as warriors. Not only does risk-free killing pose a fundamental challenge to the status of war as something morally distinguishable from other forms of violence, it also undermines the virtue of the warrior as a professional risk-taker. The traditional bargain among warriors who are moral equals is that the licence to kill may be exercised only by someone who is prepared to die. The use of armed drones is therefore arguably anathema to the warrior ethos. Unlike the pilots of in-theatre aircraft, drone operators on the ground in US territory experience no physical danger beyond what they would experience as ordinary citizens, and thus they are not required to exercise courage when using force.

Rather, with their minds away at war and their bodies safe at home, they manifest paradoxically as disembodied warriors who face only psychological risks. This paradox is confusing and potentially damaging to the military profession of which drone operators are supposedly a part, and it understandably attracts contempt both from traditional pilots and from people living in targeted countries. Uncertainty surrounding the moral status of a killer who experiences no physical risk probably compounds the emotional toll associated with feeling simultaneously abroad and at home, aloft and grounded. This, and the PTSD that has begun to be observed in US drone operators, is a subject worthy of concern and redress. More worthy still, however, is the physical suffering that occurs exclusively among humans at the other end of a drone strike.

In decades to come, will veteran drone operators march in street parades? Will any of them wear decorations for valour? Will crowds cheer and admire them as they march? As long as courage remains a military virtue, none of these things seems likely, and yet the opportunity for courageous killing is itself increasingly a casualty of this post-heroic age. Drone technology has already effected the removal of physical risk to the user of force, and it is possible in the future that killing too will be removed from human control. As pressure grows for the United States to maintain its technological edge over other international actors, there is growing attraction in military and robotics circles to the idea of autonomous drones that can operate independently in the absence of communication links. If these machines could somehow be programmed to do a better job than humans of fighting justly, there is an argument to be made that this would confer an ethical as well as an operational advantage. The advent of post-human war and post-human ethics is not, however, a likely prospect. Just as it would be difficult to have confidence in an autonomous drone's ability to navigate the uncertainties surrounding necessity, discrimination and proportionality, a robotic adjudication of competing *jus ad bellum* claims would be risible. For humans to take an autonomous drone seriously as an ethical decision-maker, they would first need to be satisfied that it could bear moral responsibility for any wrongdoing. Unless or until a non-living entity can be shown to experience punishment by suffering in a manner to which humans would be sympathetic, the idea of machines taking responsibility is nonsense and there must be a presumptive prohibition on the use/participation of drone warriors in war. Alternatively, if ever an autonomous drone could exhibit appreciable signs of pain and misery, and if they could in their own way be injured and killed, these very human-like characteristics could induce in humans a reluctance to expose their *Robo sapiens* cousins to the physical risks of combat. The technological road to post-heroic war will have come full circle.

Notes

1 Introduction

1 Joby Warrick, Joshua Partlow and Haq Nawaz Khan, 'A Psychological Blow for Pakistani Taliban', *Washington Post*, 8 August 2009. Available online at www.washingtonpost.com/wp-dyn/content/article/2009/08/07/AR2009080700271.html (accessed 28 February 2011); Peter Bergen and Katherine Tiedemann, 'Revenge of the Drones: An Analysis of Drone Strikes in Pakistan', New America Foundation, 19 October 2009. Available online at www.newamerica.net/publications/policy/revenge_of_the_drones (accessed 12 January 2011); Jane Mayer, 'The Predator War', *New Yorker*, 26 October 2009. Available online at www.newyorker.com/reporting/2009/10/26/091026fa_fact_mayer (accessed 12 January 2011).
2 Bergen and Tiedemann, 'Revenge of the Drones'; Mayer, 'The Predator War'.
3 P. W. Singer, *Wired for War: The Robotics Revolution and Conflict in the Twenty-First Century*, New York: Penguin, 2009, p. 33.
4 Warrick *et al.*, 'A Psychological Blow for Pakistani Taliban'.
5 Jeremiah Gertler, *US Unmanned Aerial Systems*, Washington, DC: Congressional Research Service, 3 January 2012, p. 7.
6 Cited in Jai C. Galliott, 'Uninhabited Systems in the Civilian Realm: Some Ethical Concerns, *IEEE Technology and Society*, Summer 2012, 13–16, at p. 14.
7 Elisabeth Bumiller, 'Navy Drone Violated Washington Airspace', *New York Times*, 26 August 2010, p. A16.
8 See Angela Gendron, 'The Ethics of Overhead Surveillance: Deploying UAVs in the National Airspace for Law Enforcement and Other Purposes', *International Journal of Intelligence Ethics* 2, no. 2, 2011, 19–44 at p. 20.
9 Singer, *Wired for War*, p. 33.
10 Max Fisher, 'Obama Finds Predator Drones Hilarious', *Atlantic Wire*, 3 May 2010. Available online at http://atlanticwire.theatlantic.com/features/view/feature/Obama-Finds-Predator-Drones-Hilarious-1171 (accessed 25 February 2011).
11 David R. Mets, *Air Power and Technology: Smart and Unmanned Weapons*, Westport, CT: Praeger, 2009, p. 60.
12 Emily Kalah Gade, 'Defining the Non-Combatant: How Do We Determine Who Is Worthy of Protection in Violent Conflict?' *Journal of Military Ethics* 9, no. 3, 2010, 219–42, at p. 221.
13 Colin S. Gray, 'Moral Advantage, Strategic Advantage?' *Journal of Strategic Studies* 33, no. 3, 2010, 333–65, at p. 345.
14 Anthony Burke, *Beyond Security, Ethics and Violence: War against the Other*, London: Routledge, 2007, p. 163.
15 Jeff McMahan, *Killing in War*, Oxford: Oxford University Press, 2009, p. vii.
16 Gian P. Gentile, 'Beneficial War', *Harvard International Review*, 24 December 2011.

Available online at http://hir.harvard.edu/india-in-transition/beneficial-war-0 (accessed 29 April 2012).
17 Charles Webster and Noble Frankland, *Strategic Air Offensive against Germany, 1919–45*, vol. IV, *Annexes and Appendices*, London: Her Majesty's Stationery Office, 1961, p. 144.
18 Michael Walzer, *Just and Unjust Wars: A Moral Argument with Historical Illustrations*, 4th edn, New York: Basic Books, 2006, p. 323.
19 Carl von Clausewitz, *On War*, London: Penguin, 1982 [1832], p. 101.
20 See Paul Christopher, *The Ethics of War and Peace*, Englewood Cliffs, NJ: 1994, pp. 87–96.

2 Post-heroic war and armed drones

1 Christopher Coker, *Humane Warfare*, London: Routledge, 2001, pp. 8–9.
2 H. P. Willmott and Michael B. Barrett, *Clausewitz Reconsidered*, Santa Barbara, CA: ABC CLIO, 2010, p. 16.
3 Michael Ignatieff, *The Warrior's Honour: Ethnic War and the Modern Conscience*, London: Chatto & Windus, 1998, p. 113.
4 Coker, *Humane Warfare*, p. 10.
5 Willmott and Barrett, *Clausewitz Reconsidered*, p. 21.
6 Coker, *Humane Warfare*, p. 52.
7 Ibid., pp. 28–9.
8 Inaugural Address of John F. Kennedy, 20 January 1961, The Avalon Project, Yale Law School, 2008. Available online at http://avalon.law.yale.edu/20th_century/kennedy.asp (accessed 5 December 2012).
9 Coker, *Humane Warfare*, p. 32.
10 John A. Gentry, 'Military Force in an Age of Cowardice', *Washington Quarterly*, Autumn 1998, 179–91 at p. 180.
11 Richard K. Betts, 'What Will It Take to Deter the United States?' *Parameters*, Winter 1995–6, p. 76 (original emphasis).
12 Quoted in Andrew P. N. Erdmann, 'The US Presumption of Quick, Costless Wars', *Orbis*, Summer 1999, 363–81 at p. 363.
13 Jeffrey Record, 'Collapsed Countries, Casualty Dread, and the New American Way of War', *Parameters*, Summer 2002, 4–23 at p. 4.
14 Mark Clegg, 'Force Protection and Society', *Defense and Security Analysis* 28, no. 2, 2012, 131–9 at p. 134.
15 Edward N. Luttwak, 'Toward Post-Heroic Warfare', *Foreign Affairs* 74, no. 3, 1995, 109–22 at p. 115.
16 Ibid., p. 115.
17 Martin van Creveld, *The Age of Air Power*, New York: PublicAffairs, 2011, p. 318.
18 Michael Ignatieff, *Virtual War: Kosovo and Beyond*, New York: Picador, 2000, p. 186.
19 Coker, *Humane Warfare*, p. 5.
20 Eliot A. Cohen, 'Kosovo and the New American Way of War', in Andrew J. Bacevich and Eliot A. Cohen (eds), *War Over Kosovo: Politics and Strategy in a Global Age*, New York: Columbia University Press, 2001, p. 56.
21 Coker, *Humane Warfare*, pp. 146–7.
22 Yee-Kuang Heng, 'The "Transformation of War" Debate: Through the Looking Glass of Ulrich Beck's *World Risk Society*', *International Relations* 20, no. 1, 2006, 69–91 at p. 74.
23 Thomas Mahnken, *Technology and the American Way of War since 1945*, New York: Columbia University Press, 2008, p. 179.
24 Cited in ibid., p. 179.
25 van Creveld, *The Age of Air Power*, p. 327.

26 William S. Cohen and General Henry H. Shelton, 'Joint statement on the Kosovo After Action Review presented by Secretary of Defense William S. Cohen and Gen. Henry H. Shelton, Chairman of the Joint Chiefs of Staff, before the Senate Armed Services Committee, 14 October 1999', Office of Assistant Secretary of Defense (Public Affairs). Available online at www.au.af.mil/au/awc/awcgate/kosovoaa/joint-stmt.htm (accessed 12 September 2012).

27 Cited in International Institute for Strategic Studies (IISS), 'Prospects for Unmanned Aerial Vehicles: The Lessons of Kosovo', *IISS Strategic Comments* 6, no. 7, 2000, 1–2, at p. 1.

28 Christopher Coker, *The Warrior Ethos: Military Culture and the War on Terror*, London: Routledge, 2007, p. 102.

29 Cited in Sarah Kreps and John Kaag, 'Unmanned Aerial Vehicles in Contemporary Conflict: A Legal and Ethical Analysis', *Polity* 44, no. 2, 2012, 260–85 at p. 277.

30 James Der Derian, *Virtuous War*, 2nd edn, New York: Routledge, 2009, p. 259.

31 Heng, 'The "Transformation of War" Debate', p. 83.

32 US Department of Defense, *Defense Casualty Analysis System*, updated 6 December 2012. Available online at www.dmdc.osd.mil/dcas/pages/casualties.xhtml (accessed 10 December 2012).

33 Watson Institute for International Studies, Brown University, 'The Costs of War'. Available online at http://costsofwar.org/ (accessed 7 December 2012).

34 Cited in Coker, *Humane Warfare*, p. 2.

35 Christopher Coker, *War in an Age of Risk*, Cambridge: Polity Press, 2009, p. 176.

36 Anne Flaherty, 'Military Bans Video Game that "Kills" US Troops', *Sydney Morning Herald*, 9 September 2010. Available online at www.smh.com.au/digital-life/games/military-bans-video-game-that-kills-us-troops-20100909-151qz.html (accessed 21 January 2013).

37 Michael Sherry, *The Rise of American Airpower: The Creation of Armageddon*, New Haven, CT: Yale University Press, 1989, p. 2.

38 Alan Gropman, 'Aviation at the Start of the First World War', US Centennial of Flight Commission. Available online at www.centennialofflight.gov/essay/Air_Power/Pre_WWI/AP1.htm (accessed 27 April 2012); Daniel Swift, 'Air Power's Century of False Promises', *New York Times*, 1 November 2011. Available online at www.nytimes.com/2011/11/01/opinion/air-powers-century-of-false-promises.html (accessed 1 February 2013).

39 van Creveld, *The Age of Air Power*, p. 20.

40 Dave Grossman, *On Killing: The Psychological Cost of Learning to Kill in War and Society*, Boston: Little, Brown and Company, 1995, p. 65.

41 Patricia Owens, 'Accidents Don't Just Happen: The Liberal Politics of High-Technology "Humanitarian" War', *Millennium: Journal of International Studies* 32, 2003, 595–616 at p. 612.

42 Keith Somerville, 'US Drones Take Combat Role', *BBC News*, 5 November 2002. Available online at http://news.bbc.co.uk/2/hi/in_depth/2404425.stm (accessed 9 December 2012).

43 Mahnken, *Technology and the American Way of War*, p. 113.

44 P. W. Singer, 'Military Robots and the Laws of War', *New Atlantis*, Winter 2009, 25–45 at p. 36.

45 IISS, 'Prospects for Unmanned Aerial Vehicles', p. 1.

46 Nick Cook, 'Leaving the Pilot on the Ground', *Janes Defence Weekly*, 3 July 1996, 34–5 at p. 34.

47 Ibid., p. 35.

48 UK Ministry of Defence, *The UK Approach to Unmanned Aircraft Systems*, Joint Doctrine Note 2/11, May 2011. Available online at www.mod.uk/NR/rdonlyres/F9335CB2-73FC-4761-A428-DB7DF4BEC02C/0/20110505JDN_211_UAS_v2U.pdf (accessed 1 February 2013), pp. 3–7.

49 Brian Burridge, 'UAVs and the Dawn of Post-Modern Warfare: A Perspective on Recent Operations', *RUSI Journal*, October 2003, 18–23 at p. 18.
50 Jeremiah Gertler, *US Unmanned Aerial Systems*, Washington, DC: Congressional Research Service, 3 January 2012, p. 5.
51 Ibid., p. 48; 'Killer App: Drones Are Lynchpin of Obama's War on Terror', *Der Spiegel*, 12 March 2010. Available online at www.spiegel.de/international/world/killer-app-drones-are-lynchpin-of-obama-s-war-on-terror-a-682612.html (accessed 1 February 2013).
52 Marc Pitzke, 'How Drone Pilots Wage War', *Der Spiegel*, 3 December 2010. Available online at www.spiegel.de/international/world/0,1518,682420,00.html (accessed 15 December 2011).
53 William Wan and Peter Finn, 'Global race on to Match US Drone Capabilities', *Washington Post*, 5 July 2011. Available online at www.washingtonpost.com/world/national-security/global-race-on-to-match-us-drone-capabilities/2011/06/30/gHQACWdmxH_story.html (accessed 25 January 2013).
54 Mahnken, *Technology and the American Way of War*, p. 31.
55 Agence France-Presse, 'Future of Military Aviation Lies with Drones: US Admiral', *Defence Talk*, 15 May 2009. Available online at www.defencetalk.com/future-of-military-aviation-lies-with-drones-18932/ (accessed 9 December 2012).
56 Statement of John F. Tierney, Chairman, Subcommittee on National Security and Foreign Affairs, Committee on Oversight and Government Reform, US House of Representatives Hearing on 'Rise of the Drones: Unmanned Systems and the Future of War', 23 March 2010. Available online at http://democrats.oversight.house.gov/images/stories/subcommittees/NS_Subcommittee/3.23.10_Drones/3–23–10_JFT_Opening_Statement_FINAL_for_Delivery.pdf (accessed 1 February 2013), p. 1.
57 Gertler, *US Unmanned Aerial Systems*, p. 2.
58 Ibid., p. 9.
59 Congressional Budget Office, *Policy Options for Unmanned Aircraft Systems*, Washington, DC: Congress of the United States, June 2011, p. vii.
60 Ibid.
61 Ibid., p. ix.
62 Gertler, *US Unmanned Aerial Systems*, p. 24.
63 Marina Malenic, 'Interview with Rear Admiral Shannon', *Jane's International Defence Review*, October 2011, p. 66.
64 Wan and Finn, 'Global Race on to match US Drone Capabilities'.
65 Daniel Brunstetter and Megan Braun, 'The Implications of Drones on the Just War Tradition', *Ethics and International Affairs* 25, no. 3, 2011, 337–58 at p. 348.
66 Somerville, 'US Drones Take Combat Role'.
67 Christopher Coker, *Ethics and War in the Twenty-First Century*, London: Routledge, 2008, p. 146.
68 Barry H. Steiner, 'What Use Overwhelming Air Superiority? A Tale of Two Campaigns', *Contemporary Security Policy* 33, no. 2, 2012, 311–36 at p. 321.
69 Somerville, 'US Drones Take Combat Role'.
70 'Obama Sends Drones to Libya', *Weekend Australian*, 23–24 April 2011, p. 20.
71 A targeted killing is 'the intentional, premeditated and deliberate use of lethal force, by States or their agents acting under colour of law, or by an organized armed group in armed conflict, against a specific individual who is not in the physical custody of the perpetrator': Philip Alston, *Report of the Special Rapporteur on Extrajudicial, Summary or Arbitrary Executions*, (A/HRC/14/24/Add.6), New York: United Nations General Assembly, 28 May 2010, p. 3.
72 'CIA "Killed Al-Qaeda Suspects" in Yemen', *BBC News*, 5 November 2002. Available online at http://news.bbc.co.uk/2/hi/2402479.stm (accessed 22 February 2011); Craig Hoyle and Andrew Koch, 'Yemen Drone Strike: Just The Start?' *Janes Defence Weekly*, 13 November 2002, p. 3.

122 *Notes*

73 Vince Crawley and Amy Svitak, 'Is Predator the Future of Warfare?' *Defense News*, 11–17 November 2002, p. 8.
74 Ibid.
75 Jeb Boone and Greg Miller, 'US Drone Strike in Yemen Is First Since 2002', *Washington Post*, 6 May 2011. Available online at www.washingtonpost.com/world/middle-east/yemeni-official-us-drone-strike-kills-2-al-qaeda-operatives/2011/05/05/AF7HrzxF_story.html (accessed 9 December 2012).
76 Mark Mazetti, 'CIA Strike Kills Top Qaeda Operative in Drone Strike', *New York Times*, 16 September 2011, p. A8.
77 Greg Jaffe and Karen DeYoung, 'US Drone Targets Two Leaders of Somali Group Allied with Al-Qaeda, Official Says', *Washington Post*, 30 June 2011. Available online at www.washingtonpost.com/national/national-security/us-drones-target-two-leaders-of-somali-group-allied-with-al-qaeda/2011/06/29/AGJFxZrH_story.html (accessed 9 December 2012).
78 Craig Whitlock and Greg Miller, 'US Assembling Secret Drone Bases in Africa, Arabian Peninsula, Officials Say', *Washington Post*, 21 September 2011. Available online at www.washingtonpost.com/world/national-security/us-building-secret-drone-bases-in-africa-arabian-peninsula-officials-say/2011/09/20/gIQAJ8rOjK_story.html (accessed 1 February 2013).
79 See, for example, David E. Sanger and Eric Schmitt, 'As Rift Deepens, Kerry Has a Warning for Pakistan', *New York Times*, 15 May 2011, p. A16.
80 Burridge, 'UAVs and the Dawn of Post-Modern Warfare', p. 19.
81 Thom Shanker and Rick Gladstone, 'Iran Fired on Military Drone in First Such Attack, US Says', *New York Times*, 9 November 2012, p. A1.
82 Fares Akram and Isabel Kershner, 'Israeli Drone Strike Kills Militants in Gaza', *New York Times*, 30 October 2011, p. A14. 'RAF Reaper Drone Squadron Stood up at RAF Waddington', *BBC News*, 23 October 2012. Available online at www.bbc.co.uk/news/uk-england-20039085 (accessed 13 March 2013).
83 Scott Shane, 'Coming Soon: The Drone Arms Race', *New York Times*, 9 October 2011, p. SR5.
84 Adam Entous, 'US Plans to Arm Italy's Drones', *Wall Street Journal*, 29 May 2012, p. A1; Veit Medick, '"Credible Deterrence": Germany Plans to Deploy Armed Drones', *Der Spiegel*, 25 January 2013. Available online at www.spiegel.de/international/germany/germany-plans-to-deploy-armed-drones-in-combat-abroad-a-879633.html (accessed 13 February 2013); Dylan Welch, 'Australia Inches Closer to Getting Killer Drones', *Sydney Morning Herald*, 31 May 2012. Available online at www.smh.com.au/technology/sci-tech/australia-inches-closer-to-getting-killer-drones-20120530-1zjej.html (accessed 13 February 2013).
85 Wan and Finn, 'Global Race on to Match US Drone Capabilities'; W. J. Hennigan, 'Drone Makers Urge US to Let Them Sell More Overseas', *Los Angeles Times*, 1 July 2012. Available online at http://articles.latimes.com/2012/jul/01/business/la-fi-drone-foreign-sales-20120701 (accessed 22 November 2012).
86 Defense Science Board, *Task Force Report: The Role of Autonomy in DoD Systems*, Washington, DC: US Department of Defense, 2012, p. 69.
87 Gertler, *US Unmanned Aerial Systems*, p. 28.
88 Entous, 'US Plans to Arms Italy's Drones', p. A1.

3 Drones and the war threshold

1 United Kingdom Ministry of Defence, *The UK Approach to Unmanned Aircraft Systems*, Joint Doctrine Note 2/11, May 2011. Available online at www.gov.uk/government/uploads/system/uploads/attachment_data/file/33711/20110505JDN_211_UAS_v2U.pdf (accessed 1 February 2013), pp. 5–9.

2 Patrick Lin, 'Ethical Blowback from Emerging Technologies', *Journal of Military Ethics* 9, no. 4, 2010, 313–31 at p. 325.
 3 Ibid.
 4 P. W. Singer, *Wired for War: The Robotics Revolution and Conflict in the Twenty-First Century*, New York: Penguin, 2009, p. 317.
 5 John Kelsay, 'Islamic Tradition and the Justice of War', in Torkel Brekke (ed.), *The Ethics of War in Asian Civilizations: A Comparative Perspective*, London: Routledge, 2006, p. 103.
 6 United Nations, Charter of the United Nations, Chapter I: Purposes and Principles. Available online at www.un.org/en/documents/charter/chapter1.shtml (accessed 10 December 2012).
 7 United Nations, Charter of the United Nations, Chapter VII: Actions with Respect to Threats to the Peace, Breaches of the Peace, and Acts of Aggression. Available online at www.un.org/en/documents/charter/chapter7.shtml (accessed 12 December 2012).
 8 The rule arising from the 1837 *Caroline* case. Letter from Mr Webster to Mr Fox, 24 April 1841, cited in D. J. Harris, *Cases and Materials on International Law*, 5th edn, London: Sweet & Maxwell, 1998, p. 895.
 9 See, for example: Alan M. Dershowitz, *Preemption: A Knife that Cuts Both Ways*, New York: Norton, 2007; Bart M. J. Szewczyk, 'Pre-emption, Deterrence, and Self-Defence: A Legal and Historical Assessment', *Cambridge Review of International Affairs* 18, no. 1, 2005, 119–35; and Terence Taylor, 'The End of Imminence?' *Washington Quarterly* 27, no. 4, 2004, 57–72.
10 *The National Security Strategy of the United States of America*, Washington, DC: The White House, September 2002. Available online at http://georgewbush-whitehouse.archives.gov/nsc/nss/2002/ (accessed 20 January 2013), p. 15.
11 Harold Hongju Koh, 'The Obama Administration and International Law'. Speech at the Annual Meeting of the American Society of International Law, Washington, DC, 25 March 2010. Available online at www.state.gov/s/l/releases/remarks/139119.htm (accessed 12 January 2011).
12 Charlie Savage, 'At White House, Weighing Limits of Terror Fight', *New York Times*, 16 September 2011, p. A1.
13 International Commission on Intervention and State Sovereignty (ICISS), *The Responsibility to Protect*, Ottawa: ICISS, 2001, p. 32; United Nations General Assembly, 'World Summit Outcome', A/RES/60/1, 24 October 2005. Available online at http://unpan1.un.org/intradoc/groups/public/documents/un/unpan021752.pdf (accessed 1 February 2013).
14 David Fisher and Nigel Biggar, 'Was Iraq an Unjust War? A Debate on the Iraq War and Reflections on Libya', *International Affairs* 87, no. 3, 2011, 687–707 at p. 701.
15 United Nations Security Council, Security Council Resolution 1973 (2011) [on the situation in the Libyan Arab Jamahiriya], 17 March 2011. Available online at www.unhcr.org/refworld/docid/4d885fc42.html (accessed 10 December 2012), p. 3 (emphasis added).
16 Ryan R. Vogel, 'Drone Warfare and the Law of Armed Conflict', *Denver Journal of International Law and Policy* 39, no. 1, 2010, 101–38 at p. 108.
17 Charlie Savage, 'Obama Adviser Discusses Using Military on Terrorists', *New York Times*, 17 September 2011, p. A6.
18 Paul Kahn, 'The Paradox of Riskless Warfare', *Philosophy and Public Policy Quarterly* 22, no. 3, 2002, 2–8 at p. 4.
19 White House, 'United States Activities in Libya', *Washington Post*, 15 June 2011. Available online at www.washingtonpost.com/wp-srv/politics/documents/united-states-activities-libya.html (accessed 8 August 2011).
20 Terry McDermott, 'Drones Won't Solve This Problem', *Los Angeles Times*, 17 June 2012. Available online at http://articles.latimes.com/2012/jun/17/opinion/la-oe-mcdermott-drones-and-cambodia-20120617 (accessed 22 November 2012).

21 Cited in Singer, *Wired for War*, p. 432.
22 *National Security Strategy*, Washington, DC: White House, 2010. Available online at www.whitehouse.gov/sites/default/files/rss_viewer/national_security_strategy.pdf (accessed 14 December 2012), p. 22.
23 Cited in Thomas Mahnken, *Technology and the American Way of War since 1945*, New York: Columbia University Press, 2008, p. 187 (emphasis added).
24 Michael Ignatieff, *Virtual War: Kosovo and Beyond*, New York: Picador, 2000, p. 4.
25 See Nicholas Fotion, *War and Ethics: A New Just War Theory*, London: Continuum, 2007, p. 19; and Thomas Hurka, 'Proportionality in the Morality of War', *Philosophy and Public Affairs* 33, no. 1, 2005, 34–66 at p. 35.
26 Daniel Brunstetter and Megan Braun, 'The Implications of Drones on the Just War Tradition', *Ethics and International Affairs* 25, no. 3, 2011, 337–58 at p. 339.
27 Ibid.
28 Colin S. Gray, 'How Has War Changed since the End of the Cold War?' *Parameters* 35, no. 1, 2005, 14–26 at p. 25.
29 Giulio Douhet, *The Command of the Air*, trans. Dino Ferrari, London: Faber and Faber, 1943, p. 219.
30 Robert W. Tucker and David C. Hendrickson, *The Imperial Temptation: The New World Order and America's Purpose*, New York: Council on Foreign Relations, 1992, p. 162.
31 C. A. J. Coady, *Morality and Political Violence*, Cambridge: Cambridge University Press, 2008, p. 94.
32 Niccolò Machiavelli, *The Prince*, trans. W. K. Marriott, London: J. M. Dent and Sons, 1958, p. 13.
33 'US Airstrikes in Pakistan Called "Very Effective"', *CNN News*, 18 May 2009. Available online at http://articles.cnn.com/2009–05–18/politics/cia.pakistan.airstrikes_1_qaeda-pakistani-airstrikes?_s=PM:POLITICS (accessed 23 February 2011).
34 Jenna Jordan, 'When Heads Roll: Assessing the Effectiveness of Leadership Decapitation', *Security Studies* 18, no. 4, 2009, 719–55 at p. 722.
35 Noel Sharkey, 'Death Strikes from the Sky: The Calculus of Proportionality', *IEEE Technology and Society*, Spring 2009, 16–19 at p. 19.
36 Jordan, 'When Heads Roll', p. 746.
37 Ibid., p. 747.
38 Ibid., p. 748.
39 See Jayshree Bajoria, 'Pakistan's New Generation of Terrorists', Council on Foreign Relations, 7 October 2010. Available online at www.cfr.org/pakistan/pakistans-new-generation-terrorists/p15422 (accessed 1 March 2011).
40 Patrick B. Johnston, 'Does Decapitation Work? Assessing the Effectiveness of Leadership Targeting in Counterinsurgency Campaigns', *International Security* 36, no. 4, 2012, 47–79 at p. 50.
41 Ibid., p. 75.
42 Ibid., p. 77.
43 Bryan C. Price, 'Targeting Top Terrorists: How Leadership Decapitation Contributes to Counterterrorism', *International Security* 36, no. 4, 2012, 9–46 at p. 46.
44 Thom Shanker and Eric Schmitt, 'Seeking Limits to "New" War', *New York Times*, 22 October 2011, p. A1.
45 H. P. Willmott and Michael B. Barrett, *Clausewitz Reconsidered*, Santa Barbara, CA: ABC CLIO, 2010, p. 174.
46 C. A. J. Coady, 'Bombing and the Morality of War', in Yuki Tanaka and Marilyn B. Young (eds), *Bombing Civilians: A Twentieth-Century History*, New York: The New Press, 2009, pp. 203–4.
47 Christopher Coker, *Humane Warfare*, London: Routledge, 2001, p. 14.
48 Jeffrey Record, 'Collapsed Countries, Casualty Dread, and the New American Way of War', *Parameters*, Summer 2002, 4–23 at p. 12.

49 Ignatieff, *Virtual War*, p. 4.
50 Daniel L. Byman, Matthew C. Waxman and Eric Larson, *Air Power as a Coercive Instrument*, Santa Monica, CA: RAND, 1999, p. 138.
51 Coker, *Humane Warfare*, p. 59.
52 See Lorenzo Zambernardi, 'Counterinsurgency's Impossible Trilemma', *Washington Quarterly* 33, no. 3, 2010, 21–34 at p. 24; Mark Clegg, 'Force Protection and Society', *Defense and Security Analysis* 28, no. 2, 2012, 131–9 at p. 132; and US Department of the Army, *Counterinsurgency*, FM 3–24, MCWP 3–33.5, December 2006. Military Field Manuals, 2009. Available online at www.militaryfieldmanuals.net/manuals/counterinsurgency (accessed 1 February 2013), para. 7–30.
53 Christopher Drew, 'Drones Are Playing a Growing Role in Afghanistan', *New York Times*, 20 February 2010, p. A6.
54 Ibid.
55 Ann Scott Tyson, 'Less Peril for Civilians, but More for Troops', *Washington Post*, 23 September 2009. Available online at www.washingtonpost.com/wp-dyn/content/article/2009/09/22/AR2009092204296.html (accessed 5 November 2010).
56 Zambernardi, 'Counterinsurgency's Impossible Trilemma', p. 25.
57 Office of the Press Secretary, 'Remarks by the President at the Acceptance of the Nobel Peace Prize', The White House, 10 December 2009. Available online at www.whitehouse.gov/the-press-office/remarks-president-acceptance-nobel-peace-prize(accessed 25 January 2013).
58 Christian Henderson, 'The 2010 United States National Security Strategy and the Obama Doctrine of 'Necessary Force', *Journal of Conflict and Security Law* 15, no. 3, 2010, 403–34 at p. 419.
59 Scott Shane, 'Coming Soon: The Drone Arms Race', *New York Times*, 9 October 2011, p. SR5.
60 Editorial, 'Too Much Power for a President', *New York Times*, 31 May 2012, p. A28.
61 Karen deYoung, 'Obama Redefines National Security Strategy, Looks Beyond Military Might', *Washington Post*, 27 May 2010. Available online at www.washingtonpost.com/wp-dyn/content/article/2010/05/27/AR2010052701044.html (accessed 29 June 2012).

4 Conducting drone warfare: the case of Pakistan

1 Seth G. Jones and C. Christine Fair, *Counterinsurgency in Pakistan*, Santa Monica, CA: RAND, 2010, p. 25; Karen DeYoung and Joby Warrick, 'Pakistan and US Have Tacit Deal on Airstrikes', *Washington Post*, 16 November 2008. Available online at www.washingtonpost.com/wp-dyn/content/article/2008/11/15/AR2008111502656_pf.html (accessed 24 February 2011).
2 Peter Bergen and Katherine Tiedemann, 'No Secrets in the Sky', *New York Times*, 26 April 2010, p. A23.
3 IISS, 'US Intensifies Drone Strikes in Pakistan', *IISS Strategic Comments* 16, no. 36, October 2010; 'CIA Pushes for Air Strikes in Pakistani City', *Sydney Morning Herald*, 16 December 2009. Available online at www.smh.com.au/world/cia-pushes-for-air-strikes-in-pakistani-city-20091215-kudx.html (accessed 22 February 2011).
4 Bill Roggio and Alexander Mayer, 'Charting the Data for US Airstrikes in Pakistan, 2004–2013', *Long War Journal*, updated 10 January 2013. Available online at www.longwarjournal.org/pakistan-strikes.php (accessed 25 January 2013).
5 John Kelsay, 'Islamic Tradition and the Justice of War' in Torkel Brekke (ed.), *The Ethics of War in Asian Civilizations: A Comparative Perspective*, London: Routledge, 2006, p. 103.
6 David Kilcullen, *Counterinsurgency*, Melbourne: Scribe, 2010, p. 173; Ishtiaq Ahmad, 'The US Af-Pak Strategy: Challenges and Opportunities for Pakistan', *Asian Affairs: An American Review* 37, 2010, 191–209 at p. 194.

7 Barack Obama, 'Remarks by the President on a New Strategy for Afghanistan and Pakistan', White House, 27 March 2009. Available online at www.whitehouse.gov/the_press_office/Remarks-by-the-President-on-a-New-Strategy-for-Afghanistan-and-Pakistan/ (accessed 24 February 2011).
8 Edward Luttwak, 'Dead End: Counterinsurgency Warfare as Military Malpractice', *Harper's Magazine*, February 2007, 33–42 at p. 42.
9 Ibid.
10 Ibid.
11 Michael Walzer, *Just and Unjust Wars: A Moral Argument with Historical Illustrations*, 4th edn, New York: Basic Books, 2006, p. 20.
12 Colin S. Gray, 'Moral Advantage, Strategic Advantage?' *Journal of Strategic Studies* 33, no. 3, 2010, 333–65 at p. 358.
13 Ibid., p. 360.
14 Mark O'Neill, *Confronting the Hydra: Big Problems with Small Wars*, Sydney: Lowy Institute for International Policy, 2009, p. 20.
15 Ibid.
16 Ibid., p. 14.
17 US Department of the Army, *Counterinsurgency*, FM 3–24, MCWP 3–33.5, December 2006 [hereafter 'US COIN Field Manual']. Military Field Manuals, 2009. Available online at www.militaryfieldmanuals.net/manuals/counterinsurgency (accessed 1 February 2013), para. 7–21.
18 Martin van Creveld, *The Age of Air Power*, New York: Public Affairs, 2011, p. 19.
19 Ibid., p. 344.
20 US COIN Field Manual, para. 7–37.
21 Ibid., para. 7–25.
22 Philip Alston, *Report of the Special Rapporteur on Extrajudicial, Summary or Arbitrary Executions*, A/HRC/14/24/Add.6, New York: United Nations General Assembly, 28 May 2010, p. 10.
23 Cited in Alex J. Bellamy, *Fighting Terror: Ethical Dilemmas*, London: Zed Books, 2008, pp. 101–2.
24 Jean Bethke Elshtain, *Just War against Terror: The Burden of American Power in a Violent World*, New York: Basic Books, 2004.
25 Walzer, *Just and Unjust Wars*, p. 144.
26 Ibid. (original emphasis).
27 Cited in Alex J. Bellamy, *Just Wars: From Cicero to Iraq*, Cambridge: Polity Press, 2006, p. 42 (emphasis added).
28 Cited in Ryan R. Vogel, 'Drone Warfare and the Law of Armed Conflict', *Denver Journal of International Law and Policy* 39, no. 1, 2010, 101–38 at p. 115 (emphasis added).
29 Avery Plaw, *Targeting Terrorists: A License to Kill?* Aldershot: Ashgate, 2008, p. 176.
30 Jane Perlez and Pir Zubair Shah, 'Drones Batter Al Qaeda and Its Allies within Pakistan', *New York Times*, 5 April 2010, p. A1.
31 Joby Warrick and Peter Finn, 'CIA Director Says Secret Attacks in Pakistan Have Hobbled Al-Qaeda', *Washington Post*, 18 March 2010, p. A01.
32 Haq Nawaz Khan and Pamela Constable, 'Pakistani Taliban Leader's Death Would Be "Fatal Blow" for Group, Analyst Says', *Washington Post*, 2 February 2010, p. A01.
33 'US Airstrikes in Pakistan Called "Very Effective"', *CNN News*, 18 May 2009. Available online at http://articles.cnn.com/2009–05–18/politics/cia.pakistan.airstrikes_1_qaeda-pakistani-airstrikes?_s=PM:POLITICS (accessed 23 February 2011).
34 John Kaag and Whitley Kaufman, 'Military Frameworks: Technological Know-How and the Legitimization of Warfare', *Cambridge Review of International Affairs* 22, no. 4, 2009, 585–606 at p. 604.

35 'Pakistan Criticises "Unjustified" US Drone Strikes', *BBC News*, 7 October 2010. Available online at www.bbc.co.uk/news/world-south-asia-11490722 (accessed 1 February 2013).
36 Pew Research Center, 'Concern About Extremist Threat Slips in Pakistan', 29 July 2010. Available online at http://pewglobal.org/2010/07/29/concern-about-extremist-threat-slips-in-pakistan/ (accessed 25 October 2010).
37 Pew Research Center, 'Pakistani Public Opinion Ever More Critical of US', 27 June 2012. Available online at www.pewglobal.org/2012/06/27/pakistani-public-opinion-ever-more-critical-of-u-s/ (accessed 18 December 2012).
38 Aleem Maqbook, 'America's Secret Drone War in Pakistan', *BBC News*, 22 July 2010. Available online at www.bbc.co.uk/news/mobile/world-south-asia-10728844 (accessed 18 December 2012).
39 Protocol Additional to the Geneva Conventions of 12 August 1949, and relating to the Protection of Victims of International Armed Conflicts (Protocol I), Geneva, 8 June 1977.
40 Cited in Timothy Garden, 'Air Power: Theory and Practice' in John Baylis, James Wirtz, Eliot Cohen and Colin S. Gray (eds), *Strategy in the Contemporary World*, Oxford: Oxford University Press, 2002, p. 150 (emphasis added).
41 van Creveld, *The Age of Air Power*, p. 101.
42 Theodor Adorno, *Minima Moralia*, London: Verso, 1993, p. 55.
43 Yuki Tanaka, 'Introduction' in Yuki Tanaka and Marilyn B. Young (eds), *Bombing Civilians: A Twentieth-Century History*, New York: The New Press, 2009, p. 4.
44 Bellamy, *Just Wars*, p. 185.
45 'US Airstrikes in Pakistan Called "Very Effective"'.
46 Scott Shane, 'US Drone Strikes Are Said to Target Rescuers at Sites', *New York Times*, 6 February 2012, p. A4.
47 Article 51(4)(c), Additional Protocol I..
48 See, for example, Erica Goode, 'Rifle Used in Killings, America's Most Popular, Highlights Regulation Debate', *New York Times*, 16 December 2012, p. A25.
49 Bellamy, *Just Wars*, p. 190.
50 Ibid., p. 189.
51 Tarak Barkawi, 'Air Power and the Liberal Politics of War', *International Journal of Human Rights* 4, nos. 3–4, 2000, 307–13 at p. 308.
52 P. W. Singer, 'Military Robots and the Laws of War', *New Atlantis*, Winter 2009, 25–45 at p. 41.
53 Walzer, *Just and Unjust Wars*, p. 156.
54 Bellamy, *Just Wars*, p. 182.
55 Martin L. Cook, *The Moral Warrior: Ethics and Service in the US Military*, Albany: State University of New York Press, 2004, p. 127.
56 Singer, 'Military Robots and the Laws of War', p. 41.
57 Bradley Jay Strawser, 'Moral Predators: The Duty to Employ Uninhabited Aerial Vehicles', *Journal of Military Ethics* 9, no. 4, 2010, 342–68 at p. 353.
58 Alston, *Report of the Special Rapporteur on Extrajudicial, Summary or Arbitrary Executions*, p. 25.
59 Robert Sparrow, 'Building a Better Warbot: Ethical Issues in the Design of Unmanned Systems for Military Applications', *Science and Engineering Ethics* 15, 2009, 169–87 at p. 183.
60 Bryan Bender, 'Attacking Iraq, from a Nev. Computer', *Boston Globe*, 3 April 2005, p. A6.
61 Roggio and Mayer, 'Charting the Data for US Airstrikes in Pakistan, 2004–2013'.
62 Peter Bergen and Katherine Tiedemann, 'The Year of the Drone: An Analysis of US Drone Strikes in Pakistan, 2004–2012', *New America Foundation*, updated 3 January 2013. Available online at http://counterterrorism.newamerica.net/drones (accessed 25 January 2013).

63 Matthew Fricker, Avery Plaw and Brian Glyn Williams, 'New Light on the Accuracy of the CIA's Predator Drone Campaign in Pakistan', *Terrorism Monitor* 8, no. 41, 2010, 8–13 at p. 8.
64 Ibid.
65 Ibid.
66 Ibid.
67 Ibid., p. 9.
68 Justin Elliott, 'Washington's Silence Creates Doubt on Deaths', *Sydney Morning Herald*, 23 June 2012, p. 22.
69 Jo Becker and Scott Shane, 'Secret "Kill List" Proves a Test of Obama's Principles and Will', *New York Times*, 29 May 2012, p. A1.
70 David Rodin, 'The Ethics of Asymmetric War' in Richard Sorabji and David Rodin (eds), *The Ethics of War: Shared Problems in Different Traditions*, Aldershot: Ashgate, 2006, p. 157.
71 Françoise Hampson, 'The Principle of Proportionality in the Law of Armed Conflict' in Sarah Perrigo and Jim Whitman (eds), *The Geneva Conventions under Assault*, London: Pluto Press, 2010, 48.
72 Anthony Burke, *Beyond Security, Ethics and Violence: War against the Other*, London: Routledge, 2007, p. 148.
73 Nils Melzer, *Interpretive Guidance on the Notion of Direct Participation in Hostilities under International Humanitarian Law*, Geneva: International Committee of the Red Cross, 2009, p. 33.
74 Ibid., p. 34.
75 Walzer, *Just and Unjust Wars*, p. 43 (emphasis added).
76 Vogel, 'Drone Warfare and the Law of Armed Conflict', p. 109, note 39.
77 Greg Miller and Craig Whitlock, 'Al-Qaeda No. 3 Yazid Reported Killed by US Drone', *Washington Post*, 1 June 2010, p. A01.
78 Stuart A. Levey, 'Loss of Moneyman a Big Blow for Al-Qaeda', *Washington Post*, 6 June 2010, p. A19.
79 Alston, *Report of the Special Rapporteur on Extrajudicial, Summary or Arbitrary Executions*, p. 19.
80 Editorial, 'Lethal Force under Law', *New York Times*, 10 October 2010, p. WK7.
81 Marc A. Thiessen, 'In CIA's Drone Mission, Who Will Protect the CIA?', *Washington Post*, 8 June 2010, p. A17.
82 Alston, *Report of the Special Rapporteur on Extrajudicial, Summary or Arbitrary Executions*, p. 8.
83 Shane, 'US Drone Strikes Are Said to Target Rescuers at Sites', p. A4.
84 Ibid.
85 John Stone, 'Technology and the Problem of Civilians Casualties in War' in Brian Rappert (ed.), *Technology and Security: Governing Threats in the New Millennium*, Basingstoke: Palgrave Macmillan, 2007, p. 140.
86 Maja Zehfuss, 'Targeting: Precision and the Production of Ethics', *European Journal of International Relations* 17, no. 3, 2011, 543–66 at p. 544.
87 Sudarsan Raghavan, 'Villagers Join Al-Qaeda after Deadly US Strike', *Sydney Morning Herald*, 27 December 2012, p. 7.
88 Stone, 'Technology and the Problem of Civilians Casualties in War', p. 140.
89 Ibid.
90 Tanaka, 'Introduction', p. 3.
91 Stone, 'Technology and the Problem of Civilians Casualties in War', p. 140.
92 Zehfuss, 'Targeting', p. 548.
93 Ibid.
94 Marc W. Herold, 'US Bombing and Afghan Civilian Deaths: The Official Neglect of "Unworthy" Bodies', *International Journal of Urban and Regional Research* 26, no. 3, 2002, 626–34 at p. 630.

Notes 129

95 Carl Conetta, 'Disappearing the Dead: Iraq, Afghanistan, and the Idea of a "New Warfare"', *Project on Defense Alternatives Research Monograph* no. 9, Cambridge, MA: Commonwealth Institute, 2004, p. 25.
96 James Der Derian, *Virtuous War*, 2nd edn, New York: Routledge, 2009, p. 193.
97 US COIN Field Manual, para. 7–30.
98 Protocol Additional to the Geneva Conventions of 12 August 1949, and relating to the Protection of Victims of International Armed Conflicts (Protocol I), Geneva: 8 June 1977.
99 Rodin, 'The Ethics of Asymmetric War', p. 157.
100 Rebecca J. Barber, 'The Proportionality Equation: Balancing Military Objectives with Civilian Lives in the Armed Conflict in Afghanistan', *Journal of Conflict and Security Law* 15, no. 3, 2010, 467–500 at p. 476.
101 Noel Sharkey, 'Death Strikes from the Sky: The Calculus of Proportionality', *IEEE Technology and Society*, Spring 2009, 16–19 at p. 18.
102 Thomas Hurka, 'Proportionality in the Morality of War', *Philosophy and Public Affairs* 33, no. 1, 2005, 34–66 at p. 37.
103 Becker and Shane, 'Secret "Kill List" Proves a Test of Obama's Principles and Will'.
104 Sharkey, 'Death Strikes from the Sky', p. 18.
105 Peter L. Bergen, 'Warrior in Chief', *New York Times*, 29 April 2012, p. SR1.
106 David Cloud, 'CIA Allowed to Kill Terrorist Suspects Without Identification', *Sydney Morning Herald*, 7 May 2010. Available online at www.smh.com.au/world/cia-allowed-to-kill-terrorist-suspects-without-identification-20100506-uh33.html (accessed 8 November 2010).
107 Ibid.
108 Amanda Hodge, 'US Kills al-Qaida Leader in Pakistan', *Weekend Australian*, 17 September 2011, p. 19.
109 Vogel, 'Drone Warfare and the Law of Armed Conflict', p. 126.
110 Harold Hongju Koh, 'The Obama Administration and International Law', speech at the Annual Meeting of the American Society of International Law, Washington, DC, 25 March 2010, US Department of State. Available online at www.state.gov/s/l/releases/remarks/139119.htm (accessed 12 January 2011).
111 Mark Landler, 'Civilian Deaths Due to Drones Are Not Many, Obama Says', *New York Times*, 31 January 2012, p. A6.
112 US COIN Field Manual: para. 7–25.
113 Editorial, 'Lethal Force under Law', p. WK7.
114 Scott Shane, 'Election Spurred a Move to Codify US Drone Policy', *New York Times*, 25 November 2012, A1.
115 Eric Schmitt, 'Pakistan Injects Precision into Air War on Taliban', *New York Times*, 30 July 2009, p. A10.
116 'US Airstrikes in Pakistan Called "Very Effective"'.
117 Koh, 'The Obama Administration and International Law'.
118 Scott Shane, 'CIA Is Disputed on Civilian Toll in Drone Strikes', *New York Times*, 12 August 2011, p. A1.
119 Alston, *Report of the Special Rapporteur on Extrajudicial, Summary or Arbitrary Executions*, p. 26.
120 Ibid., p. 27.
121 Adriana Garcia, Djemila Carron, Rashmi Chopra, Janine Morna, Alyssa Scott and Anil Vassanji, 'Targeting Operations with Drone Technology: Humanitarian Law Implications', background note for the American Society of International Law Annual Meeting, Human Rights Institute, Columbia Law School, 25 March 2011. Available online at www.law.columbia.edu/ipimages/Human_Rights_Institute/BackgroundNoteASILColumbia.pdf (accessed 1 February 2013), p. 25.
122 Kathryn Stone, *'All Necessary Means' – Employing CIA Operatives in a Warfighting*

5 Radical asymmetry and the moral equality of combatants

  Roles alongside Special Operations Forces, US Army War College Strategic Research Project 16, 2003. Available online at www.fas.org/irp/eprint/stone.pdf (accessed 1 February 2013), p. 16.

1 Thomas Hurka, 'Proportionality in the Morality of War', *Philosophy and Public Affairs* 33, no. 1, 2005, 34–66 at p. 35.
2 David Rodin, 'The Ethics of Asymmetric War', in Richard Sorabji and David Rodin (eds), *The Ethics of War: Shared Problems in Different Traditions*, Aldershot: Ashgate, 2006, p. 153.
3 Ibid., p. 159.
4 Giulio Douhet, *The Command of the Air*, trans. Dino Ferrari, London: Faber and Faber, 1943, p. 19.
5 David R. MetS, *Air Power and Technology: Smart and Unmanned Weapons*, Westport, CT: Praeger, 2009, p. 3.
6 Robert Sparrow, 'Building a Better Warbot: Ethical Issues in the Design of Unmanned Systems for Military Applications', *Science and Engineering Ethics* 15, 2009, 169–87 at p. 179.
7 Carl von Clausewitz, *On War*, London: Penguin, 1982 [1832], p. 104.
8 Suzy Killmister, 'Remote Weaponry: The Ethical Implications', *Journal of Applied Philosophy* 25, no. 2, 2008, 121–33 at p. 122.
9 Rodin, 'The Ethics of Asymmetric War', p. 159.
10 Ibid.
11 Jai C. Galliott, 'Uninhabited Aerial Vehicles and the Asymmetry Objection: A Response to Strawser', *Journal of Military Ethics* 11, no. 1, 2012, 58–66 at p. 59.
12 Ibid., p. 63.
13 Maja Zehfuss, 'Targeting: Precision and the Production of Ethics', *European Journal of International Relations* 17, no. 3, 2011, 543–66 at p. 555.
14 Ibid.
15 'Times Square Bomb Plotter Sentenced to Life in Prison', *BBC News*, 5 October 2010. Available online at www.bbc.co.uk/news/world-us-canada-11475783 (accessed 15 March 2013).
16 Killmister, 'Remote Weaponry', p. 122.
17 US Department of Defense, *Conduct of the Persian Gulf War: Final Report to Congress*, Washington, DC: Department of Defense, 1992, p. 612 (emphasis added).
18 Ibid., p. 615 (emphasis added).
19 Françoise Hampson, 'The Principle of Proportionality in the Law of Armed Conflict', in Sarah Perrigo and Jim Whitman (eds), *The Geneva Conventions under Assault*, London: Pluto Press, 2010, pp. 53–4.
20 Hurka, 'Proportionality in the Morality of War', p. 63.
21 Paul Christopher, *The Ethics of War and Peace: An Introduction to Legal and Moral Issues*, 2nd edn, Upper Saddle River, NJ: Prentice-Hall, 1999, p. 165.
22 Michael Walzer, *Just and Unjust Wars: A Moral Argument with Historical Illustrations*, 4th edn, New York: Basic Books, 2006, p. 157 (emphasis added).
23 Hurka, 'Proportionality in the Morality of War', p. 64.
24 Alex J. Bellamy, *Just Wars: From Cicero to Iraq*, Cambridge: Polity Press, 2006: 198.
25 Ibid.
26 Human Rights Watch, *Civilian Deaths in the NATO Air Campaign*, February 2000. Available online at www.hrw.org/reports/2000/nato/ (accessed 27 January 2013).
27 Martin Shaw, 'Risk-Transfer Militarism, Small Massacres, and the Historic Legitimacy of War', *International Relations* 16, no. 3, 2002, 343–60 at p. 352 (original emphasis).

28 Rodin, 'The Ethics of Asymmetric War', p. 165.
29 Thomas G. Mahnken, 'Weapons: The Growth and Spread of the Precision-Strike Regime', *Daedalus* 140, no. 3, 2011, 45–57 at p. 54.
30 Thomas Darnstädt, Marc Hujer and Gregor Peter Schmitz, 'Are Obama's Efforts to Justify Drone Warfare Aimed at Iran?' *Der Spiegel*, 15 March 2012. Available online at www.spiegel.de/international/world/obama-drone-rationale-hints-at-war-with-iran-a-821151.html (accessed 22 November 2012).
31 Anthony Burke, *Beyond Security, Ethics and Violence: War against the Other*, London: Routledge, 2007, p. 148.
32 Ibid., p. 143.
33 Ibid., p. 145.
34 Oliver Kessler and Wouter Werner, 'Extrajudicial Killing as Risk Management', *Security Dialogue* 39, nos. 2–3, 2008, 289–308 at p. 302.
35 Philip Alston, *Report of the Special Rapporteur on Extrajudicial, Summary or Arbitrary Executions*, (A/HRC/14/24/Add.6), New York: United Nations General Assembly, 28 May 2010, p. 3.
36 Kessler and Werner, 'Extrajudicial Killing as Risk Management', p. 305.
37 Ibid., p. 296.
38 Mark Mazzetti, Eric Schmitt and Robert F. Worth, 'CIA Strike Kills US-Born Militant in a Car in Yemen', *New York Times*, 1 October 2011, p. A1; Charlie Savage, 'A Not-Quite Confirmation of a Memo Approving Killing, *New York Times*, 9 March 2012, p. A16.
39 Alston, *Report of the Special Rapporteur on Extrajudicial, Summary or Arbitrary Executions*, p. 11 (original emphasis).
40 Rodin, 'The Ethics of Asymmetric War', p. 161.
41 Ibid., p. 162.
42 Walzer, *Just and Unjust Wars*, p. 155 (emphasis added).
43 Rodin, 'The Ethics of Asymmetric War', p. 165.
44 Helen Frowe, *The Ethics of War and Peace: An Introduction*, Abingdon: Routledge, 2011, p. 29.
45 Walzer, *Just and Unjust Wars*; Jeff McMahan, *Killing in War*, Oxford: Oxford University Press, 2009.
46 Walzer, *Just and Unjust Wars*, p. 38.
47 William Shakespeare, *Henry V*, ed. Gary Taylor, Oxford: Oxford University Press, 1982, Act 4, scene 1, lines 25–8.
48 Frowe, *The Ethics of War and Peace*, p. 118.
49 McMahan, *Killing in War*, p. 35.
50 Ibid., p. 5.
51 See Jai C. Galliott, 'Uninhabited Aerial Vehicles and the Asymmetry Objection: A Response to Strawser', *Journal of Military Ethics* 11, no. 1 (2012): 58–66, at p. 61; and Hurka, 'Proportionality in the Morality of War', p. 45.
52 Cited in Walzer, *Just and Unjust Wars*, p. xvi.
53 Ibid., p. 110.
54 Michael Ignatieff, *Virtual War: Kosovo and Beyond*, New York: Picador, 2000: 5.
55 Colin S. Gray, 'Moral Advantage, Strategic Advantage?' *Journal of Strategic Studies* 33, no. 3 (2010): 333–65, at p. 345.
56 Michael N. Schmitt, 'Twenty-First Century Conflict: Can the Law Survive?' *Melbourne Journal of International Law* 8 (2007): 443–76, at p. 474. Original emphasis.
57 Gray, 'Moral Advantage, Strategic Advantage?' p. 341.
58 Rodin, 'The Ethics of Asymmetric War', p. 164.
59 McMahan, *Killing in War*, p. 148.
60 Ibid., 119.
61 Ibid.
62 Ibid.

132 *Notes*

63 C. A. J. Coady, *Morality and Political Violence*, Cambridge: Cambridge University Press, 2008, p. 90.
64 Gray, 'Moral Advantage, Strategic Advantage?' p. 363.
65 Burke, *Beyond Security, Ethics and Violence*, p. 145.
66 Sarah Kreps and John Kaag, 'The Use of Unmanned Aerial Vehicles in Contemporary Conflict: A Legal and Ethical Analysis', *Polity* 44, no. 2, 2012, 260–85 at p. 278.
67 Gabriella Slomp, 'Carl Schmitt's Five Arguments against the Idea of Just War', *Cambridge Review of International Affairs* 19, no. 3, 2006, 435–47 at p. 437.
68 C. A. J. Coady, 'Bombing and the Morality of War', in Yuki Tanaka and Marilyn B. Young (eds), *Bombing Civilians: A Twentieth-Century History*, New York: The New Press, 2009, p. 199.
69 Michael Sherry, 'The United States and Strategic Bombing: From Prophecy to Memory', in Yuki Tanaka and Marilyn B. Young (eds), *Bombing Civilians: A Twentieth-Century History*, New York: The New Press, 2009, p. 178.
70 George R. Mastroianni, 'The Person–Situation Debate: Implications for Military Leadership and Civil–Military Relations', *Journal of Military Ethics* 10, no. 1, 2011, 2–16 at p. 10.
70 Christopher Coker, *Waging War without Warriors? The Changing Culture of Military Conflict*, Boulder, CO: Lynne Rienner, 2002, p. 180.

6 Drone operators and the warrior ethos

1 Roger Wertheimer, 'The Moral Singularity of Military Professionalism' in Roger Wertheimer (ed.), *Empowering Our Military Conscience: Transforming Just War Theory and Military Moral Education*, Farnham: Ashgate, 2010, p. 139. See also Ralph Peters, 'The New Warrior Class', *Parameters*, Summer 1994, 16–26.
2 Hanne A. Kraugerud, 'Shields of Humanity: The Ethical Constraints of Professional Combatants', *Journal of Military Ethics* 10, no. 4, 2011, 263–73 at p. 268 (original emphasis).
3 Helen Frowe, *The Ethics of War and Peace: An Introduction*, Abingdon: Routledge, 2011, p. 1 (original emphasis).
4 Samuel P. Huntington, *The Soldier and the State: The Theory and Politics of Civil–Military Relations*, Cambridge, MA: Harvard University Press, 1957, p. 7.
5 Ibid., p. 8.
6 Ibid., p. 10.
7 Sam C. Sarkesian and Robert E. Connor, Jr., *The US Military Profession into the Twenty-First Century: War, Peace and Politics*, Portland, OR: Frank Cass, 1999, p. 61.
8 H. R. McMaster, 'Remaining True to Our Values: Reflections on Military Ethics in Trying Times', *Journal of Military Ethics* 9, no. 3, 2010, 183–94 at p. 193.
9 Carl von Clausewitz, *On War*, London: Penguin, 1982 [1832], p. 254.
10 Christopher Coker, *Humane Warfare*, London: Routledge, 2001, p. 91.
11 Christopher Coker, *Waging War without Warriors? The Changing Culture of Military Conflict*, Boulder, CO: Lynne Rienner, 2002, p. 30.
12 Michael Ignatieff, *Virtual War: Kosovo and Beyond*, New York: Picador, 2000, p. 188.
13 P. W. Singer, *Wired for War: The Robotics Revolution and Conflict in the Twenty-First Century*, New York: Penguin, 2009, p. 343.
14 Cited in Sarkesian and Connor, *The US Military Profession into the Twenty-First Century*, p. 172.
15 Michael Ignatieff, *The Warrior's Honour: Ethnic War and the Modern Conscience*, London: Chatto & Windus, 1998, p. 117.
16 Ibid., p. 118.
17 Coker, *Humane Warfare*, p. 37.

18 Ignatieff, *The Warrior's Honour*, p. 117.
19 Coker, *Humane Warfare*, p. 108.
20 Aristotle, *The Ethics of Aristotle: The Nicomachean Ethics*, trans. J. A. K. Thomson, London: Penguin, 1953, p. 128.
21 Ibid., pp. 133–4.
22 Lionel Giles (trans.), *Sun Tzu's Art of War*, 1910. Available online at http://suntzusaid.com/book/11/32/ (accessed 8 March 2012).
23 Clausewitz, *On War*, p. 258.
24 Andrew P. N. Erdmann, 'The US Presumption of Quick, Costless Wars', *Orbis*, Summer 1999, 363–81 at p. 369.
25 Peter Olsthoorn, 'Courage in the Military: Physical and Moral', *Journal of Military Ethics* 6, no. 4, 2007, 270–79 at p. 270.
26 Christopher Coker, *War in an Age of Risk*, Cambridge: Polity Press, 2009, p. 179.
27 Artur Schopenhauer, 'On Ethics' in *Essays and Aphorisms*, trans. R. G. Hollingdale, London: Penguin, 1988, p. 135.
28 Olsthoorn, 'Courage in the Military', p. 271.
29 Ibid., p. 272.
30 See Martin Shaw, 'Risk-Transfer Militarism, Small Massacres, and the Historic Legitimacy of War', *International Relations* 16, no. 3, 2002, 343–60 at p. 356.
31 US Department of the Army, *Counterinsurgency*, FM 3-24, MCWP 3-33.5, December 2006. Military Field Manuals, 2009. Available online at www.militaryfieldmanuals.net/manuals/counterinsurgency (accessed 1 February 2013), para. 7–21.
32 Paul Kahn, 'The Paradox of Riskless Warfare', *Philosophy and Public Policy Quarterly* 22, no. 3, 2002, 2–8 at p. 4.
33 See C. A. J. Coady, 'The Morality of Terrorism', *Philosophy* 60, no. 231, 1985, 47–69 at p. 59.
34 Martin L. Cook, *The Moral Warrior: Ethics and Service in the US Military*, Albany: State University of New York Press, 2004, p. 123.
35 Ibid., pp. 123–4.
36 Cited in Dave Grossman, *On Killing: The Psychological Cost of Learning to Kill in War and Society*, Boston: Little, Brown and Company, 1995, p. 86.
37 Jeff McMahan, *Killing in War*, Oxford: Oxford University Press, 2009, p. 51 (emphasis added). See also: Thomas Hurka, 'Proportionality in the Morality of War', *Philosophy and Public Affairs* 33, no. 1, 2005, 34–66 at p. 59.
38 Michael Walzer, *Just and Unjust Wars: A Moral Argument with Historical Illustrations*, 4th edn, New York: Basic Books, 2006, p. 45.
39 Ibid., p. 36.
40 Erick Maria Remarque, *All Quiet on the Western Front*, London: Vintage, 1996 [1929], p. 133.
41 Walzer, *Just and Unjust Wars*, p. 36 (original emphasis).
42 Ibid., pp. 138–9.
43 Ibid., p. 140.
44 Ibid., p. 143.
45 Cited in Joanna Bourke, *An Intimate History of Killing: Face-to-Face Killing in Twentieth-Century Warfare*, London: Granta, 1999, p. 66.
46 Cited in ibid., pp. 66–7.
47 Frank Sauer and Niklas Schörnig, 'Killer Drones: "The Silver Bullet" of Democratic Warfare?' *Security Dialogue* 43, no. 4, 2012, 363–80 at p. 373.
48 Susan Sontag, *Regarding the Pain of Others*, London: Hamish Hamilton, 2003, p. 60 (original emphasis).
49 Christopher Coker, *Ethics and War in the Twenty-First Century*, London: Routledge, 2008, p. 147.
50 Ignatieff, *Virtual War*, p. 161.

51 D. Keith Shurtleff, 'The Effects of Technology on Our Humanity', *Parameters*, Summer 2002, 100–12 at p. 107.
52 Coker, *Waging War without Warriors?* p. 68.
53 Bradley Jay Strawser, 'Moral Predators: The Duty to Employ Uninhabited Aerial Vehicles', *Journal of Military Ethics* 9, no. 4, 2010, 342–68 at p. 343.
54 Ibid., p. 356.
55 David R. Mets, *Air Power and Technology: Smart and Unmanned Weapons*, Westport, CT: Praeger, 2009, p. 156.
56 Peter M. Asaro, 'Remote-Control Crimes', *IEEE Robotics & Automation*, March 2011, 68–71 at p. 70.
57 Mark K. Matthews, 'State Lawmakers Bag Online Hunting', *Stateline*, 28 September 2005. Available online at www.stateline.org/live/printable/story?contentId=56691 (accessed 20 March 2012).
58 International Institute of Strategic Studies, 'The Future of Unmanned Air Power', 20 April 2011. Available online at www.iiss.org/about-us/offices/washington/iiss-us-events/iiss-us-conference-the-future-of-unmanned-air-power/ (accessed 20 March 2012).
59 Nolen Gertz, 'Just and Unjust Killing', *Journal of Military Ethics* 7, no. 4, 2008, 247–61 at p. 257.
60 William Shakespeare, *Henry V*, ed. Gary Taylor, Oxford: Oxford University Press, 1982, Act 4, scene 3, lines 60–7, p. 230.
61 Coker, *Ethics and War in the Twenty-First Century*, p. 146 (original emphasis).
62 Anthony Giddens, *Modernity and Self-Identity: Self and Society in the Late Modern Age*, Stanford, CA: Stanford University Press, 1991: 99.
63 Ibid., p. 59.
64 Ibid.
65 Ibid.
66 Coker, *Waging War without Warriors?* p. 179.
67 Orson Scott Card, *Ender's Game*, London: Atom, 2002 [1977], p. 299.
68 Philip Alston, *Report of the Special Rapporteur on Extrajudicial, Summary or Arbitrary Executions*, A/HRC/14/24/Add.6, New York: United Nations General Assembly, 28 May 2010, p. 25.
69 Robert Sparrow, 'Building a Better WarBot: Ethical Issues in the Design of Unmanned Systems for Military Applications', *Science and Engineering Ethics* 15, 2009, 169–87 at p. 183.
70 Philip Alston and Hina Shamsi, 'A Killer above the Law?', *The Guardian*, 8 February 2010. Available online at www.guardian.co.uk/commentisfree/2010/feb/08/afghanistan-drones-defence-killing (accessed 21 March 2012).
71 Sparrow, 'Building a Better WarBot', p. 180.
72 See Martin van Creveld, *The Age of Air Power*, New York: Public Affairs, 2011, p. 32.
73 Singer, *Wired for War*, p. 332.
74 Greg Jaffe, 'Combat Generation: Drone Operators Climb on Winds of Change in the Air Force', *Washington Post*, 28 February 2010, p. A01.
75 Patricia Owens, 'Accidents Don't Just Happen: The Liberal Politics of High-Technology "Humanitarian" War', *Millennium: Journal of International Studies* 32, 2003, 595–616 at p. 613.
76 van Creveld, *The Age of Air Power*, p. 30.
77 Michael Sherry, *The Rise of American Air Power: The Creation of Armageddon*, New Haven, CT: Yale University Press, 1987, p. 20.
78 Cited in Jane Mayer, 'The Predator War', *New Yorker*, 26 October 2009. Available online at www.newyorker.com/reporting/2009/10/26/091026fa_fact_mayer (accessed 21 March 2012).
79 Seb Cox, 'Unmanned Aerial Vehicles: Cultural Issues', in Owen Barnes (ed.),

UAVs: The Wider Context, Shrivenham: Royal Air Force Directorate of Defence Studies, 2009. Available: www.airpowerstudies.co.uk/UAV-Book.pdf (accessed 15 March 2012), p. 88.
80 Ibid., p. 91.
81 Ibid., p. 89.
82 Ibid., p. 92.
83 Frank J. Barrett, 'The Organizational Construction of Hegemonic Masculinity: The Case of the US Navy', *Gender, Work and Organization* 3, no. 3, 1996, 129–42 at p. 134.
84 Ibid.
85 Singer, *Wired for War*, p. 253.
86 Ibid., p. 252.
87 Strawser, 'Moral Predators', p. 364, note 16.
88 Leo Braudy, *From Chivalry to Terrorism: War and the Changing Nature of Masculinity*, New York: Alfred A. Knopf, 2003, p. xv.
89 Peter Spiegel, 'Tough US Marine Gets Command', *Weekend Australian*, 10 July 2010, p. 18; Thom Shanker, 'Petraeus's Successor Is Known for Impolitic Words', *New York Times*, 20 July 2010, p. A10.
90 'What a Hoot: General Won't Be Punished', *Canberra Times*, 5 February 2005, p. 15 (emphasis added).
91 van Creveld, *The Age of Air Power*, p. 232.
92 Mark Mazzetti, 'The Drone Zone', *New York Times*, 8 July 2012, p. MM32.
93 van Creveld, *The Age of Air Power*, p. 231.
94 Jaffe, 'Combat Generation', p. A01.
95 Ibid.
96 Jim Tice, 'UAV Operators Now Can Get Aviation Awards', *Army Times*, 3 April 2007. Available online at www.armytimes.com/news/2007/04/army_UAV_awards_070403w/ (accessed 23 March 2012).
97 Karen DeYoung, 'Hagel Orders Halt to Production of Drone Pilot, Cyberwarrior Medal', *Washington Post*, 13 March 2013. Available online at www.washingtonpost.com/world/national-security/hagel-orders-halt-to-production-of-drone-cyber-medal/2013/03/12/e0e84e0c-8b30-11e2-b63f-f53fb9f2fcb4_story.html (accessed 15 March 2013).
98 Ignatieff, *Virtual War*, p. 5.
99 Quoted in Singer, *Wired for War*, p. 306.
100 Thomas G. Mahnken, 'Strategic Theory' in John Baylis, James J. Wirtz and Colin S. Gray (eds), *Strategy in the Contemporary World*, 3rd edn, Oxford: Oxford University Press, 2010, p. 77.
101 Coker, *Waging War without Warriors?* p. 6.
102 Ibid., p. 144.
103 Coker, *Humane Warfare*, pp. 121–2.
104 Singer, *Wired for War*, p. 312.
105 Jaffe, 'Combat Generation', p. A01.
106 David Kilcullen and Andrew McDonald Exum, 'Death from Above, Outrage Down Below', *New York Times*, 18 May 2009, p. WK13.
107 Written Testimony of Dr Ed Barrett, House Committee on Oversight and Government Reform, Subcommittee on National Security and Foreign Affairs, Hearing on 'Rise of the Drones: Unmanned Systems and the Future of War', 23 March 2010. Available online at http://democrats.oversight.house.gov/images/stories/subcommittees/NS_Subcommittee/3.23.10_Drones/Barrett.pdf (accessed 1 February 2013).
108 United Kingdom Ministry of Defence, *The UK Approach to Unmanned Aircraft Systems*, Joint Doctrine Note 2/11, May 2011. Available online at www.gov.uk/government/uploads/system/uploads/attachment_data/file/33711/20110505JDN_211_UAS_v2U.pdf (accessed 20 January 2013).

109 Jeffrey Record, 'Collapsed Countries, Casualty Dread, and the New American Way of War', *Parameters*, Summer 2002, 4–23 at p. 13.
110 'US Airstrikes in Pakistan Called "Very Effective"', *CNN News*, 18 May 2009. Available online at http://articles.cnn.com/2009-05-18/politics/cia.pakistan.airstrikes_1_qaeda-pakistani-airstrikes?_s=PM:POLITICS (accessed 23 February 2011).
111 P. W. Singer, 'The Ethics of Killer Applications: Why Is It So Hard To Talk about Morality When It Comes to New Military Technology?' *Journal of Military Ethics* 9, no. 4, 2010, 299–312 at p. 310.
112 Mark Mazzetti, 'The Downside of Letting Robots Do the Bombing', *New York Times*, 22 March 2009, p. WK4.
113 Walter Pincus, 'Are Drones a Technological Tipping Point in Warfare?' *Washington Post*, 25 April 2011. Available online at www.washingtonpost.com/world/are-predator-drones-a-technological-tipping-point-in-warfare/2011/04/19/AFmC6PdE_story.html (accessed 23 March 2012).
114 For legal arguments supporting this proposition, see: Alston, *Report of the Special Rapporteur on Extrajudicial, Summary or Arbitrary Executions*, p. 22; Ryan R. Vogel, 'Drone Warfare and the Law of Armed Conflict', *Denver Journal of International Law and Policy* 39, no. 1, 2010, 101–38 at p. 135; and Gary Solis, 'CIA Drone Attacks Produce America's Own Unlawful Combatants', *Washington Post*, 12 March 2010. Available online at www.washingtonpost.com/wp-dyn/content/article/2010/03/11/AR2010031103653.html (accessed 13 March 2010).
115 CBS, 'Drones: America's New Air Force', *60 Minutes*, 16 August 2009. Available online at www.cbsnews.com/stories/2009/05/08/60minutes/main5001439.shtml (accessed 16 November 2010).
116 Mazzetti, 'The Drone Zone', p. MM32.
117 Sparrow, 'Building a Better WarBot', p. 174.
118 Ibid., p. 175.
119 Statement of John F. Tierney, Chairman, Subcommittee on National Security and Foreign Affairs, Committee on Oversight and Government Reform, US House of Representatives Hearing on 'Rise of the Drones: Unmanned Systems and the Future of War', 23 March 2010. Available online at http://democrats.oversight.house.gov/images/stories/subcommittees/NS_Subcommittee/3.23.10_Drones/3-23-10_JFT_Opening_Statement_FINAL_for_Delivery.pdf (accessed 1 February 2013), p. 2.
120 Aaron Retica, 'Drone-Pilot Burnout', *New York Times*, 14 December 2008, p. MM55.
121 P.W. Singer, 'War of the Machines', *Scientific American*, July 2010, 56–63 at p. 63.
122 'It Is Not a Video Game', *Der Spiegel*, 3 December 2010. Available online at www.spiegel.de/international/world/0,1518,682842,00.html (accessed 22 March 2012).
123 David Cloud, 'Friendly Fire First as Drone Kills Two', *Sydney Morning Herald*, 13 April 2011. Available online at www.smh.com.au/world/friendly fire-first-as-drone-kills-two-20110412-1dcp2.html (accessed 23 March 2012).
124 Nick Floyd, 'Of Men v. Machines: Who Knows What Lurks in the Hearts of Man?' *Australian Defence Force Journal* 180, 2009, 78–83 at p. 79.
125 Grossman, *On Killing*, p. 195.
126 Ibid., p. 201.
127 Ibid.
128 Ibid., p. 102.
129 Ibid.
130 Ibid., p. 100.
131 David Zucchino, 'Drone Pilots Have a Front-Row Seat on War, From Half a World Away', *Los Angeles Times*, 21 February 2010. Available online at http://articles.latimes.com/2010/feb/21/world/la-fg-drone-crews21-2010feb21 (accessed 1 February 2013).

132 Walzer, *Just and Unjust Wars*, p. 142.
133 Elisabeth Bumiller, 'A Day Job Waiting for a Kill Shot a World Away', *New York Times*, 30 July 2012, p. A1.
134 Robert D. Kaplan, 'Hunting the Taliban in Las Vegas', *The Atlantic*, September 2006. Available online at www.theatlantic.com/magazine/archive/2006/09/hunting-the-taliban-in-las-vegas/305116/2/ (accessed 23 November 2012)
135 Ibid.
136 Elisabeth Bumiller, 'Air Force Drone Operators Report High Levels of Stress', *New York Times*, 19 December 2011, p. A8.
137 Greg Miller, 'Drone Wars', *Science* 336, 18 May 2012, 842–3 at p. 843.
138 Wertheimer, 'The Moral Singularity of Military Professionalism', p. 137.
139 Kathryn Westcott, 'How and Why Gardner Was Shot', *BBC News*, 18 June 2010. Available online at www.bbc.co.uk/news/10254279 (accessed 23 March 2012).
140 Joseph Heller, *Catch-22*, London, Vintage, 1994 [1955], pp. 62–3.

7 Autonomous drones and post-human war

1 Isaac Asimov, *I, Robot*, New York: Doubleday & Company, 1950, p. 11.
2 See Douglas Harper, *Online Etymology Dictionary*, 2012. Available online at www.etymonline.com/index.php (accessed 10 January 2013).
3 Peter M. Asaro, 'What Should We Want From a Robot Ethic?' *International Review of Information Ethics* 6, 2006, 9–16 at p. 9.
4 Marc Pitsky, 'Interview with a Drone Pilot', *Der Spiegel*, 12 March 2010. Available online at www.spiegel.de/international/world/0,1518,682842,00.html (accessed 11 January 2013).
5 Jeremiah Gertler, *US Unmanned Aerial Systems*, Washington, DC: Congressional Research Service, 3 January 2012, p. 48.
6 Rick Gladstone, 'Iran Shows Video It Says Is of US Drone', *New York Times*, 9 December 2011, p. A10.
7 See US Department of Defense, *Unmanned Systems Integrated Roadmap FY2009–2034*. Available online at www.acq.osd.mil/psa/docs/UMSIntegratedRoadmap2009.pdf (accessed 10 July 2012), pp. 42–3.
8 Andrea Shalal-Esa and Phil Stewart, 'US War Drones Hit with Computer Virus', *Sydney Morning Herald*, 10 October 2011. Available online at www.smh.com.au/it-pro/security-it/us-war-drones-hit-with-computer-virus-20111010-11gd5.html (accessed 13 January 2013).
9 US Air Force Chief Scientist, 'Report on Technology Horizons: A Vision for Air Force Science and Technology during 2010–2030', 15 May 2010. Available online at www.af.mil/shared/media/document/AFD-100727-053.pdf (accessed 10 January 2013), p. 106.
10 Noel Sharkey, 'March of the Killer Robots', *Telegraph*, 15 June 2009. Available online at www.telegraph.co.uk/science/science-news/5543603/March-of-the-killer-robots.html (accessed 1 February 2013).
11 US Department of Defense, *Unmanned Systems Integrated Roadmap FY2011–2036*, Reference no. 11-S-3613, 2011. Available online at www.defenseinnovationmarketplace.mil/resources/UnmannedSystemsIntegratedRoadmapFY2011.pdf (accessed 10 January 2013), p. vi.
12 S. I. Benn, 'Freedom, Autonomy and the Concept of a Person', *Proceedings of the Aristotelian Society*, new series 76, 1975–6, p. 124.
13 Andrew Reath, *Agency and Autonomy in Kant's Moral Theory*, Oxford: Clarendon Press, 2006, p. 127.
14 Armin Krishnan, *Killer Robots: Legality and Ethicality of Autonomous Weapons*, Burlington, VT: Ashgate, 2009, p. 4.
15 See Human Rights Watch and Harvard Law School International Human Rights

Clinic, *Losing Humanity: The Case against Killer Robots*, Human Rights Watch, 2012. Available online at www.hrw.org/reports/2012/11/19/losing-humanity-0 (accessed 20 January 2013), p. 2. For a ten-point scale of 'Autonomous Capability Levels', see Gertler, *US Unmanned Aerial Systems*, p. 20.
16 US Department of Defense, *Unmanned Systems Integrated Roadmap FY2011–2036*, p. 51.
17 Gertler, *US Unmanned Aerial Systems*, p. 19; Frank Sauer and Niklas Schörnig, 'Killer Drones: "The Silver Bullet" of Democratic Warfare?' *Security Dialogue* 43, no. 4, 2012, 363–80 at pp. 370–1.
18 Peter Finn, 'A Future for Drones: Automated Killing', *Washington Post*, 20 September 2011. Available online at www.washingtonpost.com/national/national-security/a-future-for-drones-automated-killing/2011/09/15/gIQAVy9mgK_story.html (accessed 1 February 2013).
19 US Department of Defense, *Unmanned Systems Integrated Roadmap FY2011–2036*, p. vi.
20 Ibid., p. 50.
21 US Department of Defense, *Unmanned Systems Integrated Roadmap FY2009–2034*, p. 10 (emphasis added).
22 See, for example: Ronald C. Arkin, 'Governing Lethal Behavior: Embedding Ethics in a Hybrid Deliberative/Reactive Robot Architecture', GVU Technical Report GIT-GVU-07-11, Georgia Institute of Technology, 2007. Available online at www.cc.gatech.edu/ai/robot-lab/online-publications/formalizationv35.pdf (accessed 20 January 2013), p. 8; and Sauer and Schörnig, 'Killer Drones', p. 374.
23 See Ryan Tonkens, 'The Case against Robotic Warfare: A Response to Arkin', *Journal of Military Ethics* 11, no. 2, 2012, 149–68 at pp. 153–4.
24 Martin Asser, 'What Happened at Haditha', *BBC News*, 10 March 2008. Available online at http://news.bbc.co.uk/2/hi/middle_east/5033648.stm (accessed 1 February 2013).
25 Tim McGirk, 'Collateral Damage or Civilian Massacre in Haditha?' *Time*, 19 March 2006. Available online at www.time.com/time/printout/0,8816,1174649,00.html (accessed 13 January 2013).
26 Mark Oliver, 'Haditha Marine "Watched Superior Kill Surrendering Civilians"', *The Guardian*, 10 May 2007. Available online at www.guardian.co.uk/world/2007/may/10/usa.iraq (accessed 13 January 2013). My thanks to Graeme Shennan for alerting me to this incident.
27 Ronald C. Arkin, 'The Case for Ethical Autonomy in Unmanned Systems', *Journal of Military Ethics* 9, no. 4, 2010, 332–41 at p. 332.
28 Ibid., pp. 334–6.
29 Ronald C. Arkin, 'Ethical Robots in Warfare', *IEEE Technology and Society*, Spring 2009, 30–3 at p. 32.
30 Arkin, 'Governing Lethal Behavior', p. 1.
31 Ibid., p. 63.
32 Arkin, 'Ethical Robots in Warfare', p. 33.
33 See Fritz Allhoff, 'An Ethical Defense of Torture in Interrogation', in Jan Goldman (ed.), *Ethics of Spying: A Reader for the Intelligence Professional*, Lanham, MD: Scarecrow Press, 2006; and Alex J. Bellamy, 'No Pain, No Gain? Torture and Ethics in the War on Terror', *International Affairs* 82, no. 1, 2006, pp. 121–48.
34 Peter M. Asaro, 'Modeling the Moral User', *IEEE Technology and Society*, Spring 2009, 20–4 at p. 22.
35 John Kaag and Whitley Kaufman, 'Military Frameworks: Technological Know-How and the Legitimization of Warfare', *Cambridge Review of International Affairs* 22, no. 4, 2009, 585–606 at p. 600.
36 Noel Sharkey, 'Saying "No!" to Lethal Autonomous Targeting', *Journal of Military Ethics* 9, no. 4, 2010, 369–83 at p. 379.

37 Nils Melzer, *Interpretive Guidance on the Notion of Direct Participation in Hostilities under International Humanitarian Law*, Geneva: International Committee of the Red Cross, 2009, p. 34.
38 Human Rights Watch and Harvard Law School International Human Rights Clinic, *Losing Humanity*, p. 1.
39 Arkin, 'Ethical Robots in Warfare', p. 31.
40 George R. Lucas, Jr, 'Industrial Challenges of Military Robotics', *Journal of Military Ethics* 10, no. 4, 2011, 274–95 at p. 284 (emphasis added).
41 Robert Sparrow, 'Killer Robots', *Journal of Applied Philosophy* 24, no. 1, 2007, 62–77 at p. 67.
42 US Department of Defense, *Unmanned Systems Integrated Roadmap FY2011–2036*, p. 43.
43 See Robert Sparrow, 'Building a Better Warbot: Ethical Issues in the Design of Unmanned Systems for Military Applications', *Science and Engineering Ethics* 15, 2009, 169–87 at p. 178; and P. W. Singer, 'Military Robots and the Laws of War', *New Atlantis*, Winter 2009, 25–45 at p. 45.
44 Lucas, 'Industrial Challenges of Military Robotics', p. 276.
45 Ibid., p. 278.
46 Sparrow, 'Killer Robots', p. 70.
47 John P. Sullins, 'When Is a Robot a Moral Agent?' *International Review of Information Ethics* 6, 2006, 23–30 at p. 29.
48 US Department of Defense, *Unmanned Systems Integrated Roadmap FY2011–2036*, p. 48.
49 Armin Krishnan, 'Automating War: The Need for Regulation', *Contemporary Security Policy* 30, no. 1, 2009, 172–93 at p. 188.
50 Sparrow, 'Killer Robots', p. 71.
51 Ibid., p. 73.
52 John Markoff, 'Scientists Worry Machines May Outsmart Man', *New York Times*, 26 July 2009, p. A1.
53 Denise Grady, 'Scientists to Pause Research on Deadly Strain of Bird Flu', *New York Times*, 21 January 2012, p. A3.
54 Robert Pepperrell, *The Post Human Condition*, Exeter: Intellect, 1995, p. 1.
55 Colin S. Gray, 'Moral Advantage, Strategic Advantage?' *Journal of Strategic Studies* 33, no. 3, 2010, 333–65 at p. 343.
56 M. G. Mullen, *Capstone Concept for Joint Operations: Version 3.0*, US Department of Defense, 15 January 2009. Available online at www.jfcom.mil/newslink/storyarchive/2009/CCJO_2009.pdf (accessed 31 January 2013), p. 9.
57 Human Rights Watch and Harvard Law School International Human Rights Clinic, *Losing Humanity*, p. 38.
58 Kaag and Kaufman, 'Military Frameworks', p. 598 (original emphasis).
59 Asaro, 'Modeling the Moral User', p. 24.
60 Tonkens, 'The Case against Robotic Warfare', p. 151.
61 Ibid. (original emphasis).
62 Ibid., p. 160.
63 Arkin, 'Ethical Robots in Warfare', p. 30.
64 For discussion of 'supreme emergencies', see: Alex J. Bellamy, 'Supreme Emergencies and the Protection of Non-Combatants in War', *International Affairs* 80, no. 5, 2004, 829–50; and Michael Walzer, *Just and Unjust Wars*, 4th edn, New York: Basic Books, 2006, ch. 16.
65 Ronald C. Arkin and Patrick D. Ulam, 'Overriding Ethical Constraints in Lethal Autonomous Systems', Georgia Institute of Technology, 2012. Available online at http://smartech.gatech.edu/xmlui/handle/1853/44653 (accessed 17 January 2013).
66 Human Rights Watch and Harvard Law School International Human Rights Clinic, *Losing Humanity*, p. 4.

67 Editorial, 'Rights for Robots', *New Scientist*, 2 April 2011, p. 3.
68 Patrick Lin, 'Ethical Blowback from Emerging Technologies', *Journal of Military Ethics* 9, no. 4, 2010, 313–31 at p. 319.
69 See Peter Menzel and Faith D'Aluisio, *Robo Sapiens: Evolution of a New Species*, Cambridge, MA: MIT Press, 2000.

8 Conclusion

1 Plato, *The Republic*, trans. H. D. P. Lee, Harmondsworth, Penguin, 1955, pp. 87–8.
2 Ibid., pp. 90–1. I am indebted to John Kaag and Sarah Kreps for alerting me to this tale in a blog post: John Kaag and Sarah Kreps, 'The Moral Hazard of Drones', *New York Times*, 22 July 2012, available online at http://opinionator.blogs.nytimes.com/2012/07/22/the-moral-hazard-of-drones/ (accessed 20 January 2013).
3 Plato, *The Republic*, p. 91.

Select bibliography

Alston, Philip, *Report of the Special Rapporteur on Extrajudicial, Summary or Arbitrary Executions*, (A/HRC/14/24/Add.6), New York: United Nations General Assembly, 28 May 2010.
Arkin, Ronald C., 'The Case for Ethical Autonomy in Unmanned Systems', *Journal of Military Ethics* 9, no. 4, 2010, 332–41.
Brunstetter, Daniel, and Megan Braun, 'The Implications of Drones on the Just War Tradition', *Ethics and International Affairs* 25, no. 3, 2011, 337–58.
Burke, Anthony, *Beyond Security, Ethics and Violence: War against the Other*, London: Routledge, 2007.
Coady, C. A. J., *Morality and Political Violence*, Cambridge: Cambridge University Press, 2008.
Coker, Christopher, *Humane Warfare*, London: Routledge, 2001.
Coker, Christopher, *Waging War without Warriors? The Changing Culture of Military Conflict*, Boulder, CO: Lynne Rienner, 2002.
Coker, Christopher, *The Warrior Ethos: Military Culture and the War on Terror*, London: Routledge, 2007.
Coker, Christopher, *Ethics and War in the Twenty-First Century*, London: Routledge, 2008.
Coker, Christopher, *War in an Age of Risk*, Cambridge: Polity Press, 2009.
Cook, Martin L., *The Moral Warrior: Ethics and Service in the US Military*, Albany: State University of New York Press, 2004.
Gertler, Jeremiah, *US Unmanned Aerial Systems*, Washington, DC: Congressional Research Service, 3 January 2012.
Gray, Colin S., 'Moral Advantage, Strategic Advantage?' *Journal of Strategic Studies* 33, no. 3, 2010, 333–65.
Grossman, Dave, *On Killing: The Psychological Cost of Learning to Kill in War and Society*, Boston: Little, Brown and Company, 1995.
Hurka, Thomas, 'Proportionality in the Morality of War', *Philosophy and Public Affairs* 33, no. 1, 2005, 34–66.
Ignatieff, Michael, *The Warrior's Honour: Ethnic War and the Modern Conscience*, London: Chatto & Windus, 1998.
Ignatieff, Michael, *Virtual War: Kosovo and Beyond*, New York: Picador, 2000.
Kaag, John, and Whitley Kaufman, 'Military Frameworks: Technological Know-How and the Legitimization of Warfare', *Cambridge Review of International Affairs* 22, no. 4, 2009, 585–606.
Kahn, Paul, 'The Paradox of Riskless Warfare', *Philosophy and Public Policy Quarterly* 22, no. 3, 2002, 2–8.

Killmister, Suzy, 'Remote Weaponry: The Ethical Implications', *Journal of Applied Philosophy* 25, no. 2, 2008, 121–33.

Kreps, Sarah, and John Kaag, 'Unmanned Aerial Vehicles in Contemporary Conflict: A Legal and Ethical Analysis', *Polity* 44, no. 2, 2012, 260–85.

Lin, Patrick, 'Ethical Blowback from Emerging Technologies', *Journal of Military Ethics* 9, no. 4, 2010, 313–31.

Luttwak, Edward N., 'Toward Post-Heroic Warfare', *Foreign Affairs* 74, no. 3, 1995, 109–22.

Mahnken, Thomas, *Technology and the American Way of War since 1945*, New York: Columbia University Press, 2008.

McMahan, Jeff, *Killing in War*, Oxford: Oxford University Press, 2009.

Plaw, Avery, *Targeting Terrorists: A License to Kill?* Aldershot: Ashgate, 2008.

Rodin, David, 'The Ethics of Asymmetric War', in Richard Sorabji and David Rodin (eds), *The Ethics of War: Shared Problems in Different Traditions*, Aldershot: Ashgate, 2006, pp. 153–68.

Shaw, Martin, 'Risk-Transfer Militarism, Small Massacres, and the Historic Legitimacy of War', *International Relations* 16, no. 3, 2002.

Sherry, Michael, *The Rise of American Airpower: The Creation of Armageddon*, New Haven, CT: Yale University Press, 1989.

Singer, P. W., *Wired for War: The Robotics Revolution and Conflict in the Twenty-First Century*, New York: Penguin, 2009.

Sparrow, Robert, 'Killer Robots', *Journal of Applied Philosophy* 24, no. 1, 2007, 62–77.

Sparrow, Robert, 'Building a Better WarBot: Ethical Issues in the Design of Unmanned Systems for Military Applications', *Science and Engineering Ethics* 15, 2009, 169–87.

Strawser, Bradley Jay, 'Moral Predators: The Duty to Employ Uninhabited Aerial Vehicles', *Journal of Military Ethics* 9, no. 4, 2010, 342–68.

Tonkens, Ryan, 'The Case against Robotic Warfare: A Response to Arkin', *Journal of Military Ethics* 11, no. 2, 2012, 149–68.

US Department of the Army, *Counterinsurgency*, FM 3–24, MCWP 3–33.5, December 2006. Military Field Manuals, 2009. Available online at www.militaryfieldmanuals.net/manuals/counterinsurgency (accessed 1 February 2013).

van Creveld, Martin, *The Age of Air Power*, New York: PublicAffairs, 2011.

Vogel, Ryan R., 'Drone Warfare and the Law of Armed Conflict', *Denver Journal of International Law and Policy* 39, no. 1, 2010, 101–38.

Walzer, Michael, *Just and Unjust Wars: A Moral Argument with Historical Illustrations*, 4th edn, New York: Basic Books, 2006.

Zehfuss, Maja, 'Targeting: Precision and the Production of Ethics', *European Journal of International Relations* 17, no. 3, 2011, 543–66.

Index

Page numbers in *italics* denote tables.

9/11 *see* September 11 terror attacks
60-day rule 26–7

Adorno, T. 44
aerial bombardment, world's first 14, 39–40
Afghanistan 98; main challenges in the US military's initial air campaign 18; military use of armed drones in 18; post-heroic flavour of drone strikes in 34; Third Afghan War (1919) 18; US counterinsurgency strategy 33–4; USAF's experience of poor intelligence and misinterpreting actions 45
Afghanistan and Iraq: combined economic cost to the United States of the wars in 14; post-war goal 14; withdrawal of US ground forces 14
Afghanistan War, US display of national partiality 63
air power, Cohen on the seductive nature of 12
air superiority, of armed drones 19
aircrews, impact of capture and exploitation on public support 15
airpower: Douhet's argument 59; early observations 40; and the relationship between combatants 73; as restrained mode of problem-solving 12
airpower technology, overwhelming advantage of in war 59
All Quiet on the Western Front (Remarque) 81–2
Alston, P. 46, 66, 86
American way of war, reliance on advanced technology as characteristic of 12

anthropomorphism, and punishment of drones 111
Aquinas, Thomas 4
Aristotle 79, 86
Arkin, R. 102–4, 110
armed drones: and the ethics of war 6–8; inventory of US *17*; only countries known to have used 20; the rise of 14; use of in Afghanistan, Iraq and Libya 19; use of in Libyan civil war 25–6, 28; *see also* autonomous drones; drone operators; drone strikes; Pakistan drone programme)
arms race, drone R&D as 20
Arnold, Henry 44
Art of War (Sun Tzu) 80
Asilomar conference 108
Asimov, I. 97–8, 111
asymmetric war, Rodin's ethics argument 58–9, 67
atomic bombs 89; *see also* nuclear weapons
atrocity, Grossman's 'spectrum' of 93
Augustine 4
Authorization for the Use of Military Force (AUMF) 25–6
autonomous, negative connotations of US military's use of the term 100
autonomous drones: Arkin's benchmark 104–5; and Asimov's Three Laws of Robotics 97–8; caution on the part of roboticists and military planners 108; child soldiers' moral responsibility comparison 108; ethical considerations 102; Fort Benning experiment 101; *jus in bello* programming and processing 102–5, 110; moral responsibility and meaningful punishment 105–8;

autonomous drones – *contd.*
  paradox of post-human war 109–11; public opinion and 101; suggested accountability mechanisms 106
autonomous weapon systems, ethical implications 102
autonomous weapons, preemptive prohibition recommendation 104
autonomy: ethical implications for non-combatants 104; etymology and meaning 100; levels of 100, *101*; moral perspective 100, 102; non-combatants and the ethical implications of 104
Avenger 16, 99
al-Awlaki, Anwar 66, 70

B-52 bombers 4, 27
Baldwin, Stanley 44
Balkan wars 15
Barber, R. 52
Barrett, Edward 90
Barrett, F. 87
Battle of Agincourt 68, 84
Battle of Fredericksburg 22
Beirut 11
Bellamy, A. J. 63
Betts, R. 11
Bhutto, Benazir 1
Bin Laden, Osama 53, 65, 67
birth rates, and tolerance for casualties 11–12
The Blitz 44
Boer Wars 39
Bomber Command 5
bomber crews, psychological perspective of WWII 93
bombing, measuring the accuracy of 51
Bonaparte, Napoleon 9–10
Bosnia, O'Grady rescue 15
Boston Globe 46
Braun, M. 28
Brennan, John 21, 26, 36, 57
Britain, use of armed drones 20
British Bomber Command, WWII survival rates 15
Brunstetter, D. 28
Burke, A. 66, 72
Bush, George W. 13, 24, 49, 54, 66
Bushey, Dean 84
Bushido 79
Byman, D. 33

Callahan, Bryan 92, 99
Cambodia 27

cannon fodder 80
casualties: aversion to 11; impact on public opinion 11, 13, 15
casualty rates, WWII bomber crews 15
Catch-22 (Heller) 95
Central Intelligence Agency (CIA): a call for transparency 57; first drone-based 'targeted killing' 19; typical use of armed drones 18
Chaput, Armand 15
chess-board image of war 58–9, 73
China: 'carrier killer' missile 18; rapid increase in drone research and development 20
chivalry 79
Christianity 4, 23
Christopher, P. 63
circular error probable 51
civilian disengagement 28
Clark, Wesley 51–2
Clausewitz, C. von 6, 78, 80
Clegg, M. 11
Coady, T. 30, 72
coercive diplomacy 12
Cohen, E. 12
COIN Field Manual (US), principle features 52
Coker, C. 10, 12, 14, 33, 73, 78, 80, 89
Cold War 10–11
collateral damage 13, 32, 42, 44–5, 52, 54, 62, 94; *see also* non-combatants
combat deaths, decline in tolerance for 11–12
combat drones, R&D 16
combatants, moral equality 68, 73
computer virus 99
concentration camps 39
conscription, ending of in the West 12
Cook: M. 46; M. L. 81
counterinsurgency (COIN) 34, 38, 43, 57, 95; ethics and 38–41; Luttwak's pessimism 38–9; moral and ethical standards for American forces 39; moral perspective 39–40
courage: Aristotelian notion of 79–80, 86; Clausewitz on 80; physical vs moral 80; Schopenhauer on 80
Cox, S. 87
Creech Air Force base, Nevada 18, 86, 99
criminal culpability, and human rights 66
Crozier, F. P. 82

decapitation strikes 30–1
decisive restraint, Ignatieff on 79

dehumanisation 73
Dela Cruz, Sanick 102
Der Derian, James 13, 51
Der Spiegel 99
Diego Garcia 18
discrimination principle: accuracy and 51–2; altitude and 45; the Israel–Palestine conflict and 48; the US COIN Field Manual on 40
disembodiment, Giddens on 85
dishonour 90
disrespect, traditional pilots feelings of towards drone operators 88
'double intention', Walzer's notion 67
Douhet, G. 29, 59
drone operator as killer: the disembodied warrior 85–7; distance and disrespect 87–91
drone operators: disrespect traditional pilots might feel towards 88; the everyday world 78; and hegemonic masculinity 87–8; military virtue and physical courage 77–80; mutual risk and war-as-contest 80–4; physical safety of US-based 91; self-respect and motivation issues 87; similarity of pre-mission routine to aeroplane pilots 84
drone operators as victim 91–5; emotional damage 93; feelings of guilt 92–3; and Grossman's 'spectrum of atrocity' model 93–4; post-combat coping mechanisms 92; psychological risk 92–5; PTSD risk 94; risk status 91–2; and the witnessing of the ordinary life of the target 94
drone pilots, medals for 89
drone programmes, global estimate 20
drone strikes: absence of a legal architecture 56; the al-Awlaki operation 66; consistency with *jus in bello* principles 29; data on non-combatant deaths from 47–8; establishing right authority for 25; ethical standards 40; expected and purported benefits 37, 42, 46; lack of transparency 44; as law enforcement 65–6; 'only game in town' 42, 44; post-heroic flavour 34; POTUS involvement 53; pre-emptive nature 24; as terrorism 91; uncertainties regarding the ethical soundness of 37; US government secrecy surrounding 35; vulnerability of a campaign of to strategic failure 30; warlike characterisation 67; weapons used 52

drone system, components and costs 16
drone technology: as prime target for foreign spies 20; Strawser on the ethics of 83
drones, classifications 3

Elshtain, J. B. 40–1
emotions, necessity of for ethical judgement 109
Ender's Game (Card) 85
ethic of responsibility, honour and 79
ethical implications, of autonomous weapon systems 102
ethical perspective, reduction in constraints against drone use 22
ethics: and counterinsurgency 38–41; war and 4–6
ethics of asymmetric war, Rodin's argument 58–9, 67
ethics of drone technology, Strawser on 83
ethics of war: armed drones and the 6–8; soldiers' treatment of enemies as the basis of 73
ethnic cleansing 25, 32–3
Europe: Peace of Westphalia 9; periods of 'total' war in 9
evil: enemies of the US as 72; eradication of and the law 72; Obama on 34; struggle of good against 41
evil doers 13–14
executioners, societal perspective 95

F-22 fighter, cost 16
F-35 Joint Strike Fighter 16
fear, Pakistan drone programme casts 'pall of' 42
Floyd, Nick 93
French Revolution 10
Fricker, M. 47
friendly fire 93
Frowe, H. 77
full-scale war 12

Gaddafi, Muammar 19, 25
game consoles, drone control units' resemblance to 46, 86
Gardner, Ronnie Lee 95
Gavotti, Giolio 14
Geneva Conventions 4, 40, 44, 52, 79
Giddens, A. 85
Global Hawk 2, 101
Gonzales, A. 40
government secrecy, surrounding US drone strikes 35

Graves, Robert 82
Gray, C. S. 4, 29, 39, 71–2, 109
Gray Eagle 16
Grossman, D. 93
Grotius, Hugo 4
ground-control stations, location 18
Gulf War 11, 15, 62; 'Highway of Death' 83
Gunderson, Scott 84
Guthrie, Charles 14

Hadi, Abed Rabbo Mansour 51
Hamas 48
Hamburg, British bomber attack 93
Harris 5; Arthur "Bomber" 5
al-Harthi, Ali Qaed Senyan 19
Hayden, Michael 91
'hearts and minds' 39, 43
Henderson, C. 35
Hendrickson, D. 29
Henry V (Shakespeare) 68, 84–5, 88
heroic war: Coker's observation on endurance 10; transition to post-heroic war from 9–14
high-value targets, Sharkey on the metric for assigning value 53
'Highway of Death' 83
Hiroshima 5, 44
Holmes, R. 81
honour: notion of within warrior ethos 79; as potential source of restraint 79
human rights: in Bush's rhetoric 13; criminal culpability and 66; impact of drone-based surveillance 2; state responsibilities 63; targeted killing and 19, 48, 67
humanitarian intervention: authorisation requirements 25; as just cause 25
hunting: ethical perspective of risk and 83–4; online 83–4
Huntington, S. 77–8
Hurka, T. 63
Hussain, Khadim 43

I, Robot (Asimov) 98
Ignatieff, M. 10, 12, 28, 33, 70, 79, 82, 89
Il diminio dell-aria (*The Command of the Air*) (Douhet) 59
The Imperial Temptation (Tucker/Hendrickson) 29
Industrial Revolution 10
information-gathering, use of drones for 15

injustice, precision munitions and the perception of 64
insect metaphor 91
intelligence professionals, lethal participation of 19
international law, Burke on America's disregard for 72
intervention, acceptability of 25
Iran 20, 99
Iraq 19, 24, 28, 71, 73, 87, 90, 98
Islam 23, 89
Islamic Jihad 48
Israel: attack on Iraq's Osirak nuclear facility 23–4; use of armed drones 20
Israel Defense Forces (IDF) 48
Italian-Turkish War 14

Japan 89
Japanese, American attitudes towards 72
jet-powered drone, development 16
Jordan, J. 31
jus ad bellum 23; evil's place 34–5; just cause 23–5; potential for tension between the principles of proportionality and last resort 29; proportionate cause and right intention 28–30; reasonable prospect of success 30–5; right authority and last resort 25–8
jus in bello 4; addressing deficits of human adherence to 110; assessment of US drone strikes 52–3; asymmetric 65–8; criteria 7, 37; drone strikes' consistency with principles of 29; emotion and 109; in US COIN Field Manual 40; and moral equality of combatants 69–70, 76; moral responsibility and 105, 111; principles 29; programming and processing 102–5, 110; proportionality 53; and prospects for peace 39; relevance of prospect of harm 61; and retaliation against the US 61–2; variability 103; WWII perspective 72
just war tradition: *ad bellum* and *in bello* connections and independence 58; default ethical position 23; historical perspective 4; religious perspective 23

Kaag, J. 42, 109
Kahn, P. 26, 81
Kaufman, W. 42, 109
Keegan, J. 78, 81
Kennedy, John F. 10
Kilcullen, D. 90
kill or be killed 83

killing: moral permissibility of in war 77; risk of developing a "playstation" mentality to 86
Killing in War (McMahan) 71
Killmister, S. 61
Kosovo campaign 13, 15, 27, 33, 45, 64, 82, 87
Krishnan, A. 107

La Marseillaise 10
last resort 23, 114; potential for tension between the principles of proportionality and 29; right authority and 25–8
law enforcement: drone strikes as 65–6; useful ambiguity between war and 67
Law of Land Warfare (US Army 2005) 41
leadership decapitations: extension of the rationale for 54; Jenna Jordan's conclusion 31–2
Lebanon 11
Lee, Robert E. 22
legitimate targets 24, 45, 48–51, 62–3, 70, 81, 116
Levey, Stuart 49
Libya 98; civil war 25; location of world's first aerial bombardment 14; US use of armed drones 19
Libyan civil war: and the 60-day rule 26–7; use of armed drones in 25, 26, 28
licence to kill 81–2
Lindh, Anna 19
Lockheed Martin 15
Lockwood, John 83–4
long-dwell capability, of drones 98–9
long-range guided missiles 16
Long War Journal 47
Los Angeles Times 94
Lucas, G. 104
Luttwak, E. 11, 38

Macchiavelli, N. 30, 78
Mahnken, T. 12, 89
Manzini, Petro 15
martyrdom 29, 89
masculinity, Barrett's research on the construction of 87
Mathewson, Eric S. 86, 90
Mattis, James 88
McChrystal, Stanley 34
McDonald, K. 94
McMahan, J. 5, 68–71, 81
McMaster, H. R. 73, 78
Medal of Honor 14
medals, for drone pilots 89

Mehsud, Baitullah 1, 49, 53
Mehsud, Hakimullah 42
The Men I Killed (Crozier) 82
military drone, range of sizes 2
military necessity: definition 41; Walzer's observation 41
military objective, self-defence as legitimate 41–2
military pilots, WWI romanticisation 87
military profession, shift in the relationship between civilian society and 12
military professionals, warriors vs 76
Mill, J. S. 70
Mitchell, William 5
moral equality of combatants 68–73; circumstances 76; and mutual respect 90; principle 58
moral permissibility, of killing in war 77
moral responsibility and meaningful punishment, of autonomous drones 105–8
moral superiority 58, 66, 68, 72, 109
moratoria, on ethically sensitive research 108
motivation 87
Mueller, Stephen P. 34
Mullen, Mike 109
mutual assured destruction 10
mutual risk, and war-as-contest 80–4

'naked soldiers', Walzer's notion 82, 94
Napoleonic war, Ignatieff's description 10
National Security Strategy, Obama Administration's 27
NATO 3, 13, 15, 25, 27, 32–4, 45, 51, 64, 70, 82
Nazi concentration camps 85
necessity principle, Pakistan drone programme 41–3
New York Times 50, 53, 91
Nicomachean Ethics (Aristotle) 79
Nobel Peace Prize, Obama's acceptance 34
non-combatant deaths: data 47–8; moral acceptability 63; *see also* collateral damage
non-combatants: and autonomous weapons 104, 106–7, 110, 115–16; and blast range of munitions 51; and the circular error probable 51; cowardly nature of cruelty against 79; deliberate targeting 41; and the ethical implications of autonomy 104; experience of physical risk in targeted territories 32; hit in first ever aerial bombardment 40;

non-combatants – *contd.*
identification issues 45–9, 51, 104 (*see also* discrimination principle); *jus in bello* prohibition on deliberately targeting 63; and *jus in bello* standards 67–8; as off-limits 81; perceptions of harm to 39; political/strategic impacts of killing 44; and radical assymetry 62, 68; and risk assessment 63; risk assessment 45–6, 52–3, 64; and Shari'a principles 37; supposed immunity from attack 44; uncertainty over who counts as 53; value judgments 53–4, 64; WWII killings 93
nuclear weapons 10, 24, 45, 89

Obama, Barack 3, 38, 44, 53–4
O'Grady, Scott 15
On Killing (Grossman) 93
On War (Clausewitz) 6, 80
O'Neill, M. 39
online hunting 83–4
Operation Allied Force 13
Operation Enduring Freedom 14
Operation Iraqi Freedom 14

Pakistan 24; consequences of political instability 38; denounces the US Government's use of armed drones 19; drone strikes 37 (*see also* Pakistan drone programme); ethical standards applicable to US conduct in 40; government secrecy surrounding US drone strikes 35; Panetta's statement on drone strikes in 30; self-defence as legitimate military objective in 41–2; US government's strategic interest in 38; US killing of Osama Bin Laden in 53
Pakistan drone programme: accuracy and proportionality 47; a call for transparency 55–7; casts 'pall of fear' 42; data on non-combatant deaths 47–8; and the discrimination principle 44–52; ethics and counterinsurgency 38–41; human rights perspective 48; necessity principle 41–3; operations base 37; Pakistani perspective 42–3; proportionality principle 52–5; public opinion 43; 'signature' strikes 54; transformation into large-scale campaign 54
Panetta, Leon 30, 42, 44, 89–90
pattern-of-life analysis 54
Peace of Westphalia 9
Pepperell, R. 109

personal privacy, impact of drone-based surveillance on 2
physical courage, military virtue and 77–80
pilots: first killed in war 15; hegemonic masculinity 87–8; risks to 83; vulnerability 16; World War I romanticisation 87
Plato's *Republic* 112–13
political risks 54
post-heroic war: allusion to in British military doctrine document 15; vs 'cannon fodder' 80; concept analysis 11–12; exemplar 13; incompatibility between COIN and 34; and the increasing estrangement between the military and civilians 26; transition from heroic war to 9–14; USAF's role in the shift from heroic to 12
post-human war, paradox of 109–11
power inequality 76
pre-emption 24–5, 55
precision, expectations of 13
precision munitions: and the perception of injustice 64; Wesley Clark on the ethics of using 51–2
precision strikes 12
Predator UAV 3, 15–16, 18, 20, 44, 46, 52, 83, 88
preventive war, justice perspective 71
prisoners of war, treatment of 40
professional armies, post-Westphalia replacement of mercenaries by 9
professionalism, Huntington on 77–8
propaganda, value of armed unmanned aircraft as 90
proportionality principle 23, 28–9, 39–41, 51–4, 63, 103, 110, 117; drones' consistency with 28; an example of 28; and the killing of Bin Laden 53–4; Pakistan drone programme 52–5; potential for tension between the principles of last resort and 29
psychological perspectives: risk to drone operators 92–5; stress and ethical performance 110; WWII bomber crews 93
PTSD (post-traumatic stress disorder) 94, 117
public support: collateral damage and 13; impact of casualties on 11

al-Qaeda 19, 24, 26, 30, 38, 42, 44, 47, 49–50, 53–4, 65–6

radical asymmetry: addressing 'fairness' objections 67; the al-Awlaki case 66; asymmetric *jus in bello* 65–8; drones and risk transfer 62–4; the problem of 58–68; war-as-contest 59–62
Reaper UAV 16, 18, 37, 44, 46, 52
Reath, A. 100
reciprocal justice 65
reciprocal risk, necessity of in war 77, 81
reciprocally indiscriminate war, al-Qaeda vision 65
recklessness 87
Record, J. 32
Red Cross warehouse, bombing of by US aircraft 45
reduced sensory perception, and the facilitation of killing 93
Remarque, E. M. 81
The Republic (Plato) 112–13
right authority: deficit of 28; relationship between combatant risk and 27
right intention, central importance to just war thinking 29
The Rise of American Airpower (Sherry) 14
risk: US Army's COIN field manual on 81; wartime necessity of reciprocal 81
risk avoidance 34
risk elimination: difference between risk reduction and 81; ethical relevance of the crossing of the line between risk reduction and 83
risk-free killing 2, 6, 26–7, 32, 76, 86, 116
risk transfer, drones and 62–4
Risk-Transfer Militarism 64
robot warriors, Arkin's 'ethical governor component' 103
robots, ethical consideration of autonomy in 97–8; *see also* autonomous drones
Rodin, D. 48, 52, 59, 67–8
Roman Empire 4, 23
romanticisation, of WWI military pilots 87
Roosevelt, Theodore 80
Rousseau, J.-J. 100
Royal Air Force, drones' implications for 87
rules of engagement, variations 103

Scan Eagle 101
Schmitt, C. 72
Schmitt, M. 70
Schopenhauer, A. 80
Schwartz, Norton 88
science fiction 85, 97, 108

secrecy 27, 35, 37
self-defence: forceful 24; just cause of 23–4; legitimacy of 83; as legitimate military objective in Pakistan 41–2; pre-emptive use of force as 24; right authority for 25
self-esteem, oldest source of warrior's 79
self-respect 87
self-sacrifice 78
September 11 terror attacks 13, 24, 38, 50, 66
Serbia 13, 27
Shahzad, Faisal 65
Shakespeare, W. 68–9, 84–5, 88
Shari'a 23, 37
Sharkey, N. 53, 104
Shaw, M. 64
Sherry, M. 14–15, 72, 87
siege warfare, Coker's likening of air-only campaigns to 33
Singer, P. W. 46, 78, 86, 90
sniper's dilemma 82
The Soldier and the State (Huntington) 77
soldiers: children's aspirations 77; Machiavelli's observation 78
Somalia 19, 24, 35, 89
sovereignty, use of armed drones as a violation of 19
Sparrow, R. 86
'spectrum of atrocity', Grossman's model 93
Star Wars (1977) 108
Strawser, B. J. 46, 83, 88
suicide bombers 48
Sullins, J. 106
summary execution, Yemen drone strike as 19
Sun Tzu 80, 89
surveillance 2–3, 16, 18, 20, 54, 98

Taliban 24, 31, 38, 42, 47, 49–50
targeted killing, legal perspective 67
technology, reliance on as characteristic of American way of war 12
teleoperated (online) hunting 83–4
Terrazas, Miguel ('TJ') 102
terrorism: characterisation of as criminal acts 66; drone strikes as 91
Thirty Years War 9
Tomahawk cruise missiles 15
Tonkens, R. 110
torture: application of rules 103; Gonzales on 40
'total' war, periods of in Europe 9

Tucker, R. 29

unarmed drones 2, 20, 99
unethical practice, source of restraint on 79
United States: 'godlike' power 59; presentation of moral superiority 66; press's aversion to US casualties 11; pursuit of heroic war 10; roots of disregard for international law 72
unjust war, temptations of recourse to for the strong 71
unmanned blimps 18
Unmanned Systems Integrated Roadmap (Pentagon, 2011) 100
US Air Force (USAF): critical role in the shift from heroic to post-heroic war 12; resistance to trend towards greater reliance on drones 16
USS *Cole* 19

van Creveld, M. 27
Vietnam War 10–11, 15, 27, 85
Virtual War (Ignatieff) 12
Virtuous War (Der Derian) 13

Walzer, M. 5, 39, 41, 45, 63, 68, 70, 81–2, 94
war: the American formula 29; centrality of the human dimension 109; chess-board image of 58–9, 83; Clausewitz's view 78; Coker's view 80; ethical implications of autonomous weapon systems for 97–8, 102 (*see also* autonomous drones); and ethics 4–6; instrumentalist understanding of 90; moral permissibility of killing in 77; necessity of reciprocal risk in 77, 81; periods of 'total' 9; useful ambiguity between law enforcement and 67; Walzer on the moral condition of 81
war-as-contest, mutual risk and 80–4
War Powers Resolution 27
War on Terror: Coker on the number of casualties 14; heroic to post-heroic transition 14; and the US rhetoric of moral superiority 65–6
warrior ethos: courage 79–80; McMaster's description 78; military virtue 77–9; moral basis 76; notion of honour within 79
warriors: oldest source of self-esteem 79; uniqueness of the experience of 78
The Warrior's Honour (Ignatieff) 79
Washington Post 86
Wasp Micro UAV 2
weapons of mass destruction 45, 71
wedding party bombing 45
Wertheimer, R. 76, 95
Western Front 80
Westphalia treaty 9
Wired 99
Wolfowitz, Paul 19
World War I 86; 'cannon fodder' 80; costly land battles 5; Remarque's novel 81; romanticisation of military pilots 87
World War II: bombing accuracy 51; German torpedoes 3; psychological perspective of bomber crews 93

Al-Yazid, Mustafa Abu 49
Yee-Kuang Heng 12
Yemen drone strike 19, 24

Zehfuss, M. 51